THE LAST DAYS OF

SHEA

THE LAST DAYS OF

SHEA

DELIGHT AND DESPAIR
IN THE LIFE OF A

Mets

FAN

DANA BRAND

Taylor Trade Publishing

Lanham New York Boulder Toronto Plymouth, UK

Published by Taylor Trade Publishing
An imprint of The Rowman & Littlefield Publishing Group, Inc.
4501 Forbes Boulevard, Suite 200, Lanham, Maryland 20706
http://www.rlpgtrade.com

Estover Road, Plymouth PL6 7PY, United Kingdom

Distributed by National Book Network

British Library Cataloguing in Publication Information Available

Library of Congress Cataloging-in-Publication Data

Brand, Dana.
  The last days of Shea : delight and despair in the life of a Mets fan / Dana Brand.
    p. cm.
  Includes index.
  ISBN 978-1-58979-457-3 (pbk. : alk. paper)
  1. New York Mets (Baseball team)—Anecdotes. 2. Shea Stadium (New York, N.Y.)
  3. Baseball fans—New York (State)—New York. I. Title.
  GV875.N45B718 2009
  796.357'64097471—dc22

                                 2009019462

∞™ The paper used in this publication meets the minimum requirements of
American National Standard for Information Sciences—Permanence of Paper for
Printed Library Materials, ANSI/NISO Z39.48-1992.

Printed in the United States of America

For my daughter, Sonia Brand-Fisher

Contents

Contents

Foreword
A Conversation with Gary Cohen

On June 5, 2009, I had the privilege of talking to Gary Cohen, who has been broadcasting Mets games since 1989, first on WFAN and now on SNY-TV. Gary talked to me about being a Mets fan, and about how he feels about Shea being gone. In our conversation I found—not to my surprise, of course—that Gary Cohen is exactly the kind of baseball fan for whom I have written this book.

DB: *When some people have suggested that the Mets might do more to celebrate their history at Citi Field, others have said, "Why celebrate Mets history? What is there to celebrate? Two World Championships in forty-six years, a lot of lousy seasons, a lot of good seasons that fell short." What do you think is worth celebrating about the experience of being a Mets fan since you started rooting for them?*

GC: Well, I think, just about everything. I think the reason people tend to discount the Mets' history is because they live in such close proximity to a team that has more history than any other major league franchise. But the Mets have their own unique history, and they have what might even be a more unique bond with their fans. Obviously the World Championships are front and center in terms of the Mets' on-the-field baseball success, but history is not built only on ultimate success. It's also built on moments and on relationships.

DB: *What do you mean when you say that the Mets have a "unique relationship with their fans"?*

GC: If you go back to the beginning with the Mets, you know that they filled the void that had been created by the departure of the Dodgers and the Giants. There were National League fans in New York who were starving for a baseball team, and even though the Polo Grounds was decrepit, people found their way there and they found a way to celebrate their team and root for their team in a way that had never really been heard or seen before. They were louder, they were younger, they carried banners. There was a palpable sense of something new being created and it was celebrated in a way that probably jibed with the changing times in society, through the sixties. And I think that that relationship has evolved over the years in many different and quirky and amusing ways. The fact that the Mets were so horrible in their early days, historically so, and yet the fan base grew and grew over those early years, I think that's indicative of what we're talking about. The relationship was never just about wins and losses. This sense may have been lost a little bit in the last few years, but I think that for most of their history, the Mets held on to their fan base in spite of their lack of success and I think that speaks volumes about the unique relationship that the Mets have had with their fans.

DB: *I agree. I think that among a lot of Mets fans and certainly among fans who have a sense of the history of Mets fandom, there's an idea that even if the Mets haven't been so successful, their fans are crazier, more enthusiastic, more involved. I did an informal survey of baseball blogs on the Web and I think that there are actually more Mets blogs than there are blogs for any other team. There is, I think, a geekiness to Mets fans which is different from . . .*

GC: What was the word you just used?

DB: *Geekiness. A lot of Mets fans are geeks. They're absorbed, obsessed. They know every detail of the history.*

GC: They might be. I can't necessarily speak to that. But I will say that the Mets have always appealed to a wide diversity of fans. I think that a team that wins all the time appeals to one type of fan.

A team that can plumb the depths and reach the heights and do so in "miraculous" ways appeals to a different kind of fan, a different kind of person. I do think that Mets fans revel in the amusing minutiae. Marv Throneberry is a piece of the Mets' past that is not disdained, but cherished. There was the Sign Man and his ability to mirror what Mets fans were thinking in any given moment in some magical way through whatever signs he happened to have brought to the game that day. There was George Theodore and his shoulders. There are so many examples of things like this over the years: of people or elements or incidents, whether it's the ball off the wall or the ball lost in the fog. These are features of the game that for an average major league baseball team either get shuffled aside or lost in the crowd of statistics and championships or other things that take priority. For Mets fans, those things are almost the substance of what it means to be a Mets fan. I mean, one of the greatest games in Mets history didn't end on a grand slam. It ended on a grand slam single. Because that's the nature of who the Mets are. There's a certain quirkiness involved in the franchise. The fact that the Mets have had some of the greatest pitching of the last half century but have never thrown a no-hitter is fittingly wacky for what this franchise is.

DB: *There is a Mets mystique . . .*

GC: Right. And I think that the Mets history that was celebrated in Shea Stadium by the official Mets Hall of Fame and by the hanging of championship banners only tells part of the story. If someone was wise enough in the Mets organization to really give this some thought, they would construct a commemoration of Mets history that included all the things that we're talking about, in addition to the championships, in addition to Seaver and Koosman and Piazza and all the great stars that the Mets have had over the years. Mets history also includes all of that strangeness and that unique quality that makes the Mets what they have been. And I think that in official Mets quarters, there may not be the understanding of how much that history means to the fan base.

DB: *I really hope that perspective does change. I think it would be great to have something like a Mets museum at Shea where you* *didn't just celebrate the greatest players and the championships, where you could celebrate the quirkiness and the unique relationship with the fans that you're talking about, where you could celebrate Marv Throneberry and George Theodore.*

GC: I also think that the Mets Hall of Fame, such as it is, was always rather hidden at Shea Stadium, but the fact is that it also suffered from neglect. The last person to go into the Hall of Fame was, I believe, Tommie Agee in 2002. You're talking seven years with no inductees and at the moment, in the short history of Citi Field, that Hall of Fame is missing. So it is my fervent hope that there is a plan in place to not only display what there is of the Mets Hall of Fame but to expand on the theme in the way that we're talking about.

DB: *I know Shea meant a lot to you. How do you feel when you see signs that Shea is no longer there?*

GC: Well, that stadium was part of my life for over forty years, so you can't help but notice that it's not there any more. You know, it's funny, I was watching some highlight clip a few days ago that featured Shea Stadium, not only what was happening on the field, but just the sweep of the stands and the very familiar contours of Shea as we've all experienced it, and I felt a pang. I felt a real sense of remembrance and loss that I didn't necessarily expect to feel. It was the first time in a while that I had seen anything that was so distinctly Shea and I think it's like anything that's associated with our childhoods and that becomes home for us: its loss and its lack eats at us in different ways and in ways that we don't necessarily expect. I remember sitting in the broadcast booth last year and thinking to myself: this space will no longer exist next year. Not only will we stop being here, but this will just be a place in the air above a parking lot. And that's a very strange way to think of something. And now as I drive by Shea, that is the case. The broadcast booth is a piece of air above a parking lot. And it's a very strange phenomenon.

DB: *It is. When I parked recently at Citi Field, I was walking around the parking lot and thinking, here I am at third base, here*

I am at home. It is remarkable how we make places so sacred to us. Obviously, that is one of the things I write about in my book: that sense of Shea's sacredness and how that's created by our imagination and our memory. Everybody knows that it wasn't such a great stadium . . .

GC: But it was a great stadium in a lot of ways. People forget what it was like before Shea came along—what older ballparks in the pre–Camden Yards retro stadium era were like. I went to games at Yankee Stadium when I was a kid and sat behind a pole and couldn't see the game. I mean, Shea was magnificent. There were no poles! It was huge. And that was a great thing in the sixties. As it came to pass, as other round stadiums joined the pantheon, whether it be Three Rivers or Riverfront or Busch stadium, it seemed that that mode of stadium became quickly outdated, and once Camden Yards came aboard and the slew of smaller retro stadiums came to the forefront, it became clear that Shea wasn't perfect. It had its own flaws—it leaked and it wasn't maintained as well as it should have been. But for its day—Shea was magnificent. And I always felt that way sitting there, even when I was sitting in the top reaches of the Upper Deck, far, far away from the field, I always felt that it was a magnificent building. And frankly, I think that in many ways it got a bad rap.

DB: *There was a sublimity to Shea. There was that sense that you were looking out to the entire universe. In Citi Field, I feel enclosed and that has a sort of cozy appeal, I suppose. But in Shea, you felt as if you were open to the world. You saw Manhattan on one side, you saw Queens, Serval Zippers, or U-Haul on the other side. It was wonderful.*

One of the things I write about in my book is the way in which baseball fandom connects you with other people: family, friends, strangers, etc. Can you talk a little about how baseball and particularly the experience of Shea Stadium provided you with a connection to other people in your life?

GC: I think that one of the joys of baseball is that it provides a great connection to people you would otherwise not be connected with. When I was in my late teens and early twenties, I would say that 90 percent of the Mets games I attended, I went to by myself. This was mostly because I found, in those days, that I needed to concentrate on the game more than the people I might have brought with me wanted to concentrate on it. In fact, it's still like this today. On the odd day that I'm not working, and I might go to the game with my family, my wife complains that I concentrate too much on the game, that I'm not a very social partner at certain times. And I think that the same was true when I was a kid. But what I did find was that no matter where I sat in the stadium, there were always like-minded souls, there were people who were just as focused on every pitch, who were as involved as I was. Inevitably there would be conversations that would arise in the course of the game that would create these instant, ephemeral friendships. To me, those connections were very important because as a geeky fan who felt this incredible need for absorption in the game it was important to me to find out that there were other people like me. Most of the people I knew, while they might have been casual fans of the game, were not as intensely interested as I was. Especially in the late seventies and early eighties, when the Mets were terrible and there'd be only four thousand people at the game, generally the people who were there were really there, not just for an event, but for the game itself. And they were as intently interested in what they were watching as I was. The connections I made with those people, and these were people I didn't know and I never knew their names, these connections were very important to me.

DB: *It's amazing the affection that fans who stuck with the Mets from '77 to '83 have for that time period. There really was no reason why we should have been going to Mets game then but . . .*

GC: Of course there was.

DB: *There was.*

GC: Baseball was still counted in the standings, it was still part of the continuum of the game. I bristle at the thought that the only reason to go watch a team is because it wins. One of the cornerstones of being a Mets fan is that you go to the game for the game.

DB: *Absolutely.*

GC: . . . for the possibility that something extraordinary might happen that day. Whether the Mets lost 120 times in 1962 or whether they were losing ninety-plus games through the late '70s, to me it didn't matter so much as the fact that here was this unscripted event that was part of the grand tradition and continuum, that everything that happened in that game would be recorded for history. It's just as important what Bruce Boisclair did in his at-bat in 1978 as what Mike Piazza did in his at-bat in 2004. I think that for people who really care about the game, especially if it involves a team that they root for, the matter of wins and losses doesn't necessarily take precedence over the sheer joy of the game itself.

DB: *From the way you talk about baseball, both as an announcer and as you're talking about it right here, I get a sense that you enjoy the game on so many different levels. And one thing I was struck by in the answers you gave to the questions on the Gary, Keith, and Ron site, where you talk about your interests and your favorite books and movies, is that you are an intellectual, which is not something, frankly, that most baseball announcers are. I know that you don't want to make a big deal out of that, but I'm curious about what you think about the fact that a whole lot of writers, artists, intellectuals have always been drawn to baseball. Do you think that being a baseball fan is a kind of cultural or intellectual activity?*

GC: Well, I don't think it has to be. I think that you can experience baseball on many different levels. Most people I know who are baseball fans just want to see their team win on a given day. They know who their favorite players are. But they don't necessarily put themselves inside the game in the way I might. And I think that's perfectly fine. I think it's no less legitimate to experience baseball in that fashion. In fact, it seems to me that for all the fervor that gets transmitted through radio talk shows and Web message boards and blogs these days, the fact of the matter is that as I look around ballparks where there is so much extraneous entertainment and activity, in addition to the ballgame itself, more people are experiencing baseball in what could be considered a superficial way than ever before. That is, a larger percentage of fans are. But I think that there is a way to look at baseball that is very lyrical and very tied to the general culture. I think that Ken Burns did a great job of espousing that in his *Baseball* series. I think that baseball is a game that lends itself to daydreaming, to musing, to thinking deep thoughts because there is a lack of action for such long stretches of time. I think it's one of the things that makes baseball broadcasting different from broadcasting any other sport, that there is so much time to make connections and to drift into other areas and to look at the game not only within itself but within the context of the world around it. And so I think all those things give baseball an appeal for people who have far deeper thoughts than I do, people who might want to expound on their experience of the game.

DB: *In the past couple of years, you and Ron and Keith have established a charitable foundation, Pitch In For a Good Cause, which is run by your wife, Lynn. Now it seems to me that in addition to doing this valuable charitable work, this foundation has created a space or opportunity for you guys to connect with the community of Mets fans. Can you talk a little about what that experience has been like for you and your family?*

GC: Well, this organization was created by Lynn for really only one purpose. The purpose was to allow Keith and Ron and myself to use our good names and whatever celebrity we might have established to do something good, to make money for charity and to help people in need. And that was really it. But I think it's evolved into something much more. I think that the GaryKeith andRon.com, Pitch In For a Good Cause community has become an entity in and of itself and it keeps getting larger and I think it really reached its apex at that event at the end of last season. It was so large, what was it, around thirteen hundred people? The whole party tent, and the bleachers, and the going on the warning track. I think that I had not realized, and I'm not sure if Lynn had realized until that point, that what she had done was not only create a charitable organization that allowed us to do some good work, mostly through her efforts, but also established almost a sub-community within the New York Mets fanbase. We had, and she had, created a cadre of people who not only had this warm feeling about the Mets and about us as broadcasters, but also about doing good for the community. From what I've seen of these events, people are thrilled to be able to be a part of that and I think that a lot of people who have attended these events have formed new friendships and new connections with other like-minded fans and I think that that's enabled the organization to take off and grow even further and spawn more good works, like what Lynn's doing this Father's Day with having kids without fathers be sponsored for a day and spoiled for a day. The kinds of things which have grown out of this organization can only breed more good.

DB: *I know that everybody who was at that GKR event at that last win at Shea will never forget it. It was . . .*

GC: The last win. I hadn't quite thought of it in that way, but I guess that's what it was.

DB: *That's exactly what it was. It was a wonderful game, but just standing on the warning track and all being together and all wearing the Gary, Keith, and Ron t-shirts, being there with my own family and with my big Mets family, the whole event was like nothing I'd ever experienced. As you say, Gary, the foundation does so much good. But it has also done all this good for Mets fans that I don't think anybody could have anticipated. Pitch In For a Good Cause has definitely become a facet of the Mets community.*

GC: I also think, Dana, your book is very much in the spirit of what we're talking about here. It's about the unique community Mets fans have and the unique relationship that Mets fans have to their team. This is a truly terrific book you've written. I was very impressed with your passion and your sincerity. I think it's very easy to be a fan. I think it is very hard to look inside yourself to see what makes you a fan, what it is that ties you to a community of people, some of whom you know and some of whom you don't, and what makes us root for the laundry over a long period of time as players come and go and what the bond of continuity is. Is it the stadium? Is it the field? Is it the laundry? Is it the ownership, the management, the announcers, what is it that ties us to this franchise year after year other than habit? I think that what I found in your book, what runs through your whole book, is some kind of deeper understanding of what underlies this thing we call "being a fan."

Preface

On April 13, 2009, the New York Mets played their first game in a new ballpark named Citi Field, after the bank that will pay $20 million a year for naming rights over the next twenty years. From April 17, 1964, to September 28, 2008, the Mets played home games at Shea Stadium, which had been named in honor of William Shea, the man who was more responsible than anyone else for bringing National League baseball back to New York. Shea was a lawyer who had been appointed by New York City's mayor Robert Wagner to find a way to replace the Brooklyn Dodgers and the New York Giants, the teams that had been relocated by their owners to the West Coast at the end of the 1957 season.

When the Dodgers and Giants left, millions of New Yorkers had something of great value ripped from their lives. Yet this was accepted as a natural consequence of the way major league baseball was structured. Fans couldn't do anything about it. The owners had the power and the money and the protection of the courts. It didn't matter what the fans felt. Using a hardball strategy that included threatening to establish a rival league, William Shea forced major league baseball to expand. New National League franchises were awarded to New York and Houston. Many if not all fans of the Dodgers and the Giants were healed by the creation of the New York Mets.

The Mets played their first two seasons in the Polo Grounds, the abandoned ballpark of the Giants. In 1964, the Mets opened their own new state-of-the-art stadium in Flushing, Queens, right next to the New York World's Fair. Designed according to the debatable architectural principles of that era, Shea was never a great or even a good stadium. But Mets fans gave it a raucous soul. The early Mets were a terrible team, mainly because the rules of the expansion draft set up by the other baseball owners made it impossible for them to be anything but terrible. Yet fans showed up for the Mets, carrying banners, screaming, and chanting.

Sensing something special about the die-hard fans of his last-place team, Mets manager Casey Stengel called them the "New Breed." Mets fans acquired a reputation for immoderate enthusiasm and intense, offbeat loyalty. They became famous for their imagination, if not always for their dignity. The myth of the Mets fan at Shea was born in the early-to-mid-1960s. Shea itself became world famous when a screaming crowd, straining at all of its limits, attended the Beatles concert there in 1965, the first stadium concert ever. The Mets myth turned to gold in the miraculous summer of 1969. It stayed alive through the first half of the 1970s, was resurrected in the 1980s, and could still be felt shaking the stadium during the wild and wonderful seasons of 1999, 2000, and 2006.

For most of its four and a half decades, Shea was a silly, joyful, passionate, and loud universe. By the time it was slated to be torn down, it contained trillions of cherished hours of human life. To those who loved it, Shea seemed to hold, in its big, blue embrace, millions of lost parents, siblings, and friends. It held some of the most precious moments of many vanished childhoods. It seemed to Mets fans as if enough energy, ecstasy, and anguish had been felt at Shea to power several civilizations for several millennia. Though the stadium was physically torn down in the winter of 2009, the immense meaning it holds for so many can never disappear. Shea is still there because millions of people will miss it forever. We can still hear it. We can still feel it tremble.

When Citi Field opened in 2009, many Mets fans had difficulty finding themselves in it. Everyone admired the comfort and beauty of the new stadium. The food was much better and Citi Field had many amenities the old stadium did not have. It takes a while, however, before a new stadium can feel like home to its fans. A spiritual transition has to take place. The team has to provide some new memories. Fans need to get used to new things, embrace others, speak up about changes they're not happy about, and make suggestions for what they'd like to see in their new home. Management needs to listen and to some degree accommodate. It is its responsibility to manage the transition well. Teams sometimes find this hard, because baseball is, as always, a business. The owners do not have quite as much power as they did in 1957, but they make even more money. Keeping the most sentimental fans happy is not their sole focus. Still, it will serve baseball well if owners understand that owning a baseball team is not just about making a profit by paying some men to play a game.

This book is about the ways baseball is a lot more than a game or a business. It is about bringing into Citi Field the essence of Shea from the rubble still piled in the parking lot at the beginning of the 2009 season. It is about telling the Mets what a lot of the fans want them to know. And it is about what we want to teach Citi Field, so it can become more than a spanking new, state-of-the-art ballpark that doesn't yet quite seem to know us.

In my book *Mets Fan*, I wrote about what I experienced as a fan from 1962 up through the ground-breaking ceremonies for Citi Field in November 2006. In *The Last Days of Shea*, I focus on the stadium itself in the context of its impending destruction. I describe attending games at Shea Stadium—how it sounded, looked, and smelled. I write about living through its last seasons and last moments and seeing the structure come down. Here I want to show how baseball fans share their hopes and how they can endure and share baseball misfortune—how they can emerge from even the most colossal disappointment without any regret about being baseball fans. If I have learned one thing by being in Shea's crowds for almost half a century, it is that the crowd that watches and responds is as important as the players who play. Baseball is a breathtakingly beautiful game. It can be experienced in solitude. But it is best enjoyed as a personal and communal experience of loyalty and love. This is why the homes of baseball are so important. Any physical space that holds so much human emotion is sacred.

Citi Field will eventually become the home of the Mets and their fans. If you doubt this, just spend a half hour watching people taking pictures of themselves and their kids in front of the old Home Run Apple, salvaged from Shea. What do you think they're doing? Check out the people finding their bricks on the walkway by the entrance to the Robinson rotunda. Read the bricks. There is something powerful here and it is looking for its home. This is where the Mets play. This is where it will have to be. But for Citi Field to become a home, some life has to be lived there. The team has to step up and give us moments we will want to remember. The organization has to step up and show that it understands our psychology, our traditions, and how much we value our history and our symbols. I am hopeful about the future.

But as hopeful as I am, I have some fear about whether the scrappy, democratic, sentimental world of baseball fandom, as Mets fans knew it at Shea, will cease to exist in an age of smaller designer stadiums, with restricted-access clubs and restaurants and many luxury boxes. This is a fear all baseball fans should share right now. I am eager for my fears to be proven groundless. I am hopeful because I refuse to believe that the story of baseball will just be the story of the greed and meanness that relocated the Brooklyn Dodgers to Los Angeles, the New York Giants to San Francisco, and Tom Seaver to Cincinnati. With the indomitable, optimistic spirit of the mythic Mets fan, I believe I will see something that my old professor Bart Giamatti always hoped he'd see—an era when what baseball fans thought and felt actually mattered to baseball, an era when each fan in a ballpark felt as valuable to the team as any other fan there.

This may be asking too much, just as it is asking too much for your one team out of thirty to beat all the other teams and win the World Championship. I don't care. We fans have to ask for this. I know baseball is a business. I know that everything in America, and arguably in the world, is run on business principles. But we still look to American business—to sports, to music, to publishing, to movies and TV—to provide us with some very important experiences. I think it is legitimate to ask these businesses to care about us. Where would they be without us, after all? I think it is legitimate to suggest that sports and sports broadcasting be shaped by something other than maximizing profit. They'll still make plenty of money in an economy that has among its goals the maximization of human happiness and the deepening of human experience.

This book is for the crowd, for those who hope beyond the bounds of reason, and who love beyond the bounds of sense. This book is for everybody who's ever had their spirits lifted by the creaky mechanism of the old Home Run Apple or the sudden appearance of Mr. Met. This is a book for people who know how to do the Curley Shuffle and know the second verse of "Meet the Mets." This is a book for everyone who still has a passionate opinion about whether George Stone should have pitched, everyone with a physical memory of Mike Scioscia's home run, everyone who knows exactly where they were when they saw the Grand Slam Single clear the fence. This is a book for those who will forever feel an emptiness when they pass a specific spot on the Grand Central Parkway or the Whitestone Expressway.

But I also hope the story of Shea can be understood by those who get excited by the Phillie Phanatic, or the Brewer's sausage race, or even the gloomy grandeur of Monument Park. I hope this book will speak to those for whom the name "Mookie Wilson" does not produce a warm glow. Underneath the most bitter baseball rivalries is a deep bond of fellowship. We baseball fans are all in the same boat now. Our precious experience is threatened by steroids and cheating, by rising ticket prices and the increasing economic stratification of our stadiums, and by the cynical manipulations of sports media. That's why we have to speak up and say why this precious game is important to us. We should not accept powerlessness. We know that we cannot always rely on the owners, the media, or the players to care about us. We will have to make ourselves heard for baseball to remain worth passing on to those who come after us.

Finally, I hope I have something to show the non-fan. A lot of people who aren't fans don't understand the point of baseball. I'm inviting these people to take a look. Yogi Berra once said that sometimes you can observe a lot just by watching. I think you can observe a lot about human beings by watching how they watch baseball, how they inhabit their stadiums, how they deal with the passage of time by responding to the destruction of a beloved ballpark. I think it is worthwhile to know what it's like to care about a baseball team, to weave the fortunes of a team into the fabric of your life, to find continuity and community in the sensory details of a game at the park, in the voices of the broadcasters, and in the emotions that are shared with others. Hundreds of millions are drawn to baseball. Billions are drawn to sport. This is a central human experience and it deserves to be treated with respect for its beauty and complexity.

I love baseball. I have survived almost half a century of rooting for the New York Mets and I will take however much more of them I can have. For almost fifty years, Mets fans have been invited to "step right up" or "come to the park" and "Meet the Mets." Well we've met the Mets. And they are us.

Acknowledgments

As a baseball fan, my greatest debt is to my family. My father, Leonard Brand, and my mother, Helen Thomashow Brand, were the ones who first introduced me to what still strikes me as the bizarre idea that paying attention to the fortunes of a baseball team is one of the things you're supposed to do with your life. I am especially grateful to my mother for letting me write about her three-quarters-of-a-century-long devotion to the Brooklyn Dodgers and the New York Mets. I am grateful to my sisters, Jennifer Brand and Stefanie Brand, who each love the Mets in ways similar to and very different from the way I do. Being a baseball fan is like being in love or believing in anything. You're doing something millions of other people are doing, but everyone's actually doing something a little different.

My wife, Sheila Fisher, and my daughter, Sonia Brand-Fisher, are the main witnesses to my life. I thank them for their patience and enthusiasm about my writing projects. I thank them for how, hearing parts of it read aloud in the car, they immediately understood the larger ambitions of the book and encouraged me to make it what it is. Sheila, a gifted writer, teacher, and translator, is the best editor I've ever known. She has an unerring sense of how sentences should and shouldn't connect with each other. I owe her a great deal, both as an editor and as a life companion. I also owe Sonia a great deal and I've dedicated this book to her. As she goes off to college, I want to say how grateful I am that she spent her childhood in our home. I've gone to more ballgames with Sonia than with anyone else. Shea was our place. And I love how there are so many other parents and kids and friends and relatives who can say that about Shea and about all the other places where people go to ballgames together. Sonia makes me excited about the future and I am looking forward to seeing what mark she makes on the world with the mind and spirit she has shown to me in all the precious times we've spent together.

I also want to thank other members of my family who've been with baseball a long time or are just discovering it: Byron Thomashow, Mitchell Thomashow, Peter Thomashow, Charlie Fisher, Sally Fisher, Danny Kessler, Sam Brand Kessler, and Sarah Brand Kessler.

I am deeply grateful to my agents: Chris Morehouse of the Dunham Literary Agency and Anne Marie O'Farrell of the Marcil-O'Farrell Literary Agency, for being so involved, smart, perceptive, and aggressive. It has also been a pleasure to work with the impressive people at Taylor Trade Publishing: Rick Rinehart, Jehanne Schweitzer, Dulcie Wilcox, and Kalen Landow.

I want to thank my Hofstra colleagues Richard Puerzer, Natalie Datlof, and Athelene Collins. Richard and I will be the cochairs of "The 50th Anniversary of the New York Mets: A Conference at Hofstra University," which will be held at Hofstra on April 26, 27, and 28, 2012. Our conference, which will be open to the public, will be held under the auspices of the Hofstra Cultural Center, which is run so well by Natalie and Athelene.

Writing my book *Mets Fan* opened up a new and fascinating world to me. I've discovered a vibrant community of Mets writers, bloggers, and blog commenters. In this world, there seems to me to be a level of intelligent, passionate enthusiasm and mutual respect that I would love to see in all enterprises in which people appreciate and talk about something they love. I'd like to thank everyone I've encountered in this world, the people I've met and the people I only know through the Internet. I would particularly like to thank fellow Mets authors Jacob Kanarek, Greg Prince, Bill Ryczek, Matt Silverman, Greg Spira, and Jon Springer; fellow Mets bloggers Matt Cerrone, Taryn Cooper, Anthony de Rosa, Jason Fry, Steffi Kaplan, Steve Keane, Deb McIver, Zoe Rice, Caryn Rose, Mike Steffanos, and Dan Ziegler; journalists Mark Healy, Jason Maoz, Howard Megdal, Matt Pignataro, Mike Silva, and John Strubel; and Mets filmmakers Joe Coburn and Kathy Foronjy. I have also been literally blown away by the quality of the comments people have left on my own blog (Dana Brand's Mets Fan Blog, metsfanbook.com/blog), and I want to take this opportunity to thank such regular commenters as Anthony, Caitriona, Chris from Staten Island, Chris Collins, Dyhrdmet, JD, MetsMom, Nava, PB, Steve, Subie, Theresa, and Vicki. I also enjoy the many excellent posters I read on such forums as thehappy recap.com, grandslamsingle.com, metsrefugees.com, cranepoolforum .net, baseball-fever.com, and even, in spite of all the crap, on the Fan Forum at mets.com.

This book owes a great deal, and all Mets fans owe a great deal, to Lynn Cohen who has founded and runs Pitch In For a Good Cause, which allows fans to help support charities chosen by her husband, Gary, and his colleagues in the booth, Keith Hernandez and Ron Darling. Pitch In For a Good Cause has also helped to create a sense of fan connection to these three guys, who are the most consistently popular aspect of the New York Mets franchise. I will be forever grateful to Lynn for making it possible for me to take my mom to a last game at Shea. It's amazing how much Lynn gets done and how much care and generosity she offers to so many in the Mets community.

I am grateful to Gary Cohen for taking the time to have the conversation he had with me that serves as the foreword to this book. As the foreword makes clear, Gary is one of us, and this is one of the things that makes him so exceptional at what he does. I thank Gary, Ron Darling, Jerry Koosman, Jonathan Lethem, Phillip Lopate, and Howie Rose for their encouragement and for the extremely kind things they have said about *Mets Fan* and *The Last Days of Shea*.

My acknowledgments wouldn't be complete without an acknowledgment of the people I write about in my book. I am grateful to the millions of strangers whose voices joined with mine at Shea. I'm grateful to those who helped me make that building shake. I thank everyone who, in stadiums and living rooms all over the world, "hope beyond the bounds of reason, and love beyond the bounds of sense."

For Shea

The Mets, as I write, are building a new stadium in Flushing. It will be called Citi Field and it looks as if it will be very nice. It will be smaller than Shea and it will resemble Ebbets Field. It will have wider seats and more legroom. And the playing field will be closer to the stands. Like most Met fans, I am impressed. Like many Met fans, I am ambivalent.

I know that Shea doesn't deserve to be mourned. But I will miss it terribly. I remember when it was young, when it opened beside the World's Fair, when it was part of the City of the Future. Who was to know that the real future would prefer Ebbets Field? Shea was so hopeful, with its big and bright modernity. It was decorated with ruffled pieces of blue and orange metal that were eventually taken down. These were replaced by gigantic, fluid neon sketches of players in action, which I always thought were bright and lovely on their background of deep Mets blue. Shea looked all right on the outside, but nothing much could be done about all the bad ideas in the interior.

As soon as you walk into Shea, you don't know what you're inside of. You feel like you've been forgotten about, or perhaps eaten. Staircases, ramps, and escalators come out of nowhere, and you can't see what they're attached to. There are no focal points or spaces, just lit ads and posters that someone seems to have put up a long time ago.

Sure the seats and rows are cramped, but I like them. You feel as if you're in the middle of other people's lives. You hear their conversations, and nothing prevents you from joining them. You are along on the dates with the girls snuggling against the guys for warmth. The nut has to be lived with. The guy next to you on the edge of his seat can't sit still and therefore you can't either. At Shea you are attached to the crowd, physically and emotionally, and when people stand up and scream, you are pulled up with them because you can't pull away from them.

In the new stadium, I will probably like being closer to the action on the field. But I'm not really convinced that smaller is good. Try getting tickets for a game at Fenway. I like how big Shea is. I like it when it has 55,000 people in it. I like how noisy it can get. I like its awkward, incoherent immensity, which never feels oppressive because so many things at Shea are so silly, like Mr. Met and the apple in the hat and the t-shirt launches and Lou Monte singing "Lazy Mary" at the seventh-inning stretch. Shea has a personality. It is big and goofy and unsophisticated. It inspires the stadium characters who come and go over the years, who make themselves famous by holding up signs or beating cowbells. It inspires vendors and ushers to be characters. It inspires sentimentality and manic energy. It is very "New Yorky" in an old-fashioned way. The smaller, stylish stadium might preserve some of what Shea has. But I'll bet it won't be the same.

I love Shea. I can't help it. It's been a part of my life for over forty years. I will miss the name: a quick syllable. I will miss what I feel every time I approach the blue bowl wrapped in its web of highways. I love to drive into the parking lot, where people are picnicking just to be near it. I love it in the sun and the wind, and I love it when the lights have turned the nighttime into magical bright green daylight. And I love it when the Mets have won the game in their last turn at bat, when the echoing exit ramps vibrate with the voices of thousands of people who can't stop chanting and cheering.

However much I love it, I can't even hope to make an argument for keeping Shea. My only argument is a selfish one. I don't want a new stadium because it won't contain my memories. Part of the reason I go to Shea is to visit my memories. I remember my childhood birthdays. I remember Tommie Agee hitting a leadoff home run into the edge of the upper deck. I remember Clendenon's long swing and Piazza's short swing. I remember Seaver's rising fastball and Strawberry's first game. I remember the intimate emptiness of the stadium in the lean years and the urgent carnival atmosphere of the good years.

When I go to Shea, I feel as if I am visiting my father and several long-lost versions of my daughter. I visit all of the different eras of my life and all of the different teams and players who gave me so much happiness as I grew up and grew older. So many pieces of my life are connected by the fundamentally unchanging experience of a game at Shea. So much of what I have known and been seems held in the great curved embrace of the stands, in the rich green symmetry of the field, and in the chaos of girders and buttresses and bathrooms and frying food on the concourse behind the seats. So much of me is here, in this thing that can be torn down but can't be replaced.

Here is where all those seasons happened. Here is where we ran onto the field in 1969. Here is where the ball went through Buckner's legs. Shea is where I've been. I will miss it as I miss a parent or a grandparent. I know it has to go. But I wish it could have been there for all of my life. I will endure its passing, but I would have loved to have been an old man in these seats, under these lights.

From *Mets Fan* © 2007 Dana Brand by permission of McFarland & Company Inc., Box 611, Jefferson, NC 28640, www.mcfarlandpub.com.

The Second-to-Last Home Opener

It's 10:15 a.m. on April 9, 2007. It's a beautiful morning, with that bright Queens morning sunlight that seems just off the ocean. I get my first glimpse of Shea from the Whitestone Expressway. It is so big. So permanent-looking, like the Roman Colosseum. And it won't be there two years from now, when I am driving on this same road. I will have to summon its bulk in my imagination. How can something as big as this disappear?

I get off at my usual Northern Boulevard exit, wondering what the parking situation is going to be. I see the cranes right up against Shea. I see why they're called cranes. They have the same sloping grace as the birds. They seem etched against the morning sky. I follow the signs, which take me to the lot on the shore of Flushing Bay. The lot is filled with bundled people hopping from foot to foot, holding beers, eating hamburgers, standing in clusters of friends and relatives. It is three hours before the game. I park somewhere I won't have to worry about running over a hibachi.

I get out of my car and walk towards the passageway under the expressway. I enjoy the smells of the burgers, dogs, and thick sausages. I enjoy all of these happy people in the windy cold. I too love the names and numbers they wear on their backs. I love the smell of their grilling meat.

On the shore of the bay, I see the futuristic bus shelters left over from the 1964–1965 World's Fair. They are so beautiful. They look like white birds of the future poised to take flight. In 1964 nobody paid much attention to them. Nobody pays any attention to them now. But they have outlasted the fair, and now they will outlast Shea. I wonder how many people walking past them even know what they are.

1

When I pass under the expressway, I am near gate A. I get as close as I can to the walled-in construction site. They are working today. Nothing stops, not even out of respect. I see towers built out of slabs of concrete. Their tops are secured with orange metal beams. There are yellow scaffolds and wooden railings. Slowly and carefully, like dinosaur robots, the big cranes feed things to men on the tops of the towers.

Along the rim of Shea I see and hear the wheezing trailers. I see the parked news vans with their big dishes. There are the ambulances at the ready, the traffic barriers soaked in the deepest Mets blue. There is the 7 train snaking along its elevated tracks. There is Mr. Met posing for pictures with fans. He swings his arms with that genial swagger he always has. He's accompanied by a group of young people in Pepsi t-shirts with their names on the back. Are they his handlers, his bodyguards, his entourage? Herb and Danielle and the rest just stand around and smile at the big man. Everybody is happy to see him. A guy walks by in a jester hat, with a t-shirt that says "No. 1 Yankee Hater." All kinds of people are entering the gates of the stadium now. There are families and groups of friends and single guys in bulging jackets and glasses and ski caps.

Inside the stadium, I pass the long line of people waiting to get into the team store. I walk right down to the field and sit in a cushioned seat, from which I can see the Mets' general manager, Omar Minaya, working the crowd. The man is so cool. He's so handsome and charismatic. He looks as pleased to be here as Mr. Met. People are as happy to see him as they are to see Mr. Met. He's as famous as Mr. Met. But he offers a very different impression. Mr. Met lets you know that you will always be a Mets fan, that you have no choice, that you are a simple being. Omar suggests to you that the people who are in charge of this show know what they're doing. The dumb loyalty you've always had to Mr. Met is going to be rewarded.

Batting practice is finally over, and it is time to leave this portion of the stadium where I never sit, where there are plaques with names on seats that make you feel as if you're in a church or a cemetery. I go up to the loge and see the big new wall of computer-faked pictures of Citi Field. I see a mysterious little clubhouse labeled "Citifield" with a doorman and a big leather sofa and flat screens and buffet tables. I go to section 9, hoping to get my usual kosher hot dog with sauerkraut and my knish, and standing in the empty space, I smack my forehead, remembering that it is still Passover. So I get some Nathan's franks that taste nothing like the Nathan's franks I remember from the Coney Island of my childhood. There are no knishes, and you can't even get sauerkraut to put on your hot dog. Why is the food so lousy at Shea, in the greatest food city in the world? It had better be different in that new little yuppie stadium they're building.

I go up the escalators with my box of food, my open Diet Pepsi bottle wedged between my not-warm-enough pretzel and my "Nathan's" franks. I find section 4 in the upper deck and climb all the way up to my seat in row Q, to the pounding rhythms of Starship's "We Built This City." I wonder why they play this. We're not playing San Francisco. Do they know that there was recently a survey that named this the worst song of all time? Obviously not. So I'm carrying this lousy lunch to eat, listening to this lousy music, on my way to my seat, which may be the worst I've ever sat in at a game. It is freezing cold. This is a real Shea experience. There is a perfect storm of misery here. And I am so happy I can hardly contain myself.

From so high up, I really get a perspective on the construction site. I see how many towers there are. One of them looks medieval, like something out of which knights would shoot arrows. I see the network of saffron girders connecting the towers. I see the ground that has been buried in obscurity under the asphalt of the parking lot for forty-five years. Soon it will be a field on which championships will be won. I see the workers milling around, and I see how the rhythm of a busy construction site is set by the slow grand motion of the cranes. What is most surprising is how close the new stadium is to the one in which we are waiting for the game. It's right up against it, crowding it. Next year, the big blank space to the left of the scoreboard will be filled with the new stadium. Shea will be completely closed in.

The Opening Day ceremonies begin as the Copiague and Lindenhurst high school marching bands, looking like toy soldiers, start coming out of the center field fence. They play what we can recognize way high up as "Meet the Mets" and "Take Me Out to the Ball Game," and so we clap and cheer in appreciation. When they're done, some Mets sprint into center field, their uniforms white and bright against the green waffle pattern of the grass. Then Howie Rose in a suit, behind home plate and up on the Diamond Vision, starts announcing the Phillies. We lustily boo their video coordinator and their assistant clubhouse manager until we realize that we need to start conserving our boos for the real Phillies, who actually seem to enjoy the boos we finally give them and doff their caps to us. Then we cheer wildly for the Mets personnel, with a bit of hesitation about the visiting clubhouse manager. Howard Johnson, our old left fielder who's just been hired as a coach, gets a hearty welcome back, and everything that the sound system says about the real Mets is drowned in a continuous cascade of cheering. Some cadets in white from the Merchant Marine Academy march in like a centipede looking really spooky, carrying a big flag. Michael Amante offers a very histrionic Star-Spangled Banner, his pant legs fluttering in the wind. After a couple of minutes waiting for an announced fly over, two fighter jets anticlimactically zoom over the stadium. Keith Hernandez throws out the first ball. Hojo catches it. Us older folk get sentimental. The new New York Mets take the field. And Jimmy Rollins, who just last week announced (outrageously!) that the Phillies were the team to beat in the NL East in 2007, leads off the game. He grounds out to the delight of everyone assembled.

The game is interesting and exciting, although it is kind of hard to watch. It's freezing and all of us were prepared for that, so we're all bundled up like the Michelin man, taking up a lot of space. Plus we're bouncing up and down to keep warm, so the stands are filled with bouncing muffled people rubbing against each other. I think of getting peanuts but I decide not to. Everyone who is eating anything is bumping into everybody around them. Our pitcher, John Maine, doesn't look like he has very much, but he is avoiding disasters. He leaves before five innings are over. The game is close. We could win it or we could lose it. The crowd is psyched, but its enthusiasm isn't confident. They lead, then we lead, then they tie it, then we go ahead again. Then there is a perfect sour silence when Ryan Howard hits a three-run home run off of Ambiorix Burgos.

Not happy. Time is running out. It's still fun to be at Opening Day. Not much is new between innings or in Shea itself. There is a big Dunkin' Donuts coffee cup in the visiting bullpen. That's it except for all of the looming, chaotic newness visible beyond the scoreboard. As the game unwinds nervously, you can't help but watch the construction that continues through the afternoon. What a view. What a mess. Expressways crossing grasslands and a grey river. Big brick apartment houses looking like broad-shouldered robots with little square heads. Piles of dirt and other stuff. Chop shops. The U-Haul building that was once the zipper factory, with its graceful green tower like a ghost from another age. Our view. Our mess. What will we see from the new stands? The seats will be wider, so we won't rub against each other on cold April afternoons. Will we see anything?

Behind 5-4, the Mets open the eighth inning with singles by Moises Alou and Shawn Green. Julio Franco walks to load the bases, and then Jimmy Rollins can't handle a ground ball hit by Jose Reyes. The crowd enjoys this and the heavens open. There's a wild pitch and then a walk and then another walk and David Wright hits a double and Moises Alou comes up a second time in the inning to hit another single. What is like a seven-run inning when eleven men come to the plate?! The runs just come and come and we all stand and yell and clap for all that remains of the game. This is a good home opener. It is filled with happy omens. It's clear that we don't need to fear Philadelphia. Atlanta's had a good first week. We fear Atlanta. None of this makes any sense, but that's how we feel now. How good this team is! This team will always have life. It will always do well. And it won't always be this cold.

Then there is the traditional victory romp down the ramps. We sing "Jimmy Rollins!" "Jimmy Rollins!" We showed him. We showed the Phillie Phanatic, who is now dangled from a ramp with a noose around his neck. Strangers slap each other's hands. We do the Jose chant. And "Lets Go Mets." We insult the Yankees and the Phillies with the usual well-worn verb. We see the afternoon gleam on the cars in the parking lot. We see the skyscrapers of Manhattan, grey and purplish, off to the west.

I walk all the way back to my car in a piercing wind off the water. The smoky picnics pick up where they left off hours ago. I join a long, slow line to leave the lot, and I open my window several times to slap the gloved hands of my happy, cheering, stumbling friends.

56,227

Between the seventh and eighth inning of the 2007 home opener, the Diamond Vision announced that the attendance in the stadium was 56,227. We were the largest Opening Day crowd in Mets history. They didn't mention this, but I thought of how we would forever rank first or second on the list of the largest crowds for a Mets home opener.

Can you imagine those 56,227 people all bundled up, cheering, freezing, and happy? Do you see them all around me up in row Q of the upper deck? Now imagine the entire upper deck sliced off and everyone in it dumped into Flushing Bay.

That's Citi Field.

According to every account, the new stadium was going to be everything Shea was not. It would be pretty, intimate, and cozy. Everyone would be close to the field because there were only going to be 42,500 seats. Now think of the 13,000 people swimming in the freezing bay.

What was in that Citi Field clubhouse near section 13 in the loge? What was the story with the doorman and the ceremonial silver shovel? When I pressed my face against the window like a Victorian street urchin, I could see deep into the enclosure. I saw a nice big room with flat screen TVs, steam tables with a buffet, and cookies and desserts. Who was this for?

As I watched the construction during the game and saw how Shea was being boxed in, I felt so bad for my dear, sweet old friend. As its replacement was being built, it was trying its best to entertain us. Maybe it was hoping for a reprieve. "Look," it said to us, "look, I can make this apple go up and down!" It showed us all of its old, worn tricks.

Cruelly, at the end of the 2008 season, after we'd had our cry, they were going to turn out Shea's lights and pluck out its parts to sell to collectors. Then they'd bring over cranes and a wrecking ball to smash whatever no one wanted.

Let's not dwell on that, the Mets say. Let's show everyone the Citi Field video between the innings! We watch a video narrated by some guy with a Hal-type voice who extols the new stadium. It reminds me of the propaganda film in Woody Allen's "Sleeper" that glorifies "our leader" and teaches us what's wrong with "The Underground." Surely the new stadium will be good for us all. We are all elevated by quality, not quantity. The largest National League city should have the smallest National League stadium. Middle-class people don't need to see as many playoff or opening day games or crucial down-the-stretch games as they've seen in the past. The Mets could use a little exclusivity. Didn't some of those tailgate parties strike you as a little dicey? At least caviar doesn't have to be cooked.

Don't show me the stupid video. Keep that baby Death Star away from me just a little while longer. I love Shea. I accept that it has to be replaced. But I hate that after the 2008 season, and for the rest of my life, there will never be a Mets crowd as big as this one.

The Curveball

For all that Mets fans enjoyed the 2007 home opener, we were still haunted by the final pitch of the 2006 season. Adam Wainwright, of the St. Louis Cardinals, had thrown a two-strike curveball to Carlos Beltran. Beltran did not swing. He saw that the pitch was high and waited for it to pass. He was waiting for the next pitch, the historic pitch, the pennant-bearing pitch. The high curve, already taken, already in the past, approached the plate at the level of Beltran's eyes. Then it fell. It dropped, like a bomb from a plane. It fell from the sky and the 2006 season was over.

In 2006, the Mets won ninety-seven games and their first division title in nineteen years. They swept the Dodgers in the first round of the playoffs. They went into the National League Championship Series (NLCS) as heavy favorites. But then, after a couple of bullpen collapses and a horrific five-run first third of an inning from Steve Trachsel, a veteran pitcher fighting to save his marriage, the inferior Cardinals had the superior Mets on the ropes, with two games to play in New York.

I still believed in my team. And after seeing the sixth game at Shea with my own eyes, having felt the upper deck bounce as I stood on it with tens of thousands of screaming people, I thought that the Mets would pull it out. By the time we reached the ninth inning of the seventh game, Endy Chavez's catch, perhaps the greatest Mets catch ever, had saved us. Oliver Perez had also saved us, giving up only one run in the seven innings he pitched. I trusted Aaron Heilman, who came in to pitch in the eighth, because I had every reason to. He had a terrific year in 2006. Then Yadier Molina hit a two-run homer off Heilman in the top of the ninth. Still, I believed that it was 1986 and not 1988. The Mets loaded the bases in the ninth with one out, and two fine hitters, Cliff Floyd and Carlos Beltran, were ready to come to the plate to give us a Bobby Thompson moment. Hope was alive until the last fraction of a second, when the curveball dropped and everything suddenly and finally took the form it would always have.

If the 2006 Mets had played a hundred games against the 2006 Cardinals, they would have won sixty or seventy. But they only played seven. And they had lost four. The 2006 NLCS, so close to having been won, would always be lost, just like the 1988 NLCS or the 2000 World Series.

Twenty years minus one week before Wainwright's pitch, the Mets had won their last World Championship. I felt those twenty years as a presence in my living room when I choked off my remote control on October 19, 2006. I wondered what I would have felt if I had known, at thirty-two, that the Mets would not win a World Championship in the next two decades. Would I waste twenty years hoping for something that wouldn't happen? Let's say I could talk to the thirty-two-year-old guy who had seen Mookie Wilson's grounder bounce between Bill Buckner's legs only two nights before. What would I say to him? What I'd want to tell him is that hoping and dreaming justify themselves. They are a pleasure, even if you never get what you want. To hope and dream, you need the idea of success. But you don't need success itself.

He already knew this. I remember that he knew this. He was a Mets fan and he had been one for twenty-five years.

As I sat in my living room at the end of the 2006 season, I asked myself what I ask myself all the time. How could baseball be worth the attention I have given it for so many years? How could it be worth the emotions I have felt for it? Many things in life are worthy of my attention. If I felt nothing for my family, if I didn't care about my career, my health, and my good fortune, my life would be much worse. But what difference would it possibly make if I suddenly decided to ignore baseball?

Look, life is filled with things you don't have to do or care about. Nobody has to listen to music, or look at art, or read a book, or walk in the woods, or care about someone else's problem, or taste food. You don't even have to love the people you love. You don't have to work where you work or live where you live or do what you do for a living. Some things are more important than other things, but everything is optional. Everything is a ride you don't have to go on. If you wanted to, you could sit and watch everything from a bench. You could listen to the screams from the roller coaster. You could watch the kids get sick from spinning around. Or you could get on the ride yourself.

Baseball is a ride I get on. It's like a lot of other things in my life. No sense of triumph justifies it and no sense of loss discredits it. It lifts me up. It drops me down. It is something I do, one of the things I live for.

Baseball is also something I share with millions of other people. Friends of mine who were at Shea for the seventh game of the 2006 NLCS tell me that they had never seen anything like the love, kindness, and sympathy that Mets fans shared at the end of that game. Even though I wasn't at Shea, I did feel that all of us were together at that moment. I had the feeling I always have at the great moments of Mets history. I feel as if I'm flying over New York with its roofs off, past apartment blocks and brownstones and long rows of small houses and suburbs spreading to the horizon. I feel as if I'm looking into the living rooms and seeing all the Mets fans in their clusters of family and friends, everyone with snacks and drinks and Mets regalia, everyone feeling the same thing at the same moment. Although the season ended with me in my living room, with just my daughter, my pretzels, and my beer, I felt as if I were with millions of people.

What sense does this make? This wasn't 9/11. This didn't qualify as a unifying triumph or misfortune. Nothing important had been lost, as it is in a war or an election. This was only the end of a winning baseball season that ended one out short of the World Series. Why value an experience like this? If something doesn't really matter, does the fact that millions of people care about it make it matter?

I don't know. I love to be with people who have the same memories I have of the New York Mets, who respond as I do to some names and numbers and events in the past, who share new things with me, as they happen. People who share these things with me are not entirely strangers, even if I have never seen them before, even if I will never meet them. I sit in the crowd at a Mets game and look around me and think, "I don't know any of these people!" Yet they are my *paysans*, my *landsmen*, my homies. This big, colorful bowl is our village. And so are all of these screens on our laps and in our living rooms with their pictures and words. I love this.

This is a good village. It's better, in lots of ways, than a real village. There's just a connection, not a lifelong interdependence. A village this big and abstract can never be a prison. While it's a part of your life, it doesn't consume or determine it. You don't really hate your rivals from other villages. You know it's all just a game. Your triumphs don't actually cost anyone anything. Your losses don't deprive you of happiness, food, freedom, or life. It's not a problem that baseball isn't real. One of the best things about baseball is that it isn't real, but it still lets you feel real love and real hope.

Real love and real hope about something that isn't real? Sure. Haven't you ever enjoyed a movie, a book, a TV show, a Broadway musical, or an opera? Baseball is part of a web of unreal things that are important to all of us. It's a story that engages us. It touches the deep things all stories touch. But no one tells it, no one controls it, and no one makes it up ahead of time. Like life, it just happens, but like a story, it is only as real as we allow it to be. It has all the indeterminacy of reality and all of the splendor of the imagined.

In this way, baseball is wonderful. And it is wonderful even when it is disappointing. But to be wonderful even when it's disappointing, baseball has to promise that someday you may have a season that is not disappointing. It offers this promise every year. Every year, I find bright shiny new reasons to hope, just as when I was a kid, I would find a stack of bright brand new pennies on top of my dresser when my grandparents came to visit. I enjoyed the twenty Mets seasons after 1986. I enjoyed them because I knew what they might have brought me but didn't. I enjoyed trying to have it, even if I didn't get it. I enjoyed the 2006 season, even though the Mets did not win the pennant. They did not win the 2006 World Series. They did not even play in it. But they almost did.

Wait Till Next Year

The ultimate goal of every baseball team in every season is to win the World Series. This is supposed to be what you're waiting for when you "wait till next year." In the 2006 World Series, the Cardinals went on to achieve their goal, beating the Detroit Tigers in five games. People must have been very happy in St. Louis and very sad in Detroit. In greater New York, I didn't watch the Series. I am not proud of this. I am a baseball fan and not just a Mets fan. But I did not have the stomach to watch the 2006 Series. I usually watch the Series if I can invent some temporary enthusiasm for one of the teams. Under ordinary circumstances, I could have become enthusiastic about the Tigers, who had gone from lousy to wonderful in a single year, just like the 1969 Mets. But I couldn't watch the Series after this Mets season. All I would have felt is that the Mets were missing.

Even after the Cardinals beat the Tigers in the Series, I refused to be impressed by them. They had also beaten the Mets. Yet the outcome of the Series did not alter the fact that the Mets and the Tigers were both better teams than the Cardinals. The 2006 Cardinals could only manage, during the regular season, to win four more games than they lost. The Mets had won thirty-two more games than they had lost. The Tigers had won twenty-eight more games than they had lost. The Cardinals won it all by getting hot at just the right time. Sure, their postseason victories were meaningful, but it didn't seem to me that they were more meaningful than the fact that the Mets had won ninety-seven games in the regular season and the Cardinals had just won eighty-three. The World Series was a joke. It was always a joke. The best team in baseball rarely wins the World Series.

If I thought that the World Series was a joke, why did I care so much about the Mets being in it? If the Mets had won the World

Series in 1973, it would not have meant that they were better than the 1973 Oakland A's. But it would have mattered a great deal to me. If Bill Buckner had fielded the famous baseball to keep the game tied and the Red Sox had won it with a rally in the top of the eleventh inning, I would not have thought that the 1986 Red Sox were better than the Mets. But I would have felt my misfortune deeply.

Whether we like it or not, the World Series means something. I don't think of 2000 as the year in which the Mets won the pennant and won seven more games than the Yankees did in the regular season. I think of it as the year the Mets lost the World Series to the Yankees in five games. This is how the World Series matters. It determines what you're going to feel and what you're going to remember by providing the end of the story of every season. Endings revise the way you feel about the beginning and the middle of any story.

Yet like a story, baseball is never just about what happens at the end. Think about National League baseball and great National League teams in the past two decades. Do you remember Atlanta's astounding and unprecedented decade and a half of dominance? Do you remember the great Astros teams of the late 1990s built around Bagwell, Biggio, and Alou; the great Cardinals teams with and without McGwire; the great Giants teams around Bonds and Kent? How about Arizona's few years in the spotlight with their one-two pitching punch of Johnson and Schilling? Or the four exciting years the Mets had from 1997 to 2000?

Quick! What National League team has won more World Series than any other in the 1990s and 2000s? The Florida Marlins. What does this tell you? What does this mean? Do you remember more about the Marlins and their glory than you remember about these other teams? Are you likely to tell your grandchildren that the turn of the millennium was the era of the Marlins?

I started following baseball in 1962. When I think back on National League baseball in the period between the first year of the Mets and their first World Championship, I cherish my memories of all the great teams: the Giants with Mays and McCovey; the Braves with Aaron and Matthews; the Pirates with Clemente, Stargell, and Clendenon; the Reds with Robinson, Rose, and Pinson. How many World Series do you think the Giants, Braves, Pirates, and Reds combined to win between 1962 and 1969? The answer is zero. Zip. Does that make those legendary teams any less legendary? The Dodgers and the Cardinals did win World Series in this period, because of their overpowering pitching, but when I remember that era, the Dodgers and the Cardinals are just part of the mix. Their World Series victories don't erase, they don't even dim my memories of these other great teams that didn't win the Series.

The World Series isn't everything. But it's something. Making a big deal of winning the World Series is a necessary fiction. You have to have goals. You have to have an occasion for the release of your emotions at full pitch. It's not enough to win or lose a poll of sports writers. It is not enough to have the highest number of anything. You have to have a decisive final moment that is either positive or negative. And then the decisive moments stay there forever, in your memory. They don't dim, and they radiate through the rest of your life. You crave moments like this, and the energy of craving them is wonderful, even if there is always a voice in the back of your head that mutters, "What the hell is this?" Even if there is a voice that asks, "So what if that curveball had hung and Beltran had hit it over the center field wall? Why should such a small change in what happened make so much of a difference?" Maybe it shouldn't make so much of a difference. But it does.

The great 2006 Mets season ended with disappointment. It ended with a sense that once again, we had to wait. But it was not enough for us to wait and to hope. As soon as the season ended, Mets fans began to clamor for the "big move" that would bring us our third World Championship. All day and night, the Internet and sports radio were filled with numbingly repetitive analyses of the team's "weaknesses." The Mets, everyone determined after a few minutes of thought and weeks on end of discussion, were in need of younger and more durable starting pitching, more bench strength, and one more decent hitter playing either in left field or at second base. We had a couple of ways to go. There were all these things Omar could do. And so the long, dreary off-season began.

Making It Through the Off-season

For a baseball fan who is not a football, basketball, or hockey fan, the first part of the off-season is boring. The leaves are off the trees, the sun slips wearily along the edge of the horizon, and it is dark most of the time. Between the end of the World Series and the arrival of pitchers and catchers at training camps in Florida, you can only think of what you don't have. All you can do is dream of the pleasure of warm evenings lit to a brightness beyond imagining in which titanically gifted grown men play a child's game for your pleasure.

The first major baseball news event of the off-season is something they call the winter meetings. I have always loved the idea of the winter meetings. You imagine general managers bundled in bright colored jackets and scarves, arriving in a fairy-tale village to discuss trades over eggnog in cozy taverns in front of roaring fires. I know that this is not what the winter meetings look like, but what the hell.

Nothing happened for the Mets during the winter meetings of 2006. Just before the winter meetings, the Mets signed forty-year-old free agent Moises Alou, but that was it. This is when the more impatient Mets fans started getting angry at Omar Minaya and the Wilpons, who owned the team, for not making any bold moves. This is when they started calling the more patient Mets fans all kinds of names like "loser" and "complacent" and the rest of it. Their discontent got worse when the Mets only made a token, flaccid bid for the player who was being billed as the mysterious Japanese pitching wizard, Daisuke Matsuzaka.

The Matsuzaka thing was fun to watch in the way that the hyping of Japanese ballplayers is always fun to watch. It should be clear to everyone by now that Japanese ballplayers, like American ballplayers or Dominican ballplayers, are merely human, with a wide range of abilities, and with skills and methods that are not very different from those that players from other countries might have. But every time there's the prospect of a Japanese superstar coming to the American big leagues, you get a sense, from the press reports, that you're right back in the days of traveling circuses and the mysterious cabinet that holds the mysteries of the Orient. Once again we heard about a ballplayer with the discipline of a samurai, who had developed strange pitches never before seen in the West, who would slice through a thick, meaty American lineup the way John Belushi used to slice the sushi in the Samurai Sushi sketch. The Mets were not sucked in. The Yankees made a serious play. The Red Sox bought.

The next big off-season spectacle was Barry Zito. If the Mets couldn't get the mysteries of the Orient, we could surely sign a pitcher who'd had a spectacular Cy Young season a few years ago and had more recently settled into a groove just north of mediocrity. Zito was undeniably the best pitcher on the free agent market who had actually pitched in the Major Leagues already. The Mets had the money for him. But working against us were the rumors that he was a real dyed-in-the-wool California guy. If the Mets were going to sign Zito, they had to figure out how to sell New York to a laid-back space cadet. They didn't put it precisely in these terms, but this was what was implied.

Earnest, New York–loving Virginian David Wright immediately offered to take Zito on a tour of New York to show him what a great place it was. A tour? Pitching all those years for the Oakland A's, hadn't he ever been here before? Isn't there an American League team in New York?

The offer by Wright was ballyhooed in the press as a kind of Mets tradition. Whenever the Mets try to sign someone who might not be a "New York guy," there's always talk about taking the player on a tour of New York to show him what a great or what a normal place it is (this depends on the player; some want great and some apparently prefer normal). According to legend, Rusty Staub helped us to hook Keith Hernandez in this way. Rusty showed Keith how wonderful the restaurants were, how terrific Broadway was, and how beautiful the women were (no one will ever know what was involved in this last bit of the tour).

Keith had played in the National League for several years at this point. He had undoubtedly been to New York. Presumably he had some idea of what it had to offer. Don't ask me how this tour could have sealed the deal. But we've always been told that it did.

Some players, usually with families, are thought to be afraid of New York. So Tom Glavine, for instance, got the "don't be afraid, your families will not be killed" tour. Like many people from outside the city, a lot of ballplayers think that New York is always as crowded, bizarre, and insane as it is around Christmastime on that one block between the tree and the Rockettes. They need to be convinced of something Phil Simms once said: that once you get outside of the craziness of the city itself, the New York metropolitan area is really not that much different from anywhere else. Phil, alas, is absolutely right. But it seems that a lot of people and a lot of baseball players think this is a good thing. They think that if you get away from all the hustle and bustle (what they like to call "the insanity") and raise kids in the normal America that begins right outside the city, the kids will not be corrupted. They will not be in danger. People who think this either have never been adolescents in American suburbs or they have forgotten what it was like.

I read all the articles about what the Mets were up against in the Zito case. If the articles were accurate, Zito was, by baseball standards, an eccentric (he did yoga, burned incense, and once dyed his hair blue). His apartment didn't have furniture, only foldable lawn chairs. I couldn't help but wonder why a guy like this needed the $16 million a year the Mets were reportedly willing to pay him.

I hoped that someone would tell Barry Zito that New York was a city that had always welcomed eccentrics. He could live in Greenwich Village, and unlike most eccentrics, he could actually afford to. Did he like music? There was a lot of great music in New York. And there really are all of the beautiful women Rusty found for Keith. If Barry Zito married one of the beautiful women, he could move to Connecticut and have kids. If he did, I could show him where to get furniture to replace the lawn chairs.

Zito signed a six-year contract with the San Francisco Giants for $18 million a year. I was happy that the Mets had not signed such a dumb contract. But the Mets starting pitching was still a question mark. It was obvious that Omar wanted to wait until the end of spring training to see what he had.

He took more crap for this from people who could not bear the thought that the Mets would enter the 2007 season without a contract from God indicating that they had a 90 percent chance of winning the World Series. In the end, though, Omar got relatively little crap. The success of the 2006 season had earned Omar the respect of everyone in the fan base who wasn't either insane or racist. I looked at the team and I was content. The guys liked each other, and with last year under their belt, they would play even better as a team in 2007. Of course the Mets had needs, but so did everyone else. What might have helped us was ridiculously overpriced. And anything we might have gotten would not have banished uncertainty. Omar was willing to go with this team. I was with him.

The Team

Fans put together their idea of their baseball team by watching the team play, and by watching them celebrate. We take into account such factors as how the guys came to the team and what they said to reporters when it was clear they were coming. We believe that candid views of the dugout on TV during a game can tell us if a team has chemistry, and that they can show us the degree to which one guy or another is important "in the clubhouse." Lots of articles are written about the players and their character and their importance to the team. Fans know that many of these articles are inaccurate and unfair, but we're never in much of a position to determine which ones are and which ones aren't. Because we know that so many of the articles are unfair, we feel that we have the right to choose to believe the ones that we want to believe and disregard the ones that we don't.

Each individual fan's idea of a team is a mosaic of personal choices. I have my own idea of the extraordinarily wonderful 1986 New York Mets. I didn't believe then and I don't believe now certain things that have been written about them. It's not as if I don't believe what people who know more than me have written. It's just that what they've written is not relevant to my life-long love affair with a talented and interesting baseball team that I saw win 116 ballgames.

The personal freedom the fan has to make his or her own team is the reason why, whenever you get a group of fans together, there will often be different opinions about the team. When a team is playing well, there is inevitably more unanimity about the character of the team and the players. In good times, reporters and fans are less likely to be trying to find the guy whose lack of some personal quality is holding down run production. Players who are a little different from other players are always a particularly important part of a fan's idea of a team. These guys are said to give a team "character" by making it easier to distinguish the team from other teams. In good times, the press and the fans focus on the "stories" the team generates, the stories that are supposed to reach their climax, or at least their next stage, in the coming season. When you start gearing up again for baseball in February, every new season feels like a bunch of stories that are restless to get out of the gate and start running down the track. In February and March, we reacquaint ourselves with the stories we'll be following, and we try to develop our own idea of the characters in them. We also like to make ourselves comfortable with the new team by finding the ways in which it reminds us of teams we've rooted for in the past. Each year, I make a Mets team for myself. And then, with the resources of memory, I make them the Mets.

Going into the 2007 season, I was very happy with the Mets. Along with other positive fans, my idea of them was illustrated by the appealing celebration we saw when they clinched the 2006 NL East division title. The team we saw through the spraying champagne that night was obviously a unit—of young guys and old guys, quiet guys and loud guys—who loved and enjoyed each other. The single most resonant image was that of David Wright and Jose Reyes with their arms around each other's necks, champagne bottles in their hands, a cigar in David's mouth, running out onto the field to spray champagne on fans who would not leave the stadium. We saw this and were determined to see it again, and there was every reason to expect that we would.

Wright and Reyes were the nucleus of the Mets in most of our minds. There was no doubt that they were fabulously talented. At the age of twenty-four, Wright had already established himself as one of the most versatile offensive players anyone had seen in a long time. He was a hitter like Stan Musial. He might not ever win the Triple Crown, but no one would get any closer than he would. Reyes was a completely unique ballplayer. In recent memory, there hadn't been a leadoff, switch-hitting, superb defensive shortstop who could run so fast and hit so well and with so much power. Jose was a player with so many talents that he encouraged you to let your imagination run wild thinking of statistical combinations he could achieve (homers, steals, doubles, triples, average, slugging percentage, etc.) that no one had ever accomplished before. Each of these appealing young men would make it into the Hall of Fame if he could stay healthy and stable. And the two of them were particularly important to the identity of the Mets because they had both emerged from our farm system at roughly the same time. In this way, they were a recurrence of an ancient Mets pattern. They were like Seaver and Koosman, or Gooden and Strawberry. One of the great pleasures of being a fan of a team is seeing something happen again that reminds you of something that made you happy long ago. Once again, twin superstars were rising at a very young age from our soil to lead us to greatness and promise us a decade of dominance.

It helped, of course, that both Wright and Reyes were so appealing as characters. David Wright was earnest, handsome, and pleasant. You could see how young he was in the way he was so restless, in the way in which all of his features were in constant motion at the plate. But then there was always the surprise of his mature swing, his steady and superb success as a hitter. Jose Reyes had strikingly expressive eyes and an immense smile. He had a way of always seeming amused by his extraordinary play. He had a way of looking as if he knew he was getting away with something. David and Jose were fine. We had no doubts of any kind about them, and we merely wondered, if they were so good so young, just how good they were going to get.

Another crucial component of the identity of our team was the several Hall of Fame–level veteran Hispanic players who had been attracted to our team by the legendary personal talents of Omar Minaya, who was the first Hispanic general manager in baseball history. Carlos Beltran and Pedro Martinez had been signed as free agents and had renewed the team's credibility when they came to the Mets in 2005. The fact that they had come at least in part because of Omar, and the fact that the Mets had been tolerant and far-sighted enough to appoint Omar, took some of the taint off of the fact that the team had improved by signing a pair of very expensive free agents. Free agents are an unavoidable part of the game of baseball, but if a rich, big-market team like the Mets signs too many of them, it can diminish the pleasure a fan takes in a team's success. Beltran was a shy, vulnerable man who had needed a season to get used to New York, but once he did, he played quietly and consistently at a level anyone else would have needed to struggle to reach. Pedro had a fine season and a half, but was going to be on the disabled list for most of the 2007 season. One of the stories we needed to follow in 2007 was whether or not Pedro would return. Would he lead us into the playoffs, or would he be in the end like Moses? Would he have led us out of the desert only to have us enter the Promised Land without him? In addition to having brought us Beltran and Martinez, Omar was credited with having made possible the trade that brought us the great Carlos Delgado. Delgado, in 2006, had been the anchor of our lineup and our clubhouse. He was a preternaturally calm and self-assured lefty slugger with a beautiful swing, great intelligence, consistency, and power. Delgado, Martinez, and Tom Glavine gave our team a gravitas that balanced so beautifully the sublime fire of youth in Wright and Reyes.

The rest of the roster was filled with interesting, talented people. There was our catcher, hot-headed fan favorite Paul Lo Duca, who was plausibly replacing the beloved Mike Piazza. There was tall, handsome chess-playing Shawn Green, who just might solve the mystery of the disappearance of his forty-homer-a-year power swing. A lot of fans didn't like him, but I loved the overenthusiastic kid Lastings Milledge, who wasn't ready for prime time but really wanted to be there. I loved the way he danced and celebrated when he wasn't supposed to. I loved the way he didn't care if he pissed people off. He was fun. He was unusual. He was interesting.

Paternal Tom Glavine, at forty-one, was our ace. And his contemporary, Orlando "El Duque" Hernandez, was right behind him in the rotation. But alongside these two guys over forty, the Mets' starting pitching staff had three developing pitchers in their early to mid-twenties. John Maine had proven himself in a strong half-season, after having come to the Mets as a throw-in in the trade that got rid of Kris Benson and his wife. Oliver Perez, who had had a near Cy Young–level season a couple of years ago at the age of twenty-two, had come to the Mets after Pittsburgh gave up on him. He pitched poorly, but all Mets fans were still excited by what should have been his pennant-winning heroic performance in the seventh game of the 2006 NLCS. Maine and Perez contributed to Omar Minaya's considerable mystique. We had gotten them for nothing because their other teams had not seen in them what Omar saw. And Omar, as always, had been right. Twenty-three-year-old Mike Pelfrey was the Mets' best pitching prospect. An enormous kid, 6'7", with a fastball approaching 100 miles per hour, he would take Pedro's spot in the rotation.

The Mets' middle relief had been an integral part of the team's success in 2006, and it promised to be even better in 2007 with the addition of the experienced Scott Schoeneweis. Duaner Sanchez, who had injured his shoulder in a taxicab accident at two in the morning on his way to get a pizza, would be coming back. There was nothing not to like about our closer Billy Wagner, the self-proclaimed and very articulate redneck whose premier season with the Mets in 2006 was worthy of the great Mets relief tradition of McGraw, Orosco, McDowell, and Franco.

This team had won ninety-seven games in 2006. When you win ninety-seven games, you're good enough to win the World Series. If you win eighty-three games, you're good enough to win the World Series. With new additions Moises Alou and Luis Castillo, the development of Pelfrey, and the steadying of Perez, the Mets could win a hundred games in 2007, even without Pedro for most of the year. There hadn't been much off-season activity, but there hadn't been much need for any. This group of guys was already a team. They still seemed to have the magnificent spirit that had taken them so far in 2006. This was the same group of friends who looked so happy to be playing together and washing their faces in champagne on the glorious night they clinched the title. They still had their calm yet sometimes disconcertingly creative manager Willie Randolph. They still had their pitching coach, Rick Peterson, with his reputed ability to turn discarded Honda Civics into Ferraris. The flukes that had tilted the 2006 Championship Series towards the Cardinals were just flukes. If our best middle relievers would have their pizzas delivered and if our starting pitchers could schedule marital problems for the off-season, we would have a successful year.

I imagined that in the future, Mets fans would think about 2006 in the way they thought about 1985 and 1999. Those were great seasons, but in the end we had fallen just short. And after each of those two years, we expected the next year to be better. And it was. The 2007 season could be just like that of 2000, or if everything broke right, it could even be like that of 1986. Sure, if you looked hard at the 2007 Mets, you could see flaws, cracks, and reasons for concern. But that was true of virtually any team. I was soaking in the optimistic mud bath of March. I couldn't look at the 2007 Mets team and think that it was destined for anything but greatness.

One thing that would be interesting about the upcoming season was that our main rivals would probably be the Phillies, rather than the Braves. Although no Mets fan of long standing would ever count the Braves out, and although the Braves had made some improvements in the off-season, the Phillies were a very impressive team. They had finished the 2006 season with an 85-77 record, six games ahead of the Braves, who had had their first mediocre season in fifteen years. The Phillies had a terrifying lineup. They had scored more runs than the Mets had in 2006. If they had any luck with their starting pitching and if they could patch together a decent relief staff, they could compete with us. And if they did, there would be, for the first time, a New York–Philadelphia baseball rivalry. The Mets had long-standing rivalries with Atlanta, St. Louis, and Chicago. The Yankees had rivalries with teams from such nearby cities as Boston and Baltimore. But no New York team had ever had a rivalry with Philadelphia, the city that has always been the second largest city on the East Coast, the city that was only ninety miles away. In forty-five years, the Mets and the Phillies had never been really good at the same time. Now they were. Now Jimmy Rollins, the Phillies shortstop, was deliberately provoking us by telling reporters that the Phillies were the team to beat in the National League East. Mets fans were outraged. I was delighted. It was going to be so much fun to see what would happen.

Waxing: How the Mets Are More Popular Than the Yankees

As the Mets geared up for their rivalries with the Phillies and the Braves, many of us were also thinking about the team's most important rivalry, with the New York Yankees. A lot of Mets fans, and some sports commentators, don't like to talk about the Mets and Yankees as rivals, since normally the Mets only play the Yankees for six interleague games a year in an exciting, sold-out, yet trivial battle for bragging rights. The only time the Mets and Yankees had ever faced each other as real baseball rivals was in the 2000 World Series. But rivalries between baseball teams aren't always about baseball. A rivalry can be a contest for love and attention, or for space on the back pages of newspapers.

The Mets-Yankees rivalry was real. It was culturally more significant, and emotionally more resonant, than the rivalry with Atlanta and Philadelphia. It hurt some that Atlanta beat us year after year for the NL East title in the late 1990s. But it really rankled Mets fans when anyone assumed that the Yankees were New York's main baseball team and the Mets were the little brother, the chopped liver, the city's second team. In the 2006 season, the Mets had won exactly as many games as the Yankees (ninety-seven) and they had gotten further in the postseason. It was time for people to understand that New York did not have a first and a second team. This idea was a misconception based on the events of the last twelve years. If New York did have a second team, it wasn't us.

Everybody knows that the Yankees are the most famous baseball team in the world. Their myth-making machine has been in overdrive for more than a century. Ours is much younger and cranks up from time to time, then it just stops. Babe Ruth is Babe Ruth. He was a deity. Joe DiMaggio was a hero to The Old Man and the Sea and to Mrs. Robinson. The Mets have had Seaver and Piazza, but they've never had the opportunity to find a way into the world's imagination in the way the great Yankees have. Probably the most famous Met in the world is Keith Hernandez, thanks to Jerry Seinfeld.

The cultural footprint of the Mets was small. We Mets fans did have those episodes of *Seinfeld* and the film *Frequency*. And there was also the episode of *Everybody Loves Raymond* where Ray and Robert go up to Cooperstown to see a reunion of the 1969 Mets. In the winter of 2007, it was announced that there was going to be a wax statue of David Wright in Madame Tussauds on 42nd street. He would be joining the wax statues they already had of Babe Ruth, Joe DiMaggio, Mickey Mantle, George Steinbrenner, and Derek Jeter. I was pleased to hear this, but I still wouldn't be satisfied until the world was convinced of something almost half of all New Yorkers believe: that the Mets, and not the Yankees, are New York's *real* team.

Obviously I'm overstating this. I know that the Yankees are just as much New York's team as the Mets are. And I know that at the end of the 2006 season there were more Yankees fans in New York than Mets fans. But the Yankee's greater popularity is not an eternal fact of New York baseball. Since the Mets have come into existence, they've normally been at least as popular as the Yankees.

In June of 1990, a New York Times/CBS-TV News poll was taken that found that three times as many New Yorkers rooted for the Mets as rooted for the Yankees. Results showed that 41 percent of the respondents to the poll identified themselves as Mets fans, 14 percent identified themselves as Yankees fans, and 6 percent said that they rooted for both teams. I know that this poll was taken towards the end of a great period for the Mets and in the middle of a lousy period for the Yankees, but if the Yankees really were always New York's number one team, you wouldn't have seen these results. I'd suggest to you, in fact, that even during the periods in which the Yankees would routinely win thirty or more games in a season more than the Mets (say, 1963, 1978, 2004) you'd never have found three times as many New Yorkers calling themselves Yankees fans as calling themselves Mets fans.

For nineteen of the Mets' first thirty-one seasons, the Mets drew more fans to their ballpark than the Yankees drew to theirs. That's almost two-thirds of three whole decades. This isn't surprising. The Mets inherited the fans of both the Brooklyn Dodgers and the New York Giants. In 1986, the Mets became the first New York baseball team to draw 3 million fans to a stadium. They broke their own attendance record, set in 1970. The great Yankee teams of the late 1970s did not draw as many fans to Yankee Stadium as the Mets teams of the early 1970s drew to Shea. The 1980s Mets drew 3 million fans three times (in 1986, 1987, and 1988) but the Yankees teams of the 1990s would not draw 3 million fans to their stadium until 1999. Even since 1999, the Yankees have not been that much more popular than the Mets. When the two teams faced off in the 2000 World Series, polls showed that New Yorkers favored the Yankees only by a slim margin. The Yankees have outdrawn every other team in baseball in the twenty-first century, but the Mets have kept close to them, even when they have been lousy. In the annual Harris Poll of baseball fandom, the Mets are almost always in the top five, often a solid second to the Yankees among all baseball teams. And in 2008, the Mets became the first National League team in history to sell 4 million tickets.

For all that you hear it repeated over and over by newscasters who don't know anything about it, the Mets are not the Yankees' little brother, always in the bigger brother's shadow. They are more like the crazy uncle who goes AWOL every once in a while to the point where the family forgets about him, but then he comes back and he's so much fun that the family suddenly remembers why they've always loved him so much. Of course, Mets fans always love the Mets, worthy or unworthy. It's their doom and their destiny. But the city, and the city media, forget about the Mets when they go away. Yet when the team comes back they jump all over them. The nieces and nephews want presents and they want to hear all the stories. They forget how completely they had forgotten about the crazy uncle they now say they love more than anyone else. This is what it's like. And to long-time Mets fans, it never stops being funny.

In 2006, a marketer of sports merchandise reported that baseball merchandise bearing the name of David Wright outsold merchandise bearing the name of any other New York athlete. Wright ended a five-year streak by Derek Jeter. I felt, and a lot of Mets fans felt, that this was just the beginning. It would not be long before all the old Mets stuff was taken down from the attic and put in the living room. The era of the millennial Yankees, which was now fully boring everyone to death, was nearing its end. The Mets were all set to own the big town again.

Pitchers and Catchers

When a baseball season ends, it is a tradition for baseball fans to comfort each other by observing that there are "only three and a half months until 'pitchers and catchers'." At holiday time, people say "only a month and a half until 'pitchers and catchers'." Not "until pitchers and catchers report to camp ahead of everybody else." Just "pitchers and catchers." It's a magic catchphrase, an incantation, with its own poetic rhythm. Pitchers and catchers. Butchers and bakers.

You know how when you're waiting on line outside a building and you think, "once I get inside the building, I'll be almost there," and you get inside the building and see that you're not almost there because there's this big waiting area where the line is compressed into a tight coil that you're going to have to snake through for the next god-knows-how-long? Well, pitchers and catchers is like when you just get into the building.

When pitchers and catchers arrives, you see pictures in the paper of guys in uniform in warm, sunny Florida. You read articles about some players not going to dinner with each other as often as they used to, or about some manager wearing a World Series ring in order to fire up his players, or about some general manager announcing that the goal of the team is to win the World Series this year. Somebody scoops the big story that the owner agrees with the general manager that the team ought to win the World Series. The players will eventually be asked to weigh in on this. You can't wait. Maybe someone will disagree?

So you've waited so long for "pitchers and catchers," and this is what you have to read about. Well, at least there's some news, sort of. A couple of guys played winter ball and you hear how they did. Some young player who hit .270 last year did really well in winter ball. So would it be fair to expect him to hit .290 this year? Sure. Why not?

What are you doing? Well, pitchers and catchers are here. So it's time to predict and speculate about the season that will start in another month and a half. You look over and over the stats of the guys we've got. You look over and over the stats of the guys we don't have. You make little adjustments on the basis of people's age, temperament, and that article about the guy in winter ball. You try to determine, with the maximum amount of precision, just how much hope it is reasonable for you to have.

How much hope it is reasonable for you to have? Are you crazy? You know, don't you, that even if you read every scouting report, every newspaper article, every blog entry, and every statistical breakdown, you still will not have *any* idea of how well the Mets will do in a coming season. You know that many things will happen that you cannot possibly anticipate in February. But, you think, this is okay. You like unpredictability. This is part of the reason you're a baseball fan. You assume unpredictability. And yet here you are trying to determine how much fear and hope you have a right to have, even though once the season starts, you will hope and fear as much as you goddamn want to, no matter what all the statistics and scouting reports have told you.

What you do during the off-season is a waste of your time. In this respect, it is exactly like what you do during the season. For even if things turn out well and your team wins a hundred games and is way ahead, nothing you have seen in the season, nothing you know about any of the other teams, nothing you know about anything, will give you any way to even begin to guess what is going to happen in the World Series.

So, pitchers and catchers arrives and your brain becomes a little command center, absorbing and interpreting information. You read, think, calculate, and compare. You may even buy some of those expensive baseball prediction magazines in the supermarket. You have something fun to do as you move slowly in the line in the lobby of the building. And to whet your appetite for the big show you'll eventually be seated for, the people who run things have set up a little television in the lobby on which you can watch that most tempting yet annoying of all spectacles: the exhibition game.

The First Exhibition Game

On February 28, 2007, I watched the first televised Mets exhibition game of the 2007 season. The first thing I saw on the screen was people on a beach. I saw guys with surfboards and one of those car-driving-under-the-palm-trees shots like you see in the opening credits of *The Beverly Hillbillies*. "Away from the cold of the Northeast," Gary Cohen tells us, "spring baseball is ready to begin in Port St. Lucie!" Old-timers like me feel a pang as we remember what it was like to hear Bob Murphy's voice, after so many months, broadcasting from "warm and sunny St. Petersburg, Florida!"

Here are Ron, Gary, and Keith, looking a year older. Gary says that "we've got the whole gang back for you," as Keith goes "ha ha." The three of them are wearing black SNY t-shirts that make too much of their bellies. Their lips are a little bit ahead of the sounds that are coming out of them. But, hey, it's spring training. Now there's a commercial about how if you buy a season ticket at Shea in 2007 or 2008, you will have priority buying season tickets in Citi Field. This makes me scowl. So does the trumpeting of the team's new slogan: "Your Season Has Come." Come? In the sense of having arrived? That makes it sound like something a butler announces. Who's announcing this? The team? To whom are they announcing this? To us? Are they telling us that our season has now arrived? What were those other seasons all about? Were they not our seasons? Were they someone else's seasons? What makes this one ours? And, really, shouldn't someone have realized that you never use the word "come" in a slogan? Who did they pay for this and how much did they pay them?

That's it for complaining. I'm here. Am I not? There, on that baseball field, are the Mets.

Some of them are the real Mets, loose, if a little out of practice. You can see how much fun it would be to come to spring training when you know you have a job. It's like a family reunion, a relaxed party in the sunshine.

Some of the players are the guys you've read about, who are trying to make the team. You see them for the very first time in three dimensions, with their current hair and sunglasses. You realize how nervous they must be and how not nervous they are trying to look.

Other players on the field are the guys who don't have much of a shot. They're a little less nervous than the guys who have a shot. But there is a sadness that goes with their high uniform numbers and their unfamiliar names and faces. They look wistfully happy to be there because they are sort of in the big time. They are like the people you've never seen before in the landing parties on the old *Star Trek*. They are the ones who will be zapped by the aliens.

Ron, Keith, and Gary go over all the reasons why Oliver Perez can be thought to have had a lousy year last year. Boy, did he. This is a little jarring since the last thing you remember him doing is starting and pitching well in the most important game of the season. You almost forgot how our starting pitching had disappeared by the time we got to the Championship Series. But for several months now, you've been thinking that Perez would be our number three or four starter because Willie likes him and you want so much to believe that he is on his way back. Perez is pretty awful in the first inning and he's pretty awful in the second. Maybe he's on his way back and maybe he's not. For the first time in a few months you have new information to absorb. You find yourself inching away a little from your hopes for Perez. And then when Alay Soler comes in and pitches a decent couple of innings you find yourself wondering, along with the announcers, why he isn't being given more of a chance to make the team. Soler looks real good. Now you've got him in the fight for fourth or fifth starter. Perez has dropped down a peg. All because of a couple of innings. What kind of stupidity is this? Haven't you ever watched a baseball season before? Don't you know how little a couple of innings means? You know. But this is what you do. This is spring training.

You listen and you watch. You hear the new buzz. All of which could be gone tomorrow or it could be the beginning of something new. There's a kid named Joe Smith you've never heard of who threw a great curveball to Lastings Milledge in an intrasquad game yesterday. Wow. Maybe he could be our number four starter.

There is Moises Alou, our newest old guy. I remember how I acted out the 1962 World Series in my basement (I was eight). I listened to the radio pretending to be each player. I remember pretending to be Felipe Alou, imitating the facial expression he had on my baseball card. I can remember this, and Moises Alou, the old guy who is Felipe's son, wasn't even born yet.

Most of the game is crappy. Most of the crowd seems to be rooting for the Tigers. At the beginning of the inning they show you shots of the landscape beyond the stadium. It looks like Gilligan's Island.

Delgado strokes a beautiful, balanced double. How wonderful to see his smooth, happy smile. The announcers praise the wonderful atmosphere on the team. Endy looks sharp. Milledge in his batting helmet looks like a child. Gary Cohen observes that he is now "like a different guy."

I like the new guys. I like Newhan, who is funny looking in a way that reminds me of George Theodore. He drives in two runs while making two outs. I like Ben Johnson's hustle. And in the eighth, Milledge's sharp little base hit makes me so happy and hopeful because I want him to do well and I want people to shut up about him, because wouldn't it be a dream come true to have a homegrown trio like Wright, Reyes, and Milledge to take us all the way up to 2020?

Newhan drives in a second run and blows a bubble. Julio Franco becomes the oldest man ever to hit a two-run single in a spring exhibition game. After that, we hear "Lets Go Mets" for the first time in the afternoon. We should have heard it earlier in the inning, but the fans don't have it together yet either.

So to end the ninth, Ben Johnson, who's looked good all game, grounds into a game-ending double play. Which is the real Ben Johnson? Gary Cohen makes a joke about the Mets' all-time February record being 0-1. Then the Mets start a series of strange little running drills, which are the occasion of much mirth for the announcers. Finally, we go to a Verizon commercial and another one of those season tickets commercials that piss me off. There are more shots of the scraggy tropical foliage beyond the stadium. The final score is up on the field. We lost. Big deal. There is a final score. There has been a game.

It has begun.

The 2007 Season Begins

As you learn anew every year, the season does not begin with the first exhibition game any more than it begins with "pitchers and catchers." It's just the next stage of the tease. And after you've watched a few exhibition games, you find yourself ready to pay for all of their tickets north. Those may look like games, but they're phantoms. Those may look like home runs and strikeouts, but they're not. Everything in Florida slips into oblivion as soon as it happens. And all four weeks of the exhibition season will not have the statistical substance, or the immortality, of a casual putout in July. March, for a baseball fan, offers only the weakest kind of fun. As soon as it begins, you are yearning for April.

But April does come. Division titles may not. Pennants may not. World Championships may not. But April always comes. Every year. As long as there isn't a strike.

April came for the 2007 Mets. And it was very good. The season started with four wins in a row, followed by two losses before the home opener. This same pattern persisted through the next two months, as the Mets would inch ahead and then fall back just a little. The Mets remained steadily on a track to win about a hundred games, but even as the 2006 season seemed to be continuing into 2007, there were some strange things happening. After forty games, going into the first Yankees series in late May, Carlos Delgado was only hitting .216, with three home runs and twenty-one RBIs. David Wright was only hitting .279, with four homers and twenty RBIs. The Mike Pelfrey experiment had flopped. Big Pelf, who had inspired such hope with a great spring training, was 0-5 with an ERA of 6.53, and he was sent down to refocus himself in New Orleans. The middle relief was wildly inconsistent, and the Mets had been blown out of three games by uncharacteristically sloppy defensive play.

Yet for every Met playing under his head, there was one playing over his head. John Maine was pitching astonishingly well, as well as Dwight Gooden had in 1985. Jose Reyes and Carlos Beltran were contending for the MVP. The old guys, Alou and Green, were playing like budding superstars. And the bench was filling in every gap, in the manner and with all the character of the great Mets benches of the past. Chavez, Easley, Castro, and Woodward certainly seemed to be the equals of our great millennial Mets bench of Agbayani, Payton, Pratt, and McEwing. If there was a weak game for the heart of the order, the bottom of the order and the bench would pick us up. If one reliever faltered, another would get hot. The Mets looked as if they had a million different ways to win. They reminded me of those metal balls on strings that nerdy guys like me used to have in our bedrooms in the sixties. They demonstrated that momentum and energy could be transferred, that one guy could do his part and move everyone else along. This was a team, and to show it, most of them shaved their heads in mid-May, not because they had to or needed to, but just because they felt like it. They did it because they were exuberant. It was their year and they wanted everyone to know it. There was no sense in anyone's mind that this wonderful team could ever be in any trouble.

And if they got into a little trouble, they would come right back. The day before the first Yankee Series, on May 17, the Mets had entered the ninth inning trailing the Cubs 5–1. Then they scored five runs in the ninth, winning the game on a two-run single by Carlos Delgado. They celebrated at home plate as if it were September.

The Yankees, in the meantime, had started off badly. They were as fun-less as they had been in their successful 2006 season, but they didn't seem to be nearly as good. They had no reliable starting pitching, and several of their overpaid sluggers were injured or slumping. More and more people were beginning to realize that the Yankee dominance of New York didn't have deep roots. The kind of fans who could switch back and forth were becoming sick of the Yankees, now that the appealing players of the late 1990s (O'Neill, Williams, Martinez, Brosius) were mostly gone and what remained was a talented yet colorless collection of hired guns. Yankees fans did not seem to have a lot of affection for their 2007 team. But they had become addicted to winning. I would listen to them on talk radio shows and occasionally I would read their blogs. None of them said: "Wow, wouldn't it be fun to see the Yankees get it together as a team and win it this year in spite of all the drawbacks they face?" They weren't saying: "I know it looks bad, but I like the looks of some of these young pitchers. They may come through, and I'm not quite yet willing to give up on Mariano. Watch them pull it out!" They didn't say: "I know the Red Sox look awfully good this year, but we've got some great young players coming along and we may give them a run for it, and if we don't, watch out for what those young players will do next year!"

Yankee fans, over the last twelve years, had lost the ability to talk like that. They were like fat, decadent Romans who could no longer rise up from their purple pillows. I felt sorry for fans who could only talk on the radio about what their team *needed* and what they had to *get*. But there was nothing the Yankees could get, especially since what they needed was pitching and there was none. So what did they do? Oh, my goodness gracious. They coughed up $25 million for forty-five-year-old Roger Clemens when they already had a payroll that dwarfed that of any other team. There was no limit to what the Yankees would spend, or how obnoxious they would be announcing the coming of a savior who would bring them the championship to which they felt they were entitled.

And so, the man who was probably the number one Mets villain of all time (more than Pete Rose, more than John Rocker, more than Chipper Jones) was resurrected once again. There he was, in Steinbrenner's box. I was delighted. Clemens was the proof, if any more was needed, that the proud pricks in pinstripes were desperate and scared. Why else would they spend $18 million plus $7.5 million in luxury tax to sign a pitcher who would turn forty-five in August and who had had no spring training? Did they think he would get them to the postseason when the rest of their pitching staff still had an ERA higher than that of the 1962 Mets? By investing so much in Clemens, the Yankees were magnifying the scale of a disaster they were powerless to prevent.

It was bad enough to have your first bad year in a long time. It was so much worse to look stupid believing that you could buy off disaster for only $25 million.

In Latin, "Clemens" means gentle and merciful. That was very funny when you thought about it. This was going to be fun for Mets fans. We would not be gentle. We would not show mercy. Comparing my fine, beautifully balanced team to the arrogant 2007 Yankees, all I could think was: "Die, suckers, die."

And so on May 18, the Yankees came into Shea for the first Subway Series. They were 18-21, already nine and a half games behind Boston. We were 26-14, a game and a half ahead of the Braves and six and a half games ahead of the Phillies. We took the first game with strong pitching from Perez and perfect relief work from Joe Smith and Billy Wagner. Endy Chavez hit his first home run of the year, a two-run blast that put the Mets permanently ahead. In the second game the Mets scored ten runs, four of them driven in by David Wright, who hit two home runs. The Yankees pulled out the third game by mystifying the Mets with a twenty-two-year-old rookie pitcher. We won the first Subway Series of 2007. The Mets had shown the Yankees why and how they were better. As I drove over the Kosciusko Bridge on May 20, after celebrating my mom's birthday in Brooklyn at my sister's, I saw the Empire State Building with its spire illuminated in royal blue and Creamsicle orange. There were the colors of my soul, rising lovely out of the heart of my city. Could it be that the grim decade of the Empire was over?

June

If there's one thing I should have learned in my forty-five years of Mets fandom, it is that just as you can never count the Yankees out, you can never count the Mets in. The 2007 Mets were 34-18 at the end of May, on a pace to win over a hundred games. They looked and felt invincible. They then lost fourteen of their next eighteen games.

I don't know how something like this happens. And neither does anyone else. It is the greatest mystery of the many mysteries of baseball. You have it and you lose it and then you have it and you lose it. Baseball, for the players, is about trying to hold on to something you can't see, grip, or understand. Baseball, for a fan, is an intense and sustained encounter with the experience of helplessness.

It's when their team is in a slump that baseball fans come closest to understanding the complete absurdity of what they're doing. Baseball fans don't do anything. We have no impact. We have the illusion that we are helping by cheering loudly, but that is for the most part an illusion. It's a nice illusion and it is part of the myth of being a Mets fan, but if we could cheer them out of funks, we would do it whenever they got into one. The truth is that we are helpless when they win, and we are helpless when they lose. We don't notice how helpless we are when they win because the world is behaving as we want it to. So we think we are doing something right. But we aren't. We are always doing the same thing: experiencing emotions about something that other people are doing.

So what were the players feeling and what impact did that have on how they were playing? If you listened to talk radio and read the newspapers during the last week and a half of June, when the Mets came roaring out of their June funk by winning eight out of nine games, you would have learned that the players' emotions were determining everything you saw. If you had only listened to the games and looked at the box scores, you might have come to the conclusion that the Mets' team defensive play had simply settled down after a rough period, and five individual starting pitchers had turned in eight pretty good pitching performances. You had to turn to the radio to learn that all of this happened because David Wright threw his glove in the dugout and Paul Lo Duca got mad at an umpire and threw his catcher's equipment around.

I have always had a hard time understanding the connection between throwing sporting equipment and getting fielders and pitchers back on the right track. Perhaps there's evidence somewhere that these two things are linked, but no one has told me where that evidence might be found.

During the Mets' streak, three of the games would have been lost had it not been for two ninth-inning at-bats by Castro and Wright on one day, one swing by Shawn Green on another day, and one swing by David Wright in a third game. The commentators and the callers were suggesting that these four at-bats would have turned out differently had it not been for the extra adrenalin that was in the blood of Castro, Wright, and Green because objects had been thrown around by others. No one tried to explain why the flying gloves and masks did not produce hits and runs during the other innings of those ballgames.

The idea that anger motivates ballplayers is based on an analogy that sports analysts like to make between sports and the psychology of fighting and warfare. I agree that anger can be a motivator in a fight or a battle. If the opposing team does or says something to show disrespect, a team can indeed get riled up. I see how that works. It may not lead to anything. And it may not be better than maintaining a sense of calm. But on occasion, I can believe that it might make a difference.

Still, how would that work here? Lo Duca was mad at an umpire for what he felt was an inconsistency in the way he was calling balls and strikes. Did El Duque also get mad at the umpire and decide, on the spot, to throw a shutout? Did Tom Glavine look at David Wright throwing that glove and think, "Hey, my teammates really want to win. I didn't realize that. I've gotta stop crapping around and go win my 296th game!" When Shawn Green hit that home run that almost went over the scoreboard, do you think he was thinking, "Thanks, David and Paulie, for waking me up and inspiring me to want to hit that home run. I wouldn't have otherwise"? Even if you don't know Shawn Green that well, from what you have seen of him, do you think it is likely that that's the way his mind works?

Look, I'm not ruling it out. I just don't know. But from what I've seen of the human race in my half century, I need to be convinced. In most instances in which I've seen people turn something around, they turn around because they've quieted down, gotten focused, and gotten serious. Sometimes they express anger before they get there and sometimes they don't. I don't think that the expression of the anger necessarily accomplishes anything in itself. And plenty of times the expression of anger and frustration derails people; sometimes it ruins everything. Older Mets fans will remember a very good late 1970s Mets pitcher named Pat Zachry who was having a very good season. One night, after a crappy outing, he kicked the dugout steps hard in anger, broke his foot, and was out for the rest of the season. Let me tell you. It didn't fire up the team at all.

I remember back in 2000, when Chris "Mad Dog" Russo said that the Mets might have won the 2000 World Series against the Yankees if Mike Piazza had charged the mound after Roger Clemens threw that piece of the broken bat in his direction. That, he said, might have woken up the Mets. Yeah, Mad Dog, the Mets didn't want the 2000 World Championship badly enough! They needed a thoughtful grown man to act in a way we teach our children not to act in order to realize how badly they wanted it! Just like you, Mad Dog, when you're constipated, you don't really want to take a crap!

Of course baseball is psychological. But it is not psychological in the way that a fistfight is. The skills that are involved are more complex and more mysterious than those that are involved in the act of punching somebody in the nose. There are grooves to get into and mysterious ways of tricking yourself to stay in them. There are boxes with no visible exits that you have to get out of. As far as I can see, it's not usually just a matter of adrenalin. I think that playing baseball is more like writing than it is like brawling. And back in 2007, I hoped that if the Mets ran into another rough patch between the end of June and October, nobody on the Mets was going to feel obligated to think of what they could throw or kick or scream at.

The Summer of Our Discontent

The Mets were 34-18 at the end of May, and then they went 4-14 up to June 20. But they finished June with an 8-1 streak. Then, to start July, the Mets won two and lost six. There was then a nice stretch, as the Mets won fourteen and lost eight between July 9 and August 3. After that, the Mets were 2-5 through August 11, but then they recovered to go 9-3 through August 25. Then they lost five games in a row, four of them against the Phillies in Philadelphia. After that awful, apocalyptic series, they won five in a row. Then they lost a game, 7–0 against Cincinnati. And then they won another four in a row.

This was all very bizarre, and the fans did not enjoy it. The inconsistency of the team was mirrored in the inconsistency of the play of each individual player. Glavine and Maine were All-Stars in April and May. But in June, Glavine dove into what would become a summer-long slump, and John Maine started pitching like a normal person. The middle relievers, Heilman, Smith, Schoeneweis, and Mota, who had been fine at the start of the season, began to pitch terribly, and they continued to pitch with maddening inconsistency throughout the summer. Reyes and Beltran had begun the season vying for the MVP as Wright and Delgado languished. But then in July, as Wright and Delgado got it together, Reyes and Beltran suddenly couldn't see the baseball. Beltran got it back in August but then Delgado slowed down. While the offense was strong overall in August and the middle relievers improved, the starting pitching collapsed, as did the closer Billy Wagner. They had been exhausted by all the extra work they had to do while the middle relievers were slumping.

In the summer of 2007, the Mets were a .500 team, anchored in first by their excellent start. But they weren't playing like a .500 team. They were playing like a first-place team that would take periodic and sudden trips into the Bizarro World. There was a surreal quality about what was going on. You knew that you had a good team on the field, but you never knew which of the good players was going to play badly today. You kept feeling that nothing good was real because you got used to seeing players play well one day and badly the next. Nothing bad was real either, because the fact that Oliver Perez walked five batters in an inning did not mean that he wasn't going to pitch six scoreless innings in his next outing. It was hard to know what the Mets were. You knew they were in first, but that didn't seem to make any sense. Still, no one else seemed to want the division so terribly much. So you just held on, hoping that the season would end with the standings looking just as they looked from May through September.

What the Mets summer of 2007 reminded me of were these wonderful black-and-white 1930s cartoons you could still see on TV when I was a kid. I remember that in one of these cartoons, there was a happy old man whose name I think was Grandpa Snazzy who was driving a car up and down these ridiculously steep hills. His car was pretty rickety. It was not what anyone would consider a hi-class ve-hic-ule. But it bounced along happily, if not entirely smoothly. Then all of a sudden the car would stop and start, lurch and belch smoke, and then all kinds of things would get coughed up out of the engine and the radiator: cats, caps, polka-dotted underwear. Grandpa Snazzy would look distressed, but then, when enough things got coughed out, the car would calm down and start running smoothly again, or sort of smoothly. Despite the fact that it was now moving forward, it always looked as if it was only a matter of time before it started to act weird again. And sure enough, after some pleasant, happy driving by the pipe-smoking and humming Grandpa, the car would start lurching and stopping and starting again, there would be explosions, and this time, out of the engine and radiator would come dogs and octopuses and Mahatma Gandhi. Then things would calm down again and Grandpa Snazzy would continue on his journey, singing and whistling, until the next time the car would decide to act up.

I don't remember how the cartoon ended. Maybe Grandpa Snazzy drove into a town where there was a fair and everybody cheered him and kissed him. Maybe the car leaped off the road after a big explosion and bounded down a hill and landed in the middle of somebody's picnic table. I don't remember.

Anyway, this is what June, July, and August were like for the 2007 New York Mets.

Ralph Kiner Night

On July 14, 2007, right in the middle of this strange summer, the New York Mets paid tribute to Ralph Kiner, the great home run hitter for the Pittsburgh Pirates in the 1940s and 1950s, who had been their television announcer since 1962. The tribute to Ralph Kiner on July 14 was great and I was there. I began to have a sense that it might be wonderful when workmen started assembling the stage in the center of the outfield to the accompaniment of Broadway music from the late 1940s and early 1950s. Ralph connected us with that era. Back then, being the home run king didn't mean that you were a big kid in shorts in a $10 million house with a gigantic PlayStation. You were one of the most glamorous men in the world, an image of masculine power, a classy grown-up getting out of a limo in a tux with a woman like Ava Gardner about to take your arm. You were a friend of Sinatra and Crosby. You were a man of the world.

So, to the music of Kern and Gershwin and Bernstein, they set up the stage in the lengthening shadows as the Home Run Apple soaked up what remained of the sunlight and a multicolored snake of people moved steadily down the subway ramp. The stadium was filling up. It was going to be an enormous crowd.

The tribute began as the Diamond Vision showed us some old *Kiner's Korners*. Not many of these old Mets postgame shows remain, as most of them, and nearly all the early ones, were taped over. Most of what we were watching was from the 1980s, and not enough of it was in the funky little original studio with the entirely implausible book shelves. The haircuts were bad and the faces and plywood paneling were green, and Ralph seemed more energetic than I had remembered him. But it was *Kiner's Korner* all right, and the audience got to see Tommy Lasorda and Davey Johnson raise their eyebrows as Ralph observed that they were so "disalike." You heard Ralph say that Johnny Bench was definitely going into the hall of fame "after he serves his five years." (What, was he going into the army, into prison?) You couldn't miss the pathos of what you were watching on the Diamond Vision. The cranes and girders of Citi Field hulked behind the screen. We were paying tribute to things that had their long and wonderful run. But new things were being built to replace them.

A moment was given to acknowledge that the mayor had passed a proclamation that tonight was Ralph Kiner Night in New York, and some wag in the mayor's office had crafted a comment about Ralph's service to "our city's favorite National League team." Ha ha. The mayor sent a deputy to represent him.

Then Howie Rose, in a suit, began the real ceremony, and a thick and slow-moving band of "friends and contemporaries" began to make their way across the field to some folding chairs near the podium set up in back of second base, right where the Beatles had played their concert. The Diamond Vision informed us that this crowd included Bob Murphy's widow, Joye, Ed Charles, Ed Kranepool, Buddy Harrelson, Rusty Staub, Jerry Koosman, Keith Hernandez, Bob Feller, Yogi Berra, and Tom Seaver. Fans were clapping and cheering and whooping and crying to see these beloved people, bent and grey but alive.

Then there was a video tribute to Ralph with Sinatra singing "Summer Wind" just as a real warm summer wind swept through the stadium. Lots of wonderful images went by too quickly, and then Ralph and his wife rode in slowly along the warning track and then down the right field line in what looked to me like a white Plymouth Belvedere from the early 1960s, a gleaming vintage car as old as the Mets.

The crowd exploded. The sound rose and held as people stood and clapped and hollered and called out to Ralph by his name. What must it be like to see a sea of 50,000 strangers calling out to you? Each of us felt that he was ours, each of us was overcome by our memories of Ralph's voice on so many summer nights, and each of us felt as if Ralph Kiner was one of the things that held our lives together.

The cranes of Citi Field seemed taken aback by all of this commotion, all of this loud celebration of so many ancient memories.

Ralph got out of his car and walked towards the podium as they played the music to Kiner's Korner in a continuous loop. The Mets announced that they were giving Ralph a cruise of his choice as a present.

Then Tom Seaver, the vintner from Calistoga, looking like Rudy Vallee in an old movie, read a tribute that had something to do with a plaque that was to be displayed in the Diamond Club. This was followed by the main event, the man himself: Ralph in all of his dignity, with his sweet, uncanny friendliness and his deceptively unsophisticated sophistication. He didn't have the clunkiness most old athletes have in situations like this because he was at home in front of a microphone. He knew that you should just talk into it. And so Ralph did the George Burns line about it being an honor to be anywhere at his age, and from Ralph it didn't sound like a cliché. He told a story about Stengel bringing down the whole set by forgetting to take off his microphone on the first *Kiner's Korner*. He made some gentle jokes about how bad the Mets were in their earliest years, and he called announcing the unforgettable 1969 season the greatest thrill of his broadcasting life.

Getting serious, Ralph quoted the most famous speech any athlete ever gave on a playing field: Lou Gehrig's farewell speech at Yankee Stadium, where Gehrig referred to himself as "the luckiest man on the face of the earth." Ralph observed that if Lou Gehrig was "the luckiest man in the world," then he, Ralph, was "a close second." This was certainly pure Ralph Kiner. Everybody knows the context of the Gehrig speech. Gehrig was saying goodbye to his fans and teammates because he had just received the terribly unlucky news that he had only a few months to live, but he was defying death and asserting that the love and loyalty of others made him lucky. It doesn't really make sense to say that if Gehrig was the luckiest man, he, Kiner, was a close second. It's actually kind of a bizarre thing to say. But you know what Ralph meant, and he is who he is. And if he says it, it's true. It makes sense because he says it. And Ralph, when you think of his life, has truly been the luckiest man on the face of the earth.

Ralph and his wife walked to the white Plymouth as the sound system played "Nobody Does It Better." The car glided away to the lovely, tender beauty of Sinatra singing "The Way You Look

Tonight." I looked through my binoculars at Jerry Koosman and Rusty Staub walking off the field with each other, catching up. I could hardly hold the binoculars steady.

The car disappeared behind the left field wall. And then, as if from some hidden, inexhaustible source, the 2007 Mets welled up out of the dugout and ran out onto the field.

The Real Meaning of
Ralph Kiner Night

Every day of the strange midsummer of 2007, fans felt something different about the Mets. We were confident when the team took three out of the first four games played after the All-Star break, but then our confidence would be lost in a single lousy evening. A pitcher would pitch well against us and we'd be certain that our offense, raucous just a few days before, was still in its deep June slumber. We'd win a beautiful game with flawless pitching and plenty of offense. We'd be on top of the world, but then the loss of a game in which we'd had a brilliant comeback would be enough to bring us back down. There always seemed to be just one Joe Smith pitch between joy and despair. Then we'd clobber the Dodgers. Our offense is alive! Are we having any fun yet? Hey, now what's happening to our starting pitching?

There was no getting happy and staying there. And so none of our pleasures were felt very deeply. We had hope, of course. Mets fans always have hope. But in the stands at Shea, on the radio, in the blogs and forums, I didn't hear belief. Tug didn't say "Ya Gotta Hope." Ya gotta do more than hope.

We Mets fans were having an identity crisis. Who were we? Were we still the loony diehards of Mets history and myth? Or were we turning into the one in twenty at Shea on Ralph Kiner Night who booed Carlos Delgado when he flied out weakly after he had earlier hit two balls to the warning track? Were we getting to be like the guy sitting behind me who sagely observed, after four or five beers, that in no other profession would this "not doing your job" be tolerated. Had no one explained to Carlos Beltran that his job is to hit .300 with runners in scoring position, the same way that my job is to teach my classes and my plumber's job is to fix my pipes? Why did no one tell him that? This wasn't really happening, was it?

The real meaning that I took away from Ralph Kiner Night was that it is possible to feel something steadily. We may not have known what to think about the 2007 Mets from game to game, but was there any one of us who didn't know what to feel about Ralph? Was there any one of us who didn't know what to feel about the permanent Mets, the Mets who are always in our soul, whom we love as we love Ralph, because they've always been with us and we can't imagine our lives without them? Have the Mets ever been anything but imperfect? The closest they ever came to being perfect was in 1986, and do you remember how close that team came to losing the playoffs and the World Series?

Truth be told, was Ralph ever anything but imperfect? He told wonderful stories and he's had wonderful insights and we loved the old *Kiner's Korners*. But did fans love *Kiner's Korner* because Ralph was such a skilled interviewer? Did Mets fans love the Mets because they've always been such a terrific baseball team?

One of the things Ralph Kiner and Bob Murphy accomplished is that they taught millions of people to be a little like them. Like Ralph and "Murph," lots of Mets fans are among the nicest people you could ever hope to meet. We're hopeful, friendly folk with a tolerant and bemused attitude towards imperfection. We're Ralphs. We're Murphs. We see the good in others. If we don't, others aren't likely to see the good in us. I knew, as the 2007 season was playing out, that not all Mets fans were like this. I knew that in the fan base, a culture was developing that despised any sign of weakness or failure. I tried to blame this on the influence of the fans of the Yankees, but I knew that this wasn't fair. A lot of Mets fans were coming up with this on their own. Still, I really hated this. And I wanted it to stop. And I didn't know how to stop it.

In the summer of 2007, Mets fans needed to remind themselves of the unselfconscious teachings of Ralph. Year after year, he won home-run titles while playing for a last-place team. Year after year, with generous equanimity, he announced games for another last-place team. But he wasn't reconciled to losing. In his speech, Ralph called the 1969 Mets the greatest thrill of his broadcasting life. Boy, did he deserve that. But the whole point of Ralph is that he didn't absolutely have to have it. He would still have been the second luckiest man in the world if 1969, or 1986, had never happened.

When I drove out of the parking lot after Ralph Kiner Night, I was happy. We won, we had seen Ralph honored, and we had seen all his wonderful friends there with him on the field. I replayed the ceremony in my head as I was driving home. Then I turned on the radio and heard fans complain about the Mets doing their exercises during the Kiner ceremony. I turned off the radio. I wanted to be alone. With my memories. And my belief.

Saving the Apple: We're Mets Fans, We're Goofy, Get Over It

Throughout the summer of 2007, many Mets fans were getting more and more nostalgic. Part of this may have been caused by the identity crisis produced by the emotionally confusing baseball. Part of it may have been sparked by the wonderful tribute to Kiner. But the main reason, of course, was that as the new stadium continued its relentless growth beyond the center field wall, fans were realizing more vividly than ever that we were soon going to lose Shea. What would happen to us when we were no longer in the ballpark that had been our home for four and a half decades?

Few of us felt a desire to fight to save our old stadium. It was too late for that. And there was a lot of genuine excitement about the new stadium. Still, even the most partisan advocates of Citi Field knew that something was going to be lost when Shea was torn down. And as comic or as trivial as it may seem, many fans who felt this way began to focus on the unspoken likelihood that when the Mets moved out of Shea, the Home Run Apple was going to be left behind.

The Home Run Apple is a precious painted apple of wood that rises out of a big, black top hat over the center field wall whenever a Met hits a home run. It has a Mets logo on its front that lights up and pulsates with happiness. It seems to be alive. It is not very professionally made, but this is a crucial part of its considerable charm. It looks like folk art or a school project. It has been where it is and it has done what it does for almost thirty years. How was it possible that the Mets could not find room for such a thing in their new stadium?

A movement was launched on the web to "Save the Apple." I signed the petition and so did thousands of others. You may ask,

"Is this an appropriate political concern?" and, "Are these appropriate elegiac emotions for grown-ups?" The answer is yes. The Home Run Apple defines the Mets fan. It is the sort of thing that inspires fans of other teams to make fun of us. Let them make fun of us. What do they know?

As the "Save the Apple" movement was getting off the ground, an individual named Colin Cowherd (no comment) ranted, on ESPN, about the tackiness of the Mets' theme song "Meet the Mets" and the bush-league quality that he felt characterized the entire Mets' media presentation. Cowherd said, "Give me a break. Step up Mets. This is the most bush-league stuff I have ever heard in my life. I mean, honestly, you turn on the Yankees and it's regal—maybe it's pompous, but it sounds New York. . . . You turn on the Mets, it's horrible—and as good as the Mets are, get rid of dorky Mr. Met, get rid of that stupid apple in center field after the home runs, your nine tacky uniforms. . . . You sound bush league, and you're not. You've got Disneyland players and you sound like the traveling carnival."

This is so stupid I don't know where to begin. First of all, the superiority of Mets broadcasting to Yankees broadcasting has been so consistent and so overwhelming for four and a half decades that that should have at least been considered by anyone trying to compare the media presentation of the two teams. But leaving that aside, what is most amazing, and I suppose most interesting, about what Mr. Cowherd said is how completely he misses the point of being a Mets fan. Has it really never occurred to him that there are people who find traveling carnivals more compelling than Disneyland?

At the very center of "Mets-ness" are three things: "Meet the Mets," Mr. Met, and the Home Run Apple. These three things share an essence. They establish an atmosphere that is the permanent atmosphere of our team. It is a traveling carnival atmosphere, and it is distinguished by the fact that it has none of the prepackaged corporate sterility one might associate with Disneyland, or the New York Yankees for that matter. It is tacky, corny, and sweet. It is actually very New York, as Jerry Seinfeld, the quintessential Mets fan, has demonstrated to the world. The holy silliness, the happy sixties-retro tackiness of "Mets-ness" is the same quality of loving irony that so many New Yorkers have, New Yorkers who love what is familiar to them even when they know it is ridiculous—things like Pez dispensers, Shea Stadium, or the diner where they've always hung out. We love what we love because it is familiar, because it is what we have always had and always will have. We don't love it because it wins championships and has triumphal music and ceremonial graveyards and thinks it's so great and prances around in pinstripes.

The Mets, according to the mythology of the Mets fan, are the other side of New York. We are the not-Yankees, the aspect of the metropolis that doesn't take itself quite so seriously. This side of New York has given the world some of its greatest humorists and some of its finest recorders of simple, ordinary, humble, and ridiculous detail. When "Meet the Mets" was written, and when Mr. Met was conceived, the new franchise struggling to climb out of last place would have looked ridiculous with dignified, triumphant theme music. It would have seemed humorless without a silly mascot. It had no choice but to try to charm fans with good-natured nuttiness.

We who became Mets fans grew to love that nuttiness. To us, it has become indispensable. We can't live without it. We won't live without it, however good the Mets become.

If they were not going to bring that apple from Shea to Citi Field, I was going to offer to bring it over myself. I'd round up some of the people who signed the petition and we'd get a lot of rope and some station wagons. We'd have a big tailgate picnic in the parking lot and then we'd get down to work. I wanted to bring the apple over so that people in the new stadium, in the new century, would understand that for a Mets fan, nothing is more important than affectionate, unconditional loyalty. It is loving the old neighborhood, for all of its drawbacks. It is appreciating Ralph Kiner. It's wanting to win but being able to cheer for spirited losers from time to time. It's loving your parents even when they're being neurotic and falling apart. This is what New York really means, Mr. Cowherd, not the regal pompous stuff you think it means. New York Mets fans will want the Home Run Apple forever, because it's what makes us *us*, and it's what distinguishes us from them.

The Mystery and Myth of Motivation

At the start of September, the Mets universe recovered its balance as the Mets won nine out of ten games, right after the devastating loss of all four games of a series in Philadelphia. When this happened, I heard Joe Benigno, in a radio ad, boasting that he had single-handedly turned the Mets around by dissing them in an opening monologue on his morning talk show on WFAN. Why, I wondered, would the Mets have needed Joe Benigno to motivate them? Weren't there already sufficient reasons for the Mets to want to win the National League East title?

At the end of Philadelphia's four-game sweep of the Mets, I came to the frightening conclusion that the Phillies really wanted the division title and it might be impossible to deny it to them. Then I wondered if the epic 11–10 game that ended the series, when the Mets kept coming back and coming back, had lit some special fires under our team. When the Phillies dropped three out of four games to the Marlins in their next series, I marveled at this sign that perhaps the Phillies didn't want to win after all. As the Mets swept Atlanta in three games at Turner Field while the Phillies were losing three to the Marlins, I marveled at how little the Braves seemed to want something that was now plausibly within their grasp.

Why would Philadelphia want to win the division title so badly during the weekday series with the Mets, and then lose their desire in the weekend series against the Marlins? Why wouldn't the proud Braves want to grab this unanticipated opportunity to regain their title as New York and Philadelphia slumped? Why wouldn't Philadelphia, on the verge of virtual elimination, really want the Wednesday game they played against Atlanta, the game in which they blew a six-run lead? Now that Atlanta had virtually eliminated themselves, why would they want Wednesday's game so much that they'd stage a titanic comeback, scoring seven runs in the last two innings to beat the Phillies 9–8? And if the Braves wanted it so badly on Wednesday against Philadelphia, why did they show so little sign of wanting to come back when they played the Mets over the weekend? If the Braves could score seven runs in two innings against the Phillies, why could they only manage three runs in a whole three-game series against the Mets? Why, I couldn't help but ask, do we talk so much about "wanting?" Surely the degree to which the Mets, the Phillies, and the Braves wanted the NL East title didn't vary *that much* from day to day. Why would it? How could it?

Many Mets fans were convinced that the 2007 Mets, good as they were, had had a motivation problem all year. I wasn't convinced of this. Nobody had ever said that the 1986 Mets had a motivation problem. So why couldn't they, with all their scrap and guts and nails, beat Mike Scott in the playoffs against Houston? Didn't they want to? The 1986 Mets came, as you may remember, *this close* to losing to Boston in six games. What if they had lost that series? Would you have said that they didn't want it? How could you have said that? Well, you say, the Mets beat the Red Sox in seven games; didn't that show that they wanted it? Maybe, or maybe that simply showed that Stanley was tired and Schiraldi was inexperienced. I have to be honest. I think that the amount that the Mets wanted to win the 1986 World Series would have been the same if they had lost it in six as it was when they won it in seven.

When a player or a team is trying really hard to break out of a slump and can't do it, we say that they are pressing, that they need to relax. But if they relax when they're doing badly, we say that they don't want it. This makes no sense.

I think that motivation is important in baseball, as it is in everything in life. But I think that we rely too much on the idea of a lack of motivation to explain disappointing performance, and too much on the idea of motivation to explain good performance. It's not that motivation is irrelevant. It's just that there are too many other factors involved. When an enormously talented pitcher gets into the right groove, no amount of motivation is going to make it possible for you to hit him. When a batter gets so keyed in that you can't get him out, motivation is not going to make it possible for you to get him out. Somebody could say that motivation accounts for what Atlanta did to Philadelphia on Wednesday, but to me it had all the marks of a Philadelphia bullpen meltdown. If motivation could do what we sometimes say it can do, players would get out of slumps when they wanted to. Everybody would win the pennant when they really, really wanted to. It doesn't work that way. The universe does not bend so easily to human will.

As the 2007 season went into its final months, I was getting tired of listening to all the speculation about how much the Mets wanted or didn't want to find their way to the postseason. I was convinced that they wanted to win the World Series. And I suspected that the same was true of all of the other teams in contention. I thought that the World Series would eventually be won, not by the team that wanted it most, but by the team that somehow managed to win the most games. It would be won by the team that managed to grab and hold on to the slippery beast that would try to slither away. It would take desire to do this, but it would take a whole hell of a lot more than desire.

A Sunday in September

As the Mets won nine out of ten going into September, it began to look as if their season was going to turn out exactly as I had hoped after all. The inconsistency of the summer would be forgotten in the future, as forgotten as the midsummer collapse of the 1969 Mets, the incredible awfulness of most of the 1973 season, or the September swoon of the 1999 Mets. All of these things actually happened, but they are not remembered; or when they are, they are only remembered as stuff that made what you do remember more exciting.

On September 9, when everything appeared to be solid and safe once again, I went to the stadium to witness the return of Pedro Martinez to Shea. He was back after having been on the disabled list for almost a year. A great pitcher and a wonderful guy, Pedro, in 2005 and 2006, was the symbol of the team's return to respectability. I wasn't sure what he was now, whether he would be any good, whether he could help us. But I wanted to see him because I liked him, and because I dreamed of him rejuvenated, leading us to the World Championship he practically promised us when he came in 2005. I went online and bought tickets for myself and my daughter Sonia. We drove down and entered the stadium as soon as they opened it, two and a half hours before game time, on a slow, hot, and lazy Sunday morning.

First we went down to the Mets dugout to see batting practice, but there was no batting practice because there had been a night game on Saturday. A few people stood around, to be close to the sacred earth, even though there were no Mets in sight. We could see Howie up in the WFAN booth, looking over some papers. We saw Ron, Gary, and Keith, relaxed and looking out over the blue and orange seats from their perch in the press level. In the meantime, we heard an organ concert just like Jane Jarvis used to give us back in the days before Diamond Vision. Where else can you spend a Sunday morning listening to an organ playing the Monkees' "Pleasant Valley Sunday" or the Four Seasons' "Oh, What a Night" followed by "Talkin' Baseball"? You can do it right here, in this very American place on the edge of the American metropolis, in this big, old stadium near the airports and the marshes.

Finally some Mets started running back and forth out by the bullpen in right field. But they weren't the regulars and they weren't today's pitcher. Sonia and I were hot so we went and got chocolate ice cream in plastic baseball helmets. Then we went up to where we could look out over the Mets. We got our hot dog and knish lunch, and just as we finished it, just after our picture was taken by one of those people who walk around with the cameras, Pedro appeared in right field.

There he was, amazingly back, drawing everybody's attention away from some girls in red costumes banging drums for Taiwan Heritage Day. We all looked at the broad, friendly, and familiar outline of number 45. We thought we had lost him forever, but here he was, returning on the wave of win streaks that made us feel, once again, that we had a right to the postseason. Pedro was back. We were ready to be happy. We were calm and unequivocally pleased with the Mets for the first time in three and a half months.

As he ran back and forth and chatted with pitching coach Rick Peterson, the girls in red danced and waved red scarves as tall, brooding, swaying god and monster puppets looked on. Out in right, everyone saw Pedro doing his loosening up under the gaze of the Home Run Apple who, I suddenly noticed, had just been given a new coat of paint. The paint was lighter and brighter. Apples weren't that color. When it finally sank into the hat for the game to start, it looked for all the world like the Home Run Tomato.

We cheered and stood for Pedro when the lineup was announced. We did the same when the Mets took the field. There he was, and we watched as he stymied the Astros hitters with 69 mph curveballs, 81 mph sliders, 78 mph changeups, 80 mph cutters, and wham, 87 mph fastballs. They got some hits. But they didn't score runs. And in one inning in which a passed ball allowed a runner to reach first, we almost saw Pedro tie the all-time record of four strikeouts in one inning. There were lots of pop-ups, lots of groundouts, lots of pitches, but Pedro always seemed ahead in the count. Carlos Beltran and Moises Alou gave us some runs but nothing gaudy, no more than we needed. Pedro was two for two, with a double and an infield single. Magical Mets Pedro, the Pedro who pitched so well in 2005 and the first half of 2006, was back. He was different from lightning-perfection Red Sox Pedro. This was mysterious, slow-pitch Pedro. They couldn't hit him any more than they could hit the other one. When his five shutout innings were up, we demanded a curtain call and he gave it to us.

We sat down to watch the relief pitchers. We were on a short fuse for Guillermo Mota, who had been lousy lately, coming off his fifty-game suspension for steroids. But Mota didn't give Pedro's ballgame back. Feliciano, Wagner, and Heilman pitched well to close it down. The ending was happy. We were even rewarded with the distraction of the actress Julia Stiles taking a seat during the fifth inning just two rows in front of us, in a blue Mets hat, with a friend, like a perfectly normal person in a sea of normal people.

Normal Mets fans, on that September Sunday, were very happy. We were coasting to a new clinching. We would return to the postseason, but this time we would have a starting pitching staff that was not crumbling and tearing their calf muscles. On a hot and perfect September afternoon, I dreamed of the cool bracing nights of October.

No Choke

By winning their game on September 9, the Mets completed a three-game sweep of the Astros. Then the Braves came into town and the Mets took two out of three from them. On September 12, when the series with the Braves was over, the Mets were 83-62. The Phillies were 76-69. The Mets were seven games ahead of the Phillies with seventeen games to play. If the Mets were to go 9-8 over those seventeen games, a below average performance for an 83-62 team, the Phillies would have to win all seventeen of their remaining games to beat us. A Phillies record of 16-1 would only tie us. How hard was it for a Mets team that had just won nine out of ten to go 9-8? And if they achieved this very modest goal, what were the odds that the Phillies would win seventeen in a row? Wouldn't that be something like one over two to the 17th power? Seriously. The regular season was over. If there was to be a choke, it would have to be the worst choke in history. And it would take more than the Mets choking to give the division title to Philadelphia. The mediocre-all-season-long Phillies would have to come up with an incredible streak. It wasn't going to happen. To worry would be like worrying about getting hit by lightning or being in a plane crash. You could do it, but the odds were such that it was a waste of your time.

It was funny, I thought. The Mets had done almost everything in their forty-five seasons, but they had never choked. In the thirty-seven years of divisional play, the New York Mets had won five division titles. Three times, in 1986, 1988, and 2006, they had done it by building an early insurmountable lead and holding it. In 1969 and 1973, the Mets won their division by coming from far behind and passing everyone else with a strong final month. In 1970, 1984, 1985, 1987, 1989, 1990, 1999, 2000, and 2001, the Mets were in contention for the division title into at least the final month, and often into the last few days, of the season. But they never held a first-place lead of more than two games after April in any of those seasons, and of course they did not win any of those division titles in the end. Mets fans knew the experience of greatness (which they valued because of its rarity). They knew the experience of coming from behind. They knew the experience of fighting the good fight and losing with dignity in the end. They did not know, and they did not therefore fear, the collapse when you're way ahead, the bottom falling out of what appears to be a safe and happy universe. Mets fans were not like fans of the Phillies, or the Red Sox, or the Cubs, or the Dodgers, or the Blue Jays, or the Giants, or the Angels, or even the Yankees.

It's true that the Mets had experienced some dramatic September collapses in the puzzling, tired-Piazza, crazy-Valentine years of the late 1990s. In 1997, we could have had the Wild Card, but we fell just short. In 1998, we had had a small Wild Card lead but we lost it. In 1999, we won the Wild Card after losing another Wild Card lead and then having a miracle comeback. So the Wild Card races of the late 1990s, to be honest, did have moderately choke-suggestive aspects. But they didn't really count as chokes. We had never had that much of a lead to begin with, and, let's face it, although the Wild Card is as good a route to a World Championship as a division title, it is still just the Wild Card. Wild Cards aren't things you fight for. They're things you settle for. The crazy Wild Card seasons hadn't taught Mets fans about the psychology of collapse any more than they had taught them about the psychology of triumph.

Mets fans knew disappointment. Boy did they. But going into the final weeks of 2007, they were choke innocents, choke virgins. We had been through just about everything else, but we had not been through that.

My Birthday Party

On September 14, the Phillies came to town for a three-game series at Shea. They swept us, just as they had swept us in the four-game series at the end of August. The odds against them doing that were at least 8:1, I figured. But they did it, and the Mets were suddenly only four games ahead, with fourteen more games to play. The odds were still on our side. But the unlikelihood of the worst possible outcome had been reduced by a factor of eight. If the Mets were to win seven and lose seven, the Phillies would now have to win twelve and lose two to pass us. Okay. That still sounded good for us. And Mets fans could take some comfort in the fact that the two remaining series were at home, against the Nationals and the Marlins, two teams well under .500 who were fighting with each other to stay out of last place.

After the sweep by the Phillies, the Mets went to Washington and lost two games to the Nationals. The Phillies, at the same time, took two from the Cardinals. The Phillies had gained five and a half games on the Mets in six days. Then on the nineteenth, the Mets beat the Nationals and the Phillies lost to the Cardinals. But on the twentieth, the Mets lost to the Marlins and the Phillies beat the Cardinals. After the Marlins game on September 20, the Mets were 84-68. The Phillies were 83-70, a game and a half behind us. On the twenty-first and the twenty-second, both teams won. On Sunday, September 23, we still had a game and a half lead. The Mets had eight more games to play and the Phillies had seven.

On September 23, 2007, I celebrated my fifty-third birthday, and for the first time since I was thirteen, I had a birthday party. But it wasn't just a birthday party. It was a book launch. I had written a book called *Mets Fan*, and I was throwing a party to promote it at a little bohemian joint on Avenue A in the East Village called Mo Pitkin's House of Satisfaction. A reader of the blog that I had set up to promote my book was an investor in the place, and he recommended it for the book launch party. It turned out to be perfect for the occasion. A book launch party has always been a fantasy of mine, a part of my dream of myself as a writer and not just a professor. I had always imagined that they were glamorous affairs, either glittery or funky. We were obviously going to go for funky here. But they don't really have book launch parties anymore, certainly not for obscure little books by nobodies, books like my *Mets Fan*. They're things of the past, things from the days before the corporate acquisition of publishing houses, things from the days when the world, irrationally, had more on its mind than making money.

They also don't really have funky and cheap little joints in the East Village anymore. Yet Mo Pitkin's was trying to be the kind of mythical place where hip, offbeat, and not very rich people could gather and eat comfort food and hear great music and watch performance art. It was a dream of the Hartman brothers, Phil and Jesse, big Mets fans who had founded the Two Boots pizza empire. Mo Pitkin's would be out of business by the end of the year. It just seemed to me to be appropriate that we were having the kind of party they don't have anymore in the kind of place they don't have anymore, to celebrate a book about being a baseball fan in ways that didn't fit what baseball was anymore. The whole thing was an exercise, on every level, of wistful yet idealistic romanticism. It was perfect for a fifty-third birthday. It was perfect for an aging professor who was trying to reinvent himself, before it was too late, as the writer he had dreamed of being ever since he was fifteen.

I had invited my friends and colleagues, my blog readers, and my fellow bloggers to the party. And of course my family was there, including my mother Helen, who had made it up the one flight of stairs with considerable difficulty, and my father-in-law Charlie, who was bravely going out into the world less than two months after losing his wife. My sisters, Jennifer and Stefanie, my wife, Sheila, and my daughter, Sonia, were there. Sonia wore a cool, hip new dress and had gotten a bohemian gamine haircut, thinking that she was going to a big literary event in Greenwich

Village. A lot of people came. I was particularly moved by the turnout of fellow bloggers. There was Steve Keane of the Eddie Kranepool Society, Mike Steffanos of Mike's Mets, and Kathy Foronjy, who had made a documentary film about Mets fans called *Mathematically Alive*. Mike Silva, the first guy to interview me on a radio show, came with his dad. There were MetsGrrl and three other women bloggers (Zoë Rice, Taryn Cooper, and Stefi Kaplan) who called themselves the Joan Whitney Paysons, after the woman who was the Mets' first owner. I knew my friends, family, and colleagues, of course, but I had never met any of the Mets people in person before. I felt like a kid in a cartoon whose imaginary friends have come to life. Sure I knew that people I knew from the Internet really existed, but you're never really sure, you know what I mean? For all I knew, these people were inside the worn laptop with the F8 key missing on which I had written my book, and on which I composed my blog and my website.

Everyone was so nice and so supportive. Everybody made me feel as if I had done something worth doing. Everybody made me feel as if we were all in this together, trying to build an alternate world of blogs, podcasts, and films about the Mets, an alternate world in which the hopes and dreams of millions and the joys and sorrows of fandom were treated with respect. For that one afternoon, the Mets did not exist simply to soak up irritating condescension from Mike and the Mad Dog. They were part of a family that included many fine, generous, and imaginative people.

All through the afternoon, as we ate Two Boots pizza, drank, and talked, people kept track of the game that was being played in Florida. The Mets finally won, 7–6, on a David Wright home run in the eleventh. The Phillies had lost, 5–3, to the Nationals. We were two and a half games up with seven more to play. The Phillies had six more games to play. If we could win four of our seven games, the Phillies would have to win all six of theirs to tie us. If we only won three, they would have to win all six of their games to beat us. If we won two and lost five, they would have to go 5-1 to beat us. We were okay. Everyone in the assembled company felt good. When the game was over, I read a few pieces from my book to my fellow Mets fans.

You know, in the end, I am convinced that the most amazing thing about the New York Mets is not the inconsistent baseball franchise by that name. It is the millions of people who continue to root for them, through years of frustration and disappointment, even though they are geographically entitled to root for the most successful of all baseball franchises. We fans had been dangling over a precipice ever since the Mets had dropped those four games in Philadelphia. Now we could breathe just a little bit easier. We could rest. We would find out soon enough how we would remember this strange moment in Mets history. Whatever happened, though, I knew that I would never forget my fifty-third birthday. I knew I would never forget my sense of wonder at how I was celebrating my fifty-third birthday. I would never have imagined any of this on my fiftieth birthday. Life was full of surprises. Life is nothing but surprises. It is one thing that might have been different after another thing that might have been different. That's what it is.

This Team Does Not Suck

The eleventh-inning victory in Florida launched the Mets into the final week of the season. The team was 87-68 and it was about to play three games against the 69-87 Nationals, a makeup game against the 73-82 Cardinals, and then three games against the 66-90 Marlins. On Wednesday, September 26, I went to Shea to see the final game of the series against the Nationals. The Nationals had won the first two games of the series, and they won the game I went to, 9–6, for a sweep at Shea. The game, as you might imagine, was a genuinely lousy experience.

But do you know what was even worse than the Mets losing? What was worse was having to listen to people's mouths. Not everybody's mouth. I'm talking about the brain-dead 10 percent. That's all it is. It's never any more than 10 percent. It's even less. But you could hear them loud and clear. If the Mets were going to lose a playoff spot by a game or two, others could blame the team. I was going to blame the loud minority of morons in the stands. I have other folks to blame too. They posted the attendance for this game as 51,940. I didn't see any 51,000 people. I'd guess that there were 35,000 people in the stands. So I also blame the 16,000 people who had tickets and weren't there. And I blame the several hundred thousand people who could have bought any of the 4,000 unsold tickets to that game and didn't take the trouble to do so.

On his way out of the stadium at the end of the game, one of the booing losers, on our sacred ramps, observed that "this team sucks!" If this team sucked, how would you have liked to have rooted for the twenty-eight teams in the major leagues that hadn't won as many games as the Mets had won by September 26? Go down the lineup, moron. Sure, Jose Reyes was having a mysteriously unsatisfying second half, but taking everything into account, would you really want to say that Jose Reyes sucks? Did Luis Castillo, who was hitting over .300, suck? Did David Wright suck? I'm surprised Wright wasn't booed when he popped up and when he hit into a double play, but I think I heard some of the booers thinking about it. Did Carlos Beltran suck? You know, for a guy who ended the 2007 season with 32 home runs and 109 runs batted in, he'd heard an awful lot of boos in the course of the year, so maybe he did suck. Did Moises Alou suck? Did Carlos Delgado? (The answer is no, don't even think about it.) Did our bench suck? Did Pedro or El Duque? Glavine was giving us the same year he gave us last year. Ollie was having a terrific comeback season. Maine slumped in the second half, but surely he'd had an excellent second year in the majors. Wagner had had a spectacular year. Heilman and Feliciano had done decent jobs, just as they did last year. So who sucked? Well, our middle relief staff was nowhere near as good in 2007 as it was in 2006. That was the crux of it and it was perfectly obvious. Sure, some of our starters slumped or were incapacitated as we got to the end, but that happened in 2006 as well. The most significant difference I could see between the 2007 Mets and the 2006 Mets was that the middle relievers in 2007 did not measure up to the previous year's Mota, Bradford, Oliver, Sanchez, and Hernandez.

There was the reason, right there. That explained it; that would account for the seven-game difference. That's all you needed to explain it. Oh yeah, and the other difference is that the Phillies and Braves were better than they were in 2006, which created a race. And in 2007 we were used to the Mets being good, so it wasn't a novelty. So, when the mediocre middle relief could not hold a lead built for a tired starter who imploded, we felt anguish because there were consequences, and nothing causes a fan to lose faith more than repeatedly blowing leads when a team is fighting to stay in first place. It gives you a sense of total insecurity.

No matter what was happening, I could not bring myself to believe the theory that most Mets fans were coming to accept during that dark September: that the 2007 team just didn't want it enough. They didn't suck. We sucked and we didn't want it enough. They were an excellent team, probably the best in a relatively weak league, and they had one particular glaring flaw. And that flaw was difficult to correct, because if someone really shines as a middle reliever, there is a logical temptation to turn him into a starter or a closer.

As Donald Rumsfeld once observed, you go to war with the army you have. I liked these guys. I was tired of hearing the impression of fans that they lacked this or that intangible manifestation of "guts" or "spirit" or "heart." The booers and carpers didn't really know that. Willie Randolph was a quiet, undemonstrative guy. He wasn't going to change his personality just so that fans and talk show hosts wouldn't say that he had no heart.

I was going to cheer them on. Others would join me. We would pull this one out. It would not be like the Cardinal series that ended 2006. I loved the Mets. They would have to wave white flags and kiss the Marlins' shoes before I would ever dream of booing them.

Washington at Valley Forge

To support my team, I showed up at the stadium on Thursday, September 27. And from the very beginning of the game, you could feel how insecure people were. They were hopeful, but they were terrified. You could tell this when you heard the relief in the crowd's throat, when the first pitch Pedro Martinez threw was a strike. You heard the nervous fear when the second Cardinal at-bat was a single. And you knew what you were up against when you heard the fatalistic groan after Castillo's first-inning error. Pedro looked good. I thought things would be all right when I saw his 72 mph curveball, that slow, sneaky strikeout pitch. I felt as if the Cards would not score many runs. We might be okay.

Nobody really thought we would be. I saw the Mets come up, and I couldn't imagine what it would be like for them to get a few hits in a row. I felt as if I had looked into the future and seen nothing. I would stay for the whole ballgame of course. I would cheer and chant "Lets Go Mets!" and glower once again at the booers. Those guys are loud, let me tell you. I think the part of their brain that has been removed has been replaced with extra lung tissue.

What really gave me the sense of deepest sadness was the fact that, perhaps for the first time ever, I took no pleasure in the festive goofiness of the stadium. I found it distracting. At one point Mr. Met popped into the crowd right next to where Sonia and I were sitting. Sonia whooped and ran after him shouting, "Dad, take a picture! Take a picture!" I took a beautiful picture of my beautiful daughter and my favorite Hall-of-Famer. But for the first time in my life, Mr. Met could do nothing to cheer me up.

I didn't want to have fun. Yet all around me people continued to have fun. The young couple sitting in front of us made me feel as if I was behind the Kiss Cam. Boy did they have a lot of beer, and pretzels, and hot dogs, and ice cream, as if being able to eat all this food and kiss in the bright lights was a kind of foreplay. They made me wonder, in my sourness, if they should think of setting up little booths in the concourse of the new stadium. I think the Romans had things like that. Oh, was I miserable! I saw people leaving before the end of the game, with no emotions on their faces. They weren't numb, just indifferent.

The ironies of the season flashed before me as I sat there waiting for the runs that never came. We were good and the Yankees were bad. And then that all changed. We were a .500 team since what now seemed like an impossibly distant Memorial Day. And now it looked as if we had forgotten how to be anything but a .500 team. We did, as a crowd, enjoy a moment of pride when, just when he should have been taken out, Pedro insisted on pitching to Albert Pujols and got him out. We cheered Pedro. He did his job. But it wasn't enough. He left us alone with our thoughts and our bullpen. Oh why, pray tell, would we want to stand up and sing "Take Me Out to the Ball Game"? Why did I have to hear Lou Monte singing "Lazy Mary"?

After we made a lot of noise through a feeble ninth inning, it ended. The 0-3-1 that had been on the board for so long stayed there and froze. It was stuck. It was humiliating. We were tied for first. Our lead was gone. And here we were in this mocking semblance of a familiar reality, in our beloved stadium where the lights were still bright and kids were still cute. But nothing was the same.

Most of the people in the crowd on the ramps were anguished. I was with them. Some were indignant. Screw them. The season was down to three games.

I thought of how strange it was that in four days, we would know what happened. I remembered reading about Washington at Valley Forge in a book I had when I was a kid. I remembered wanting to go back in time to tell the Continental Army that even though things looked as bad as they could possibly be, they would win and their victory would create our wonderful country. I wanted to tell the Mets something like that. But I couldn't. I had to leave them in the snow, with their crutches and bandages and grey, blank faces, just like the pictures in my book about Valley Forge.

Remember the Maine

On Friday, the Mets lost to the Marlins, 7–4, to drop into second place for the first time since May. There were only two more games to play. Then on Saturday, after having lost eight games in the standing in just sixteen games, after having lost five games in a row to three teams that were well below .500, the Mets played one of the best games they ever played. John Maine came within four outs of a no-hitter, giving up one hit and two walks, and striking out fourteen Marlins in seven and two-thirds innings. The Mets offense, in the meantime, scored thirteen runs on nineteen hits. Lastings Milledge hit two home runs. Was there ever a better, more inspiring, more energizing Mets game than this? Had a losing streak ever been broken in a more dramatic fashion at a more important moment? The Mets were back in a tie for first with the Phillies.

Retelling this doesn't capture what it felt like, because all we can feel now is the irony. There was no irony after that blessed, hopeful innocent Saturday. There was what comes before irony, what always comes before irony. There was the true substance of life, its existence in the present. If that isn't real, then nothing is real, because the irony is that the earth is going to be burnt to a cinder when the sun expands as it cools out and dies. What is real is what was there. It is what gets lost when we look back on something, after we know what didn't last and what got ruined.

It Isn't Fair

On September 28, 2007, Tom Glavine, a certain Hall-of-Famer, took the mound in the hope of winning his 303rd game, in the hope of returning the Mets to the postseason. He faced nine batters. One grounded into a fielder's choice. Five singled. One doubled. Two walked. One batter, the opposing pitcher, was hit by a pitch. Seven runs were scored by the Florida Marlins in one-third of an inning. It was the worst appearance of Glavine's twenty-year career. The Mets got a run in the bottom of the first. They didn't score again, although I begged and I pleaded with them in every inning. The Marlins scored another run in the fifth. The final score of the game was 8–1.

When the game was over, I thought of how it isn't fair that you live through 162 games and are left with this.

It isn't fair that after that golden spring and that irritating restless summer filled with good things and bad things, all you have now is this.

It isn't fair that I got to have that warm September Sunday with a seven-game lead and Pedro on the mound. It isn't fair that I got to have that now impossibly distant day before this one, when it looked as if everything might be all right, when we had thirteen runs and nineteen hits and almost our first no-hitter.

It isn't fair that after all of the pleasure and excitement of comebacks and renewals, after all of the promise of a baseball season that was always on the point of redeeming itself, all we had now was this thing that could no longer change or be redeemed. It was already hardening into an unpleasant memory. It might have lived. If one-third of an inning had been different, we might have had one last historic game, which we might have won, which might even have led to the World Series. All of the lousiness and weirdness might have been forgiven and forgotten. But now we were done, one game out of first in the NL East, one game out of the Wild Card. And we would always look back on this exciting, exasperating season through the dirty glass of one rotten Sunday.

The 2007 season would always be like a love affair or a marriage that had its ups and downs, but that had lots of wonderful moments, too, even though all you can remember now is one awful final argument. It would be like the wonderful productive life of a friend whom you can't remember without thinking of the awful circumstances of his death. The 2007 season would always be like any good and hopeful thing that is stamped forever by the awfulness of its end.

Years from now, Mets fans wouldn't want to think about this thing that made them so excited on the morning of September 28. It would be like 1988 and 2000, such wonderful seasons! But it would be much, much worse. It wouldn't just be a disappointment. It would be something shameful. Because we didn't even make it to the postseason, despite having been in first place since the middle of May. We had it and we lost it. Something solid turned to sand and our fingers couldn't hold it.

One reason fans love baseball is that the death of a season is not really the end. The Mets, like the earth, come back to life in the spring. The Mets, weirdly enough, are eternal. But each season is mortal. And each is preserved in a numbered box in our closet. Some boxes we open and look at over and over. And some never get opened.

This one won't be opened much. Even though it had its treasures. There were the emergence of Perez and Maine and the return of Pedro. There was the magnificence of Reyes in the first half and Wright in the second. There were the steady brilliance of Beltran and the aging grandeur of Moises Alou. There were all these great things, and some of these things would never be seen again. This was the last time we'd see Tommy Glavine, or Paul Lo Duca, or Shawn Green in Mets uniforms. The Mets who would come to life in the spring would not be the Mets who left the field, showered, and dressed that Sunday. Nor should they be. What would come back to life would be different. It would be new. But it would also be old. And we would follow it to the end of its arc across next summer's sky, just as we followed this one.

So there it is. Say goodbye to it. It was a good season that ended horribly, and the future will always be unfair to it. Give it a last kiss. And remember that you once loved it, just as you'll remember forever how and why you hated it. There it is, pale and cold on that slab. Isn't it pitiful to see it like that?

Explanations

The 2007 season, which still had plenty of redeeming features all the way up through the 161st game, was turned overnight into the worst thing that had ever happened to the New York Mets. Any way you tried to calculate it, the odds of losing a seven-game lead over seventeen games were more than a thousand to one. The Mets had done something that no team is likely to do again for more than a century. For the rest of my life, whenever people talk about a choke, or even just the possibility of the choke, they will mention the 2007 Mets. They won't talk about the 1964 Phillies as much. The 2007 Mets were going to become a touchstone, one of the markers of baseball possibility. Just as the 1962 Mets still set the standard for baseball lousiness, and just as the 1969 Mets were still the most famous Cinderella team ever, the 2007 Mets, a very good team that got run over by a truck they may or may not have been driving, would always be the team that lost a seven-game lead with seventeen games to play.

The Mets only won five of their last seventeen games. The Phillies had won thirteen of their last seventeen. No answer could be made to the Phillies fans' taunts. All you could do was hang your head. And what was worse, after that May series against the Yankees that gave me the sense that the city was ours again, the Mets won sixty games and lost fifty-nine. The Yankees won seventy-five and lost forty-five. The Yankees, and not the Mets, had made it to the playoffs in 2007. And there was no comfort to be had in the fact that the Yankees were eliminated in the first round of the playoffs. At least they had been there to be eliminated.

The mood in Metsville was ugly. I wish I could say it wasn't, but it was. Mets fans didn't sit around and hug each other and cry together into our beer. It wasn't like 2006. We couldn't mythologize ourselves or our team. We howled. We complained. We

What Did I Want?

The irony wasn't lost on me that I had published a book about being a Mets fan in what turned out to be the worst month in Mets history. I wasn't afraid of the book being a flop and not making any money. I was not planning to live off the profits from the book, let me tell you. But I was hoping that people would read my book and understand what I felt were the particular pleasures of being a baseball fan and being a Mets fan. It was a good thing I had also written about the redemptive pain of being a Mets fan.

On November 11, 2007, Mark Herrmann, a writer for *Newsday*, did a piece about me. Herrmann wrote, "As a literature professor at Hofstra with a PhD from Yale, Dana Brand has spent his career studying the great authors who have shaped American thought and culture. Now he has taken on a much deeper, thornier topic: Why on Earth would anyone be a Mets fan? So far, he has no rational explanation." This is fair enough. *Mets Fan* does begin with the sentence, "There is no good reason why I should care about the New York Mets." Near the end of my book, I return to this sentence and observe, "There is still no good reason. It won't be found." What I also said in the opening paragraph of my book was that "I enjoy my loyalty. I enjoy the irrationality and intensity of my loyalty." The Mets had just done something, however, that called into question the idea of enjoying any such irrational loyalty. This was not like last year. Last year's loss to the Cardinals in the NLCS made Mets fans feel wistful, tragic, loving, and philosophical. Rooting for a team that has just lost a seven-game lead with seventeen games to play can just make you feel like a moron.

But of course I wasn't going to give up on the Mets now. This too had to be lived through. This had to be thought around and thought through, felt around and felt through. I couldn't abandon the Mets. I certainly couldn't abandon them because they had failed to win something. The only way I could imagine abandoning the Mets is if they became like the Yankees, if they became a team that paid too much money all the time in a desperate and selfish belief that they had to win all the time. I could imagine abandoning the Mets if they won too much, not if they lost too much.

This is essentially what I told Mark Herrmann in his article, and as I read the article, I wondered, and I'm sure plenty of *Newsday* readers wondered, "What the hell does this guy want?" It didn't come through clearly enough in what I was quoted as saying, but I really did want the Mets to win. Did I want them to spend $300 million on a ten-year contract for A-Rod? No, I told Herrmann, I didn't. But that would certainly help them win. A-Rod was one of the best ballplayers in the history of the game. Why wouldn't I want him?

Well, I wanted to win in a certain way. Without free agents? No. I had no trouble signing Glavine or Beltran or Martinez. Did I have a problem with very high-priced free agents? Probably not. If I could get Johan Santana for $25 million a year, I'd do it. So I suspect that I really would be willing to do it with money if I could, even though I always say I don't want to do it with money. Of course, I don't want to spend too much money on players who aren't worth the money. Well, yeah, duh.

As I said in the interview and as I said in my book, I really liked the idea of rooting for the underdog. That's part of the Mets tradition. I lived through 1962–1968 and 1977–1983, and I enjoyed those seasons. But how serious was I about all this underdog stuff? Let's say the Mets did absolutely nothing to improve themselves over the off-season, and Philadelphia and Atlanta made some major moves. That would make us underdogs. Would I like that? No. Well, actually I would like it if we ended up winning anyway. Would it be worth taking the risk? No.

So did I want the Mets to do something in the off-season or did I want them to do nothing? Something. What? Something that would make the team better. How do you like the level of thinking here? Maybe I should have been a general manager.

This was my quandary: I didn't know what I wanted. Wait, I did know what I wanted. I wanted a fun rooting situation. Did that mean winning? Yes, but not necessarily. You have to be able to enjoy rooting for a baseball team even when they don't win. To have a fun rooting situation, it helps to have a chance of winning. And it helps to have a team you like. So, I asked myself, which do you want: nice guys with interesting personalities, or guys with high averages with runners in scoring position? The answer is guys with high averages with runners in scoring position who you can manage to convince yourself are nice guys with interesting personalities. They don't all have to be nice guys with interesting personalities. Just some of them is enough, as long as a lot of them have high averages with runners in scoring position.

Who knows what can create a fun rooting situation? When it happens, it happens. It's a hard thing to plan in advance. You can assemble a bunch of good guys, but how they hang together is hard to predict and depends a lot on how many games they're winning. Winning creates chemistry at least as much as chemistry creates winning.

You also have to have that other thing: the hype, the myth, what gets created by the interaction of the fans and the press. Fun rooting situations aren't just a product of what happens on the field, or in the dugout and the clubhouse. You have to have scores of people writing the same stuff over and over again to the point where the millions of people reading the same stuff over and over again start believing it.

We didn't believe in 2007, and this may even have had an impact on what happened. When they don't believe, we don't believe, and when we don't believe, they don't believe.

I know what I wanted. I wanted belief.

What Reggie Jackson Said to Me About the Mets' Collapse

On December 8, 2007, I went to sign copies of *Mets Fan* at the Magic Monikers Autograph and Memorabilia show at the Crowne Plaza Hotel in Secaucus, New Jersey. I sat at a table with Kathy Foronjy and Joe Coburn, the filmmakers who made *Mathematically Alive*, the genuinely wonderful film about New York Mets fandom as a metaphor for successful psychological adaptation to the trials of human existence.

We were sitting in an exhibition hall filled with tables of vendors selling baseball cards, framed pictures of ballplayers, memorabilia, and limited and numbered editions of god-knows-what. The exhibition hall was one of these vaguely underwater-seeming seventies-looking, broad, vast, cramped, windowless spaces. People walked by in team jerseys, jackets, and caps clutching precious baseballs, bats, and posters that had been signed over in the distance by people you couldn't see behind a bank of people in jerseys, jackets, and caps who were taking pictures from cameras in hands raised hopefully high above everyone else's head. Every once in awhile I would walk over and peer above the bank of flashing hands. Against the blank and undecorated wall, you saw lunchroom tables and lunchroom chairs. In front of the tables and chairs was an inner line of people in jackets, jerseys, and caps holding tickets and precious objects. Beyond this inner line, sitting at the lunchroom tables, were silent, unsmiling men writing on the objects, listening to and following instructions from the people standing in front of the tables.

If you looked carefully at the silent men, they reminded you of men you had always known about but had never seen except on screens or in photos or down on the flat, green, distant plane of a ball field. They didn't really look like these men. They were smaller, and older, and wearing shirts and sweaters. Eventually, I allowed myself to understand that these really were the men they seemed to look like, but their silence, the awkward ordinariness of the lines of people in front of them, the flashing of the cameras, and the dim, windowless room, gave me a sense that I was in Plato's cave. I wasn't sure that what I was looking at was real.

As several of the men who had been signing at the tables finished their tedious yet absurdly well-compensated work, they would walk down the aisle where our table was. I saw them close up, surrounded by people who were somehow attached to them. I saw, in some sense, Bob Gibson, Steve Carlton, Eddie Murray, Ozzie Smith, Yogi Berra, Tom Seaver, Ron Guidry, and Don Zimmer. I saw them with my own eyes. It was like a dream, which is the only other place you will ever see so many people you have mainly imagined. It was also like a dream in that it was freaky that it didn't seem strange that they were all there. Somehow I don't really think I saw them, just as I don't really think that a signature on a baseball you've paid to get in a hotel in Secaucus is actually an autograph.

The high point of the day was a genuinely wonderful and strange encounter. Kathy, Joe, and I were sitting at our Mets table, and we saw a cluster of men coming down our aisle, an entourage that must have someone at its center. As the cluster came closer, we saw the man at the core of it: a medium-sized man in ordinary clothes and a black cap and glasses, whom you would not necessarily recognize on a sidewalk in Manhattan. You had to overcome some significant doubt before you could accept the eventually undeniable fact that the man you were looking at was Reggie Jackson. It's been a deep, dark secret, but I've always liked Reggie Jackson. I like ballplayers who are great and who get pleasure from the fact that they are great. We watched him come closer and then we saw him stop and look carefully at the big poster blow-up of the cover of my book that I had set up in front of me. "Mets Fan," he proclaimed. He looked at us. "You folks are Mets fans?" He stared at us and then asked, with a perfect sense of timing and emphasis, "WHAT HAPPENED?" We laughed as his entourage waited patiently for him to have the moment he had chosen to address people he didn't need to address. We scrambled in our minds for something to say to him in response. But we didn't need to do this. He had something to say and he wanted to say it. "What was it, they only needed to win one more game?" "Something like that," we ruefully mumbled. "You know," he said as if he was giving us the benefit of hard-earned wisdom, "people used to call me egotistical, but I tell you, if I had been playing for them, I would have won that one game, even if I had to do it all by myself." "You would have," we agreed, struck dumb by the fact that he had said this to us, that he had said anything, that he had chosen us, strangers who had not been his fans, to give us an idea of what he believed about himself.

Maybe Jackson was right. Maybe you could just will it. I remembered watching that World Series game back in the 1970s in which he hit the three home runs in three swings of the bat. I remembered his cocky face. I remembered pounding the bar I was sitting at when he hit the third home run. I remembered the intensity of my excitement. I was cheering for a non-Met, for a Yankee, the defining Yankee of his time. I was cheering because, with his grand egotistical energy, Jackson knew just where the balls were and how to hit them. He did it three times in a row. In three split seconds.

Say It Ain't So: The Mitchell Report

It is difficult for a fan to enjoy an off-season when his team has just offered up the biggest choke in baseball history. So to distract myself, and perhaps to remind myself of what there was to love about baseball, I bought George Vecsey's new book: *Baseball: A History of America's Favorite Game.* I was reading it just as the Mitchell Report, on the abuse of steroids in baseball, was released on December 13, 2007. Reading Vecsey's book, I was struck by how typical a moment this was in baseball history. It was a typical moment in American history too. And as many people have said, baseball is the best metaphor there is for American life. I almost wish it wasn't.

F. Scott Fitzgerald was one of the many who understood this fact. After Nick and Gatsby have lunch with Meyer Wolfsheim (a character modeled after Arnold Rothstein), Nick asks Gatsby who Wolfsheim is. Gatsby "coolly" replies that this is the guy who fixed the 1919 World Series. Nick says he remembered, of course, that the 1919 World Series had been fixed, but the idea still "staggers" him: "It never occurred to me that one man could start to play with the faith of fifty million people—with the single-mindedness of a burglar blowing a safe." "How did he happen to do that?" Nick asks Gatsby. "He just saw the opportunity," Gatsby replies. Nick and Gatsby could have been talking about the Mitchell Report.

In order to understand America, you have to understand why Gatsby is so cool and matter-of-fact when he explains that the man who fixed the World Series just saw an opportunity. You have to understand why Gatsby has an imperishable dream and is indifferent to any scruples that could get in the way of achieving it. You have to understand how Nick can manage to believe that he's the only honest person he's ever known even though you can see how dishonest he is. You have to understand why journalists and a nation could get all sentimental about the damage the underpaid and exploited champion 1919 White Sox did to America's innocence when they threw the Series. You have to understand what was in the minds of the U.S. Supreme Court when they decided that baseball is a game and not a business and so it's all right for the owners to keep all the money and treat the players like slaves. You have to understand how baseball managed to keep African-Americans off the field for sixty years with hardly anybody complaining, even though it was no secret that some of the greatest players in the world were being excluded. You have to understand how apparently intelligent people sitting next to you in a ballpark will wax lyrical about how baseball players used to care about loyalty and the game itself and now all they care about is money. You have to understand why Roger Clemens eats a big breakfast every morning without anything interfering with his digestion. You have to understand why you still take baseball seriously.

We are a nation of suckers. This is our greatest strength and our greatest weakness. It amazes me, and it amazes the rest of the world, how many times Americans can lose their innocence without losing their innocence. We are a country of dreamers and innovators with a competitive and imaginative energy that has done the world a lot of good. And yet, no matter what we do to gain our blessed "competitive edge," we are incapable of ever believing that we are either deluded or corrupt. No matter how many mistakes we make, we don't believe we can make a mistake. We only acknowledge mistakes as an effort to limit damage, and then we explain and glorify the mistakes by saying that they came from a noble excess of our desire to achieve our dream. We are not a stupid people. We know that cheating is rampant in our culture and in our games. We know that there isn't really much competitive balance in our competitions. But once we get those stars in our eyes and those lumps in our throats, we never get them out.

That's what we are. As Americans and as baseball fans. I'm not saying I'm going to change or that you're going to change. We're suckers.

If they build it, we will come.

The Signing of Johan Santana

After reading the Mitchell Report and venting my outrage at the rotten eggs who had tried, by cheating, to alter the competitive balance of baseball, I turned my attention to the efforts of the Mets to trade for Johan Santana, a pitcher who would receive and deserve the most expensive contract ever offered to a pitcher. Santana was eligible to become a free agent at the end of the 2008 season, so he could be had for less than his full value. The Twins could certainly not afford what he would cost. The Yankees and the Red Sox could, and they were the Mets' competition. On January 29, 2008, the Twins accepted the Mets' offer, and so we got the best pitcher in the American League for four decent but not spectacular prospects.

The Mets had to make this trade because they needed to do something to get people's minds off the 2007 season. For three months, they had done virtually nothing, because there was nothing to be done. The Mets had to give their fans something to believe in again. There had to be a change that would give the team something of a new character. It was also necessary to replace Tommy Glavine in the rotation. Glavine was going home to Atlanta, after disappointing Mets fans by telling reporters that he was disappointed but not devastated to have blown the last game of the 2007 season.

Santana was a genuinely big deal. He was one of the two or three pitchers who could lay legitimate claim to being considered the best in baseball. He was a remarkably consistent lefty. He had several seasons with an ERA below 3 in the American League. He pitched a lot of innings, got a lot of strikeouts, and gave up very few hits and walks per innings pitched. His statistical profile was a lot like Seaver's. He was about to turn twenty-nine. He was a genuine reason to get excited, and with him, the Mets certainly had the best pitching staff in their division, and they arguably had the best in the league. There was no reason to think that they couldn't make it to the playoffs now, and with someone like Santana as their ace, they would be favored in any postseason series they would play in.

When Santana was introduced to the press at Shea, everyone was impressed with how stable, solid, and centered he seemed. He was articulate, and he came across as dedicated and very intelligent. He was a good man who helped out the little town high in the Andes where he was born and grew up. He was likeable and would get along with the guys on the team. He said he wanted to win a World Series with the Mets. He said New York was the center of the world.

I still didn't know much about Johan Santana, but as his press conference ended, I felt I knew enough to start rooting for him. I knew his statistics, and now I could add a character to the statistical contour (consistency, toughness, nice guy, an unselfish player). I offered my conditional allegiance to the character I'd made. I knew that sometimes we find out that the characters we make up for our baseball heroes are nothing like the people themselves (this was the case, say, with DiMaggio or Mantle). And sometimes we run up too hard against what they actually are as human beings (this happened with poor Steve Trachsel). But being a baseball fan involves this pact we make with a person we create, as we project onto players our hopes and dreams and fears.

Johan Santana, a pleasant, exceptionally talented man, was ready to accept his role and responsibilities. He knew that we had a story here and that he was expected to provide a compelling and very necessary turn of the plot. Like Gary Carter in 1985 and Mike Piazza in 1998, Johan Santana would assume the mantle of our dreams. Depending on what happened, his calm demeanor, his changeup, his consistency, and his unusual skill as a hitter would all acquire meanings. They would all become part of our collective memory. He would earn his enormous salary by becoming part of each of us, just as Carter was part of us, and Piazza was. We were ready to love him. And we would love him, if he did what he knew he had to do.

The Sign Man

In February, right after Santana signed his contract with the Mets, it was reported in the press that Karl Ehrhardt, "the Sign Man," had died at the age of eighty-three. From 1964 to 1981, Ehrhardt, an ad designer, had a season ticket in the field boxes at Shea. At his feet, he kept a bag of homemade professional-quality signs. When something significant happened in a game, Karl would stand and hold up a sign that would comment on the action. He had 1,200 signs in all, the most famous of which were "There Are No Words," which he held up when Cleon Jones made the catch that ended the 1969 World Series, "Grant's Tomb," which he held up in the empty stadium after M. Donald Grant dealt away Tom Seaver, and "Ya Gotta Believe." Tug McGraw was responsible for that last slogan, which expressed the spirit that brought the Mets the 1973 pennant. But it was the Sign Man who made that phrase into the slogan of the Mets and the city that loved them.

In the beginning, you see, we didn't have Diamond Vision. We fans had to figure out for ourselves when and how to express our excitement. We didn't have Peter Finch telling us to open all the windows. No recorded voice from a pop song insisted that we all had to clap our hands. Don't get me wrong. I've come to love the programmed cheerleading as much as anyone else, but it's nice to remember when we didn't have any of it. Well, we did have the organ going "bump bump bump Bump bump bump bump Bump" and then a trumpet going "da da da Da da Da." But that was it. The rest of it was pretty much up to us.

So we invented a chant: "Lets Go Mets!" Nobody told us to do that. We did it ourselves. And we had banners. You should have seen them. Going to Shea in the early years could feel like visiting the Lower East Side or Little Italy in the early years of the century, with crowds of people and all of these sheets hanging over everybody's heads, flapping in the wind. On the sheets, or on what art teachers used to call "oak tag," were witty and clever drawings and slogans, all desperately seeking a TV camera. People would walk through the stands to look at the banners. And there was even a Banner Day, when proud banner-makers would parade on the field between games of a scheduled doubleheader.

The Sign Man came out of that early Mets world. Being a Mets fan in the 1960s was very interactive, although I'm not sure we had that word back then. Or if we had it, we didn't use it. But we were all in the game, and we had to make up our own ways of loving and cheering for the Mets. We didn't just sit there and do what they told us. We talked back to the Mets. With signs. With words. We were an articulate mob. And Karl Ehrhardt was our leader.

I guess you could say that Karl was the first Mets blogger. The people who brought their homemade banners to the game couldn't vary their message. What they had to say was determined before they entered the stadium. But the Sign Man could respond as things happened. He'd hold up his sign and look around for people's approval. We gave it. He spoke for us. And he spoke for himself. Just like a good blogger. And like a good blogger, he loved the Mets unconditionally, but he wouldn't pretend that he liked everything he saw.

Holding up his signs, Karl Ehrhardt became the first Mets fan famous just for being a Mets fan. He anticipated Cowbell Man and Doris from Rego Park. We need people like this so that we don't become an undifferentiated mass in our own minds or in the minds of the Mets. We are all individual people. And a few of us have to stand out as representative individuals so that we don't all lose sight of this fact.

The Sign Man disappeared from Shea around the same time that a lot of us were disappearing. But the rest of us came back, although he didn't. I don't know what the story was and I've read several different versions. He did disappear around the time the banners disappeared. I've heard that insurance companies and the Mets didn't like them because they were dangerous (foul balls aren't dangerous?). Diamond Vision came around this time too. Everything changed.

In the 1980s and 1990s I missed Karl Ehrhardt, and I wish I could have seen his signs from 1981 onwards. We need Karl Ehrhardts, like we need Cowbell Man and the guy with the Metsmobile. We need the folk art of emotion.

I hope the Mets appreciate and understand this. I hope there will be room for this in the new stadium. I hope the museum in Citi Field will have some sort of acknowledgement of the contributions of Mets fans. Because if a bunch of guys play a game on a baseball field and nobody holds up signs or bangs cowbells or paints their faces or gets to the park hours early to cook on a hibachi and sit on a very old lawn chair, then nothing has really happened. If no one is around to watch or care, then the Mets don't really exist. Okay, maybe they exist.

But it is because of us that they matter.

Going into the 2008 Season

The historic collapse of the Mets at the end of the 2007 season created a sense of urgency. And desperation. What had happened could only be tolerated as the unpleasant part of a story that would have a happy ending. Without a season of redemption to follow it, 2007 would just dangle. It would be the most dramatic of our many disappointments. It would not be the dark wood in which we wandered before we climbed the sunlit mountain.

As the 2008 season began, I was worried and fearful. I was not worried about whether the Mets were good enough to win. As far as I could tell, they were still one of the best teams in the National League. They had a good but not a reliable chance of making it to the postseason, and maybe even all the way to the end. I was worried about Mets fans. I was worried whether we were going to be able to enjoy the season.

The ability to enjoy a baseball season depends on context. The 1984, 1997, and 2005 seasons were not the most successful Mets seasons, but they were fun because after years of misery, an exciting and sympathetic team was performing above our expectations. The Mets won more games in 1987 than they did in 1984, but 1984 was much more fun. It wasn't following 1986. It was following 1983. Every new season picks up the thread of the previous season. This was a problem. After the just miss of 2006 and the collapse of 2007, there were only a few ways to finish the story so that fans would be happy.

Would their fans be satisfied if the Mets just made it to the postseason? How would fans react if it looked, at *any point*, like they might not? Would fans cheer on this great bunch of guys to show that they still had faith in them? Or had their faith been so abused by what happened in 2007 that at the first sign of trouble, they would just boo or throw up their hands and stay home? What would happen this year if the Mets stumbled and the fans booed? On the one hand, I would want to leap out of my seat and strangle my fellow fans. On the other hand, I would know exactly where they were coming from. The same bile would churn in my stomach and the same screech of pain would rise from my gut, only to be stopped by the clenching of my teeth.

If the Mets won the division, would fans be satisfied with any postseason that did not at least take us one game further than we got in 2006? Hell, would the fans be satisfied with any postseason that did not take us further than we got in 2000?

This wasn't good. I wished I could say, on the verge of what I hoped would be a happy season, that I was pumped and psyched and all that. I was, kind of. But I couldn't help but acknowledge that 2006 and 2007 had done a number on my head. I wasn't even thinking about 2000 and everything that followed it, and well, maybe even 1973 and everything that followed it, or 1962 and everything—oh, forget it. I thought that the Mets had an excellent chance of having a successful season in 2008. But I didn't know what the chances were that Mets fans were going to have any fun.

There was also the serious problem of the fact that, except for the addition of Santana and the subtraction of Glavine, Trachsel, and Green, we were being asked to love the same team that had blown the 2007 season. We knew Wright, Reyes, Beltran, Perez, Maine, Wagner, and the rest of them were good, but wasn't there a problem of tarnish? Few people wanted the Mets to clean the team out and replace it with a new one. Everybody understood that these players had the talent to be successful. But if we had seen them go down so dramatically once, could we shake our fear that they would go down again?

The 2007 season had changed our sense of who these guys were. We knew Wright was a great ballplayer, but we had seen that frustrated, helpless look on his face so many times that we didn't have the confidence in him that we wanted to have. Reyes was still Jose Reyes, but if he hadn't inexplicably dropped off at the end of 2007, nothing would have happened as it had happened. There was an arrogant defensiveness on Jose's face while he was in his slump. We didn't recognize him when he looked like that. Beltran was the same as he ever was, but Beltran did not contribute as much to the team's personality and spirit as he contributed to their run total. Beltran's steady, superb play was not enough. *We* needed more, and where were we going to get it? Carlos Delgado, with his injury-plagued, sub-par season, was now something different from what he had been. He couldn't be the same leader in the clubhouse without that awesome swing he used to have. I still loved Delgado and I didn't believe any of the negative rumors about him. I wanted him to come back, but I thought of him as the leg of a chair I hoped would just hold out until we had the time to get it replaced. Paul Lo Duca was no longer here. The Mets had gotten rid of him, and then it came out in the Mitchell Report that he had used steroids. Lo Duca was going to be replaced by Brian Schneider, about whom I knew nothing. Schneider was coming to the Mets along with Ryan Church in a trade for Lastings Milledge, whom I had really wanted to see grow up and develop into a fun, nutty, bad-boy superstar. Now instead of Milledge we had this Church guy, who, according to the first reports, had been scared witless by some fundamentalist preacher the Nationals had hired who told Church that his Jewish ex-girlfriend was going to go to Hell. Did I have to root for somebody like that? Perez and Maine looked fine, but Mike Pelfrey was no longer anybody we were counting on. In our mind, he was already one of these prospects who becomes a trivia question. Glavine was gone. We were counting on Santana, but I was sheepish about that, since he was such a great pitcher and the Mets had essentially bought him. In the meantime, Willie Randolph looked calm and determined. But how you feel about a manager who is calm and determined depends on what has just happened. It also depends on what you think is going to happen.

The Mets were tarnished. I felt as loyal as ever, but I felt as if my loyalty required effort and concentration. I did not have the happy, expectant, innocent excitement I had at the start of the 2007 season. Something had to bring that back. A good start would bring that back. Maybe Jose Reyes would go back to what he had been. Maybe Delgado would too. David Wright could make me feel confident again. Pelfrey might improve. And if they played well, Schneider and Church wouldn't have a hard time winning me over. But could it happen? What was it going to take for these guys to become the 2008 team and not the 2007 team? What was going to renew them?

The VW Bus and the Maserati

Going into the 2008 season, one thing was certainly new. There was a stadium in the parking lot. It was impossible to ignore and it was big enough to block the traditional view of Flushing from the seats at Shea. On March 30, just before the season started, the *New York Times* ran an article by Ben Shpigel entitled "Shea in '64: The Planes Above, the Mets Below." In it, Ron Darling was asked what it was like to come to Shea this year, with Citi Field looming over the outfield wall. Ron said: "It's like driving a VW bus with a Maserati in the lot."

Exactly.

A Volkswagen Bus is built to contain as much as it possibly can. It is made with an optimistic sense that it's good to be big, that big things contain more, that they encourage the forming of a community, the inclusion of everybody. They beckon. They say, "Come on, everybody, hop in! We don't know where we're going, but we're going for a ride!"

It was for this reason that the Volkswagen Bus, like Shea Stadium, became a symbol of the 1960s. The 1960s were all about getting everybody in, getting everybody together. Until the Beatles played for 55,000 people in Shea Stadium, no one had even thought of having a concert in a gigantic stadium. It wouldn't sound as good as a concert in an acoustically perfect little hall. It certainly wouldn't look as good. But it would get lots and lots of people in so that they could all be part of the experience. This was the idea behind the Summers of Love, which is exactly what we had in Shea Stadium in the 1960s. And even after.

Volkswagen buses were automotive Shea Stadiums. And they had faces. They looked a little like Mr. Met. They were goofy, tacky, and silly. Just like dear old Shea.

A Maserati is smaller. It can't hold more than a couple of people who have to be very rich to have the privilege of getting into it. It doesn't say, "Hop in!" It says, "Aren't I cool? Get out of my way." A Maserati is prettier than a Volkswagen bus, but it would be harder to live in and harder to love.

In order to love something, it helps if it is not state-of-the-art and super cool. It helps if there's something pitiful, bedraggled, disappointing, and fallible about it. You have to root for it to do well. You have to put it in first place yourself, in your heart. It can't come into existence looking as if it deserves to be in first place.

Shea is the Mets. Maybe the Mets will be something different now. Maybe they'll be a Maserati, a reliably superior product. Maybe that would be good. And maybe it wouldn't.

The Last Home Opener

At 8:30 a.m. on April 8, 2008, I began my drive down to the last home opener at Shea Stadium. It was also the home opener of the 2008 season. These were two separate events, even though they were the same baseball game. I was grim and nostalgic about the first, fearful and desperately hopeful about the second. I knew that today I would see Citi Field for the first time close up. I was bracing for that. It was a bright morning. It was cold, and I was not feeling the enthusiasm that all of these new beginnings called for.

I turned on WCBS-AM 880 to get the news, weather, and traffic. They were having a little sequence about the last home opener at Shea. The reporter asked one of the construction workers, a Mets fan, about his best memory of Shea. "Some girl," the construction worker says. "Did it work out?" the reporter asks. "Yeah," the construction worker says with a kind of chuckle. That's it. I thought of how I should be mad that that's all they have about this very big event in the lives of so many people. But then I think of how this interview kind of sums it up. Who knows what happened to that guy? Maybe he married the girl, maybe they had dinner, maybe they spent a wild night in bed with each other. What means the most to us about Shea Stadium is what has happened to us there: what has happened over forty-four years to tens of millions of people who've gone to the stadium to spend a few hours looking for something more than what life usually gives them. Is it any wonder that people love stadiums and amusement parks and bars and restaurants and all these other places where things happen that aren't the things that just happen at work?

I turned off my ignition in parking lot A around 10 a.m. So many people were here already, eating hamburgers and sausages and drinking beer at ten in the morning. People were playing catch just for the symbolism of it. There was, as always, wind off the bay, and party tents shook and banners fluttered. There was Citi Field. And there was Shea. Both of them were together now, side by side, for one year only. Shea was tall, all sharp blue angles and curves, still silly and funny as always. Citi Field was short, broad, and graceful, with classical columns and arches. It was a lovely thing, I admitted sadly to myself. It was even prettier than I thought it was going to be.

I walked all the way around the two stadiums. Shea looked as it always did. It looked as if it had no idea that it was not going to be there forever. Citi Field looked exactly like pictures I'd seen of Ebbets Field. It looked as if it should be on a street corner in Brooklyn in the 1940s or 1950s. It didn't really belong on this windy plain off Flushing Bay. But it was here because Ebbets Field meant a lot to someone. This is what stadiums are. They are things that, by containing our lives, become part of what we are. And when they die, they live only in our memories, like dead people. Unless we own a baseball team. Then we can bring the dead back to life. If I owned the Mets twenty years from now, would I rebuild Shea in the parking lot of Citi Field? No, I wouldn't. But I guess I'd want to.

So there was the new thing, with slender arches like waves. It looked like the Baths of Caracalla. Look at the keystones on top of the waves. Look at how, where the waves ended, a stately colonnade continued the march and the movement. Here was beauty. Here was architecture. And there behind it was my big old friend Shea in his stupid clown costume. What taste in clothes my big moron friend has! Who let him in the building? Oh, how embarrassing it is to be related to someone like him. How do I explain him? Did he even have an architect?

I'm sorry, I thought. I would be loyal to Shea unto death. And when I finally got into the stadium and saw that Citi Field was only as tall as Shea up to the top of the mezzanine, I was angry as I had been angry for two years. Citi Field was too small. I didn't want to hear what the accountants have figured out about profitability. So they hired good accountants. They also hired good architects. The goddamn thing was beautiful. I hadn't changed my mind about it. But it was beautiful. And my new ambivalence did not make me feel any better.

I went inside and did my Shea things. I stood on the field level and looked around. The arches overlooked the apple. I got my hot dogs and knish and found my seat and sat and had lunch with my sister Stefanie. We talked and watched all the goings on. There was the New Milford High School Marching Band. There was a ceremony to honor the Shea family, who would now no longer have a stadium named after them. There was a very good little documentary narrated by Gary Cohen on the Diamond Vision about how William Shea forced Major League Baseball into expanding by threatening to found a new league and had a stadium named after him for his efforts. The teams were introduced, and as always, the Phillies clubhouse staff took the brunt of the booing because they were announced before the players. Jimmy Rollins got it because Mets fans still couldn't get over him saying that the Phillies (the Phillies!) would be the team to beat in the NL East in 2007. I thought we should just shut up about that already. "Friend of the Mets Michael Amante" sang the Opening Day national anthem *again*. And then some super duper Hornets or something wowed us by flying over the stadium (Stefanie says to me, "Yeah, like what Shea Stadium needs is a flyover.") The game began. The crowd was into it. Fists pumped into the air when Oliver Perez ended the first half inning with a strikeout.

Delgado hit a long home run and was now a fan favorite. The season was already different. The 2008 Delgado was going to be 2006 Delgado and not 2007 Delgado! You felt the hunger of the crowd for a great season. You felt the desperate hopefulness. How glorious it was to be at the ballgame! How perfectly Perez was pitching. From my seat in the mezzanine, far back in the cold dark shade under the upper deck, I watched as flatbeds of blue cotton candy floated over the field and the boxes. They looked so bright in the early spring sunlight. I was at the last home opener at Shea—the beginning of a bright new season of memories, hope, and redemption.

The game was good and the crowd was happy. And then it all turned bad. And then we felt once again that feeling that was left over from last year: that sense that a three-run lead by the opposing team is simply insurmountable. We cheered and clapped when the Mets came up. But although I didn't join the stream of people leaving between the eighth and ninth innings, I knew that it was not going to happen. The crowd was not filled with the despair you saw at the end of 2007. But as the Mets fell behind, the crowd became sullen, glum, hopeful, and fearful. It was a hard year already. We weren't going to lose hope this early. But it felt as if there was something around our neck, something as big and as awkward as the blue and orange horseshoe of flowers presented to Willie Randolph by the Shea family at the start of the game.

What would get the yoke off? Jose Reyes flied out deep to end the game. The last home opener was over. The season was just beginning.

The Last Days of Carlos Delgado?

The Mets played reasonably well over the next few weeks. They were 10-6 on April 19. But then they lost five out of six and quickly fell into the sort of pattern they had been in for the final two-thirds of the 2007 season. They stayed close to .500, with little winning streaks following little losing streaks. Once again the competition was lackluster, and so through April and May, the Mets were able to stay within a game or two of first place. We waited for the team to break away, and it looked as if, with a lost look in their eyes, they were waiting for themselves.

Willie Randolph just played his players, but he could not, apparently, think of anything that might suddenly move the team forward. The one thing he did, in May, to try to improve the team's performance was drop Carlos Delgado from the fifth spot in the batting order to sixth. No one disagreed with this decision. Everyone else on the team was playing adequately, and there was hope that, in time, they might each break out. Delgado, however, was not hitting at all, and batting fifth, he was keeping the Mets from scoring runs. His 2007 numbers had been seriously, if not disastrously, below his career-high level, and he was now about to turn thirty-six. Some players continue to hit well past that age, but most don't. Some Mets fans wanted Delgado off the team right away. I wanted the Mets to be patient with him. I was willing to make excuses for him. It certainly seemed to me that if he had only had a physical chance to get into a groove during a 2007 season interrupted with minor injuries, he might have brought his numbers up to respectability. But I was not fully convinced of my own faith in Carlos. I had seen myself do this before, with players like Hernandez, Carter, and Piazza. I knew that I mainly wanted the Mets to be patient because I like it when teams are patient, out of loyalty, to older guys on the way down. Still, I knew that in baseball, as in many things in life, patience out of loyalty is not always the right move. Like everyone else, I knew in my heart of hearts that Carlos Delgado was washed up.

As a baseball fan, I always hated to see this familiar drama. Here you had a marvelously gifted individual, big, strong, smart, and handsome, owning the world and owning the fans at thirty-three as he leads the team during a glorious season. Carlos was spectacular in 2006, with his 38 home runs and 114 RBIs in the cleanup spot. I remembered his gorgeous blasts high up into the night sky to right. I remembered the line drives slapped almost awkwardly yet with great strength over the center field wall. I remembered Carlos cool and smiling and totally at ease in the fine, fun 2006 dugout.

But then there was 2007. And our questions. If Moises Alou could be so good after forty, why couldn't Carlos be really good at thirty-five? But you knew that Alou was the exception. Piazza had been thirty-five in 2004. Keith Hernandez had been this age in 1989. It was weird. They looked the same as ever. They were still young men. In each case, I believed they would come back. But they didn't.

I remember the first time I saw an unambiguous sign that I was getting older. I was in my late twenties. One night, after a party, I had a hangover. It was my first hangover ever. I had been drunk before, but this was the first time my body ever said to me, "Hey, now things are different. You are not capable of what you were capable of last month." Of course, it was no big deal. Or not much of one. I could still drink, but not like I used to. I still do a lot of things I've always done. I do some of them differently, but I'm not that old. In early 2008, I was a healthy fifty-three years old. I was the same age as Keith Hernandez. I could still do my job, and I still felt as if I was pretty far away from death.

Carlos Delgado was young enough to be my son. He was born on the day I graduated from high school. But look at what he was dealing with at the age of thirty-five. It wasn't the same for him as it was for me. He was making millions, so I didn't feel sorry for him. But you know those small drop-offs in your thirties that don't mean that much to you? For him it meant being knocked down out of the realm of the immortals. For him it meant still being big and strong and fit and young and yet still struggling to get something back that was small, that was going away, and that made all the difference in the world. A millisecond of a reflex, an ability to heal just this quickly, the tiny advantages that made him so much more than an ordinary human being.

Big-league ballplayers, as they begin to go into their tailspin, are terrifying to watch. They are fighting with death at the first moment it appears on a distant horizon. We don't have to fight it this early, but we watch them do it for us. Because they look the same as they did when they were so great at thirty-three, they look as if they are fully equipped for the battle. They look as if they can win it. We have to watch them fight. Do you remember Mike Piazza's face when he would throw to second base and not even come close to throwing the runner out? Do you remember Keith Hernandez in 1988 and 1989? They fought for us and for themselves. They had such dignity and nobility, and every once in a while they'd have a great game and look as if they were going to come back to us, just as they had been. But it wasn't happening. They couldn't do it. Our heroes looked the same, but they had come to mean something different. And you felt something different when they came to the plate. You felt the triumph of time and the need to move on. You saw strong young men losing the struggle that everyone loses.

I was rooting for Carlos Delgado. When I have a sense that things may be over for a player, I am desperate to be proven wrong. Baseball, as I've said before, is about belief. I believed in Carlos. But I didn't think it was going to happen.

My Mother and the Mets

A couple of weeks after my first birthday, my parents' baseball team, the Brooklyn Dodgers, did something they would only do once. They beat the New York Yankees in the World Series. My father, an intern, was at work. My mother was alone with me in an apartment at 163rd street and Riverside Drive. When the game ended, she couldn't stand the silence in the middle of Giants and Yankee country. She called her brother in Flatbush and asked him to hold the telephone receiver out the window so that she could listen to Brooklyn.

Obviously I don't remember this, but I sure wish I did. And I wish that I had been in a position to help my mother celebrate what was probably a once in a lifetime event. On May 19, 2008, my mother turned eighty. We celebrated her birthday, watching the Mets clobber the Yankees in the same den in our house in New Jersey where we had watched the Mets win the 1969 World Series. I thought of how grateful I would be if my mother could see her team beat the Yankees in the World Series one more time.

My mother is the most dedicated baseball fan I know. She remembers going to her first baseball game over seventy years ago with her older cousin Naty. Ebbets Field, she remembers, "was just a place in our neighborhood." My mother grew up at 823 President Street, at the corner of Seventh Avenue. In what is now, I think, an optometrist's shop, my grandparents had a "candy store," called Thomashow Brothers, from 1913 to 1960. You could get a soda in the shop, or ice cream, a newspaper, a comic book, a pack of cigarettes, a roll of lifesavers, and you could always, during the summer, hear the Dodgers game on a radio. In the late 1950s, I used to sit in the phone booth to the right as you came into the store and I'd watch all the people. My most vivid memory is of the time the phone rang and I jumped out of the booth in terror. I can still bring up images of what I watched from that phone booth. I remember men in hats and women with bright red lips. I remember my grandmother in a grey jacket, solemnly making ice cream sodas for pimply teenagers with too much Brylcreem in their hair. I'm glad I have these memories. It makes me feel a part of old-time Brooklyn, which I always think of as the soil from which the New York Mets have sprung.

It used to be that you could take a trolley from Grand Army Plaza to Ebbets Field. Brooklyn used to have trolleys. That's how the Dodgers got their name. "Trolley-dodgers" were what they called Brooklyn street urchins around 1900. Before they were the Dodgers, the team was called the Brooklyn Bridegrooms. What were they thinking? Since you had to walk a few blocks from Seventh Avenue to get to Grand Army Plaza, and Ebbets Field was not that much further, it was not considered to be worth the nickel it cost to take the trolley to the stadium. So my mother used to walk down Flatbush Avenue to see a baseball game. She remembers how cozy and fun the stadium was. Ebbets Field, she says, was like a circus. She loved the band that walked around the stands playing commentary (like "Three Blind Mice" when the umpires made a bad call). Her favorite player as a kid was Cookie Lavagetto, and she remembers the lady who sat in the stands and screamed and held up signs about being crazily in love with him. Later her favorite player was Dixie Walker, "the People's Cherce," as he was called in the papers, though she was saddened when he was one of those who wrote the letter asking Branch Rickey not to let Jackie Robinson play. Before Robinson came in the late 1940s, the Dodgers were generally a pretty dismal team. I asked my mother if she minded this, and she said, "Of course not. We didn't care if they were good. They were the Dodgers." I asked her what it felt like when the Dodgers went from very bad to very good. She said, "You know what it was like. It was just like the Mets." During the great years, her favorite player was Roy Campanella, and she remembers how devastated she was when he was in the accident that crippled him. She also remembers how awful she felt when her team left her to move to Los Angeles. She says that only the coming of the Mets made it possible for her to get over it.

My mother loves the Mets. She watches every game. In the minds of many old Dodger fans, the Brooklyn Dodgers and the Mets are one team that represents the scrappiness of old New York life, one team that represents the highs and lows of life as it is actually lived. She asks me who my favorite Mets have been and I tell her Seaver, Koosman, Hernandez, Strawberry, and Piazza. She says, "you see, those are the good ones. I like the good ones too, but I also like the other ones." I say I like the other ones too, and I ask her who her favorite Mets are. She tells me Mookie and Hubie. To her, I guess, these are the heirs to Cookie and Dixie. I don't think it's just the funny nicknames. I think what she likes is the guys who are "The People's Cherce," guys who come through in really special moments and who are not necessarily great or even good all the time.

I've been to a lot of ballgames with my mother. She gets very emotional at them. We used to go to Shea as a family on Mother's Day, when my mother and sisters would get these little makeup kits from Maybelline. My mother never went to any games with her parents. They were immigrants who did not understand what the younger generation saw in this American game that was so obviously a waste of time. They thought watching baseball was like playing cards. Still, all of my mother's brothers and cousins became die-hard baseball fans. The ones who lived in the Bronx even became die-hard Yankee fans. Baseball, I guess, was one of the first things that really let us in. Here was this American thing that everybody could love alongside everyone else. There were all these people living side by side in New York, eating their own foods in their own houses, going to their own churches and synagogues and mosques and union meeting halls, living their own different senses of the world. But baseball gave them a sense of what it was like for everyone to feel the same about something. No matter who you were or where you came from, you felt the same thing as everybody else did when Carl Furillo made a great catch, or Gil Hodges hit a home run, or Jackie Robinson stole a base. The importance baseball had in making Americans all feel like Americans probably can't be understated. When my mother asked her brother to hold the phone out the window in 1955, what she wanted to hear was the voice of all of Brooklyn.

My mom doesn't walk very well. I had hoped to go with her to one last game at Shea, but I knew that she wouldn't want to go to a game in a wheelchair. She watches all the games on television. She says that's good enough. She talks about Gary Cohen, Ron Darling, Keith Hernandez, and Kevin Burkhardt as if they were her other sons. She is very proud of them because she thinks they do such a good job. They carry on the Mets tradition of great announcing, and that's important to her. She says she's content to listen to them. She doesn't need to go to the ballpark. Still, even if she doesn't expect to go there again, she is very sad that Shea is coming down.

The Dodgers and the Mets have been an important part of my mother's life. For this reason, I have to admit that one thing I do like about Citi Field is that by resurrecting Ebbets Field, it brings my mother's baseball life around in a kind of circle. I imagine this little girl walking down big, broad Flatbush Avenue between Prospect Park and the Botanic Garden in the 1930s. I remember my family seeing the big new stadium right by the cool World's Fair in 1964. Baseball gives us a certain relation to time and to place. We're all Americans now in my family. We're here in this one place. And we're still moving through time, watching and caring about the Mets.

What Willie Said

As the Mets continued their disappointing play into the middle of June, many people started to blame the anguished but still apparently unflappable Willie Randolph. I didn't want to see this, because I really liked Willie and I did not think he deserved much of the blame for the lackluster way in which the Mets were playing. Still, given what they had been through and were going through, it was hard for a lot of Mets fans to be generous. The fact that Willie Randolph was the first African-American manager in the history of New York baseball complicated this situation. Not everyone who criticized Willie was a racist, and not even everyone who was being unfair to Willie Randolph was a racist. But some were. There were jerks, Mets fans who said overtly or implicitly racist things about Willie on Internet forums, talk radio, or in the privacy of cars and houses. Not all Mets fans are paragons of virtue.

Willie noticed. And during the height of his understandable frustration, on the day after an 11–2 rout of the Yankees, an interview with Willie appeared in the *Bergen Record*. The reporter, Ian O'Connor, interviewing an angry Randolph in the clubhouse before the game, wrote that Randolph

> wanted to know why the traits often admired in the calm, cool and collected likes of Joe Torre are portrayed as flaws in Torre's former third base coach.
>
> "Is it racial?" Randolph asked. "Huh? It smells a little bit."
>
> Asked directly if he believes black managers are held to different standards than their white counterparts, Randolph said: "I don't know how to put my finger on it, but I think there's something there." (Ian O'Connor, "Randolph Bares His Pain," *The Bergen (NJ) Record*, May 19, 2008)

In the article, Randolph went on to complain about how he was not being understood, how he was not being given credit for what he had accomplished, and how his managing was not being represented fairly by the SNY cameras.

Obviously, Willie should not have said any of this.

You would have to be naïve to believe that racism didn't play a part, for some people, in the anger and bitterness that had been directed at Randolph. But you'd have to be unfair to think that it was a prominent reason. Mets fans, after the historic choke and through the continuing troubles, had a legitimate sense that their team lacked fire and direction. It was plausible to put some blame on the man who is supposed to lead and set the tone for the team. Any manager with a laid-back manner and a controversial managing style is going to get crap from the fans when a team is playing lackluster ball. This happened with Art Howe too. Race was not the main issue.

What really got me, and everyone else, was the bad timing of these comments. The Mets had just had a meeting a few days before in which they all vowed not to create off-the-field distractions and not to be distracted by off-the-field stuff. Finally it looked as if they might have gotten their heads together. They clobbered the Yankees in the two games of the May Subway Series at Yankee Stadium. All attention was on the upcoming series against the Braves. And then, before you could blink, we were all back in the media stew. We were not in the glorious green world of the ballpark. We were in a jam on the Long Island Expressway, listening to Mike and the Mad Dog in an endless loop. What a complete and total bummer.

Willie must have known that he had picked the wrong time to say this. Why would someone who hated off-the-field distractions want to go and create such a big one? There was only one answer to this question.

Willie must have meant it.

You know how sometimes you're having a fight with someone and everybody's finally calmed down and things are all right and then you just can't help but say something that shows how hurt you were that the other person said what they said before things calmed down? I think that's what happened with Willie. I don't think that Willie thought racism was the big issue. But my guess is that he couldn't help but feel as if it was. I think that like most African-Americans, Willie had had to deal all his life with people who just didn't like him for some reason and didn't want to give him a chance. And I think that when you've had to deal with crap like that, it is sometimes hard to put things in perspective when you are suddenly the object of so much intense hostility, when you've been doing your job with a pretty fair amount of success for three years. If you looked at the Internet boards and if you listened to the radio, you knew how over-the-top the blame-Willie, we-hate-Willie stuff had been. I know it wasn't necessarily racist. I know it bubbled up out of the angst of being a Mets fan at this particular moment. But I could see why Willie mistook one kind of unfair hostility towards him for another. That may not have been fair of him, but I could understand why he felt that way.

His problem, I thought, was similar to the problem Tom Glavine had when he said that he was disappointed and not devastated to lose the last game of the season in the first inning. Tom was trying to tell us to back off, to understand that baseball is only a game. His comment was foolish. Tom should have known how much that last game meant to Mets fans, and he should have been devastated, not merely disappointed. But I could see where Tom and Willie were coming from. These guys must wonder how all of these strangers could be so emotionally involved in what happens as they try their best to do their job. Why, they must wonder, if things go bad for me, do people go so far as to hate me? It's a reasonable question, but it's also a dumb question. That's what this thing is. Baseball is something a baseball fan is passionate about. Sometimes our passion will come after you guys, and sometimes it will look like some of the worst things in the world. At other times our passion will lift you to the heavens.

People talked for days about how unfair and unwise Willie's comments were. I wished that they would also say something that showed that they respected the anguish that would have prompted Willie to say what he shouldn't have said. It must not be easy for these guys, no matter how much money they make or glory they get. Yeah, they should put up with it, yeah, heat, kitchen, all that stuff. Yeah, and they're human beings too.

We should treat them with some understanding. And they should understand where we're coming from. It is true that baseball is just a game, that it isn't real. But that's like saying *American Idol* isn't real, or Harry Potter. The statement is true, in the most obvious and literal way. But it isn't true.

Day Game

After Willie's comments, the limp Mets got limper. I'm not saying that there was a cause and effect relation, but I will say that the Mets did not take advantage of their opportunities after sweeping the two games of the Yankees series. The Braves won all four games of a series against the Mets in Atlanta, and from May 20 to June 10, the Mets won eight and lost fourteen. On June 10, back from a West Coast road trip that featured a four-game sweep by the Padres, the Mets were 30-33, three games below .500, in fourth place, seven and a half games behind the division-leading Phillies. In another couple of weeks, the Mets would be halfway through the season. Now they were to play a seven-game homestand before heading right back out to the West Coast to play the Angels. I went to the third game of that homestand, a day game on a Wednesday afternoon.

As much as I love the drama and brilliance of a stadium lit up at night, there is always just something about a day game. There are all these kids. There are all these groups of kids and teenagers in matching t-shirts. There are all of these grown-ups who feel as if they're playing hooky, even if they're not. There is innocence and generosity. And so the day game of June 12, 2008, felt terrific as people came in off the ramps into the bright sunlight of the stadium plaza.

It wasn't just an ordinary day game, though. The crowd that poured into Shea had the giddiness of a death-row prisoner who had just been reprieved. The night before, we had come so close to what felt like the worst possible disaster when Billy Wagner gave back Mike Pelfrey's three-run lead in a game that seemed on the point of giving us back our season. Carlos Beltran had come through, hitting a game-winning two-run homer in the thirteenth. The Mets were not playing well, but they were surviving, and it was still spring. We were coming to this game so that Johan Santana could show us that there were reasons to be glad we were still Mets fans, sixty-four games into a mostly joyless season.

Things felt surprisingly good in the crowd. Ramon Castro hit a home run, and Santana went through all of his innings with precision and grace. He was as untouchable as the DIRECTV blimp that plowed the cloudless sky all afternoon. I noticed that the apple, for some reason, didn't come up when Castro hit the home run, and I worried that there was something wrong with it. I also noticed when a boy in a wheelchair won an autographed baseball. He was up on the Diamond Vision as his father smiled sweetly at the camera and adjusted the boy's head in his headrest. The father rubbed his son's shoulder with an absolutely tender gesture of affection and it really moved me, although this was off the screen in a few seconds.

David Wright drove in a second run with a double he tried to turn into a triple. Fernando Tatis drove in two more in the seventh. And so, as the Mets established a decent lead behind a great pitcher, the mood of the fans stayed calm and wonderful. How little it took to make Mets fans happy! If this crowd could feel this good on the few crumbs the Mets had thrown us, imagine what we would be feeling if we were actually having a good season.

Santana came out after seven innings for a pinch hitter. It was time for the relievers to start righting their own ship. A four-run lead, no doubt, was enough. Wagner had only given up three the night before. Joe Smith then gave up two runs in the eighth. He was relieved by Scott Schoeneweis, who threw two balls outside the strike zone to the first batter he faced. I thought it was strange how two balls could produce such a funny sound from the crowd. It was a kind of frightened moan, not the sort of thing you'd normally hear after two balls. Since he was having a pretty good season so far, I didn't want anyone to start booing Schoeneweis for two balls, and I was relieved to hear the affirmative pleasure of the crowd when the batter popped up to short left to end the inning.

Two runs, by all rights, should be enough. The crowd sang "I'm a Believer," and the loud "ooooohhhhhs" suggested that we were still happy with our ballgame. And when they did the whole

Wagnerian photo montage to "Enter Sandman" at the start of the ninth inning, most of the crowd stood and applauded. There were a few boos, but the booers were greatly outnumbered.

Wagner walked a batter and brought the tying run to the plate. I heard the same frightened moan I had heard in the eighth. Then there was an infield hit and you had to realize reluctantly that you were watching a significant moment that would take all of your concentration. Now I worried that the crowd would boo Wagner, and there was a kind of muted booing when he threw a ball to the next batter. But the crowd was still with him. You heard that in the cheers of encouraging delight when the next pitch Wagner threw was a strike. Oh great, I thought, we're down to booing and cheering every ball and strike. The next pitch was inside, but the crowd acted as if it was affronted when the umpire called it a ball. This isn't good, I thought. And then the batter hit a double down the left field line. A run came in and there were now two runners in scoring position with nobody out and a one-run Mets lead. The boos were real boos now. They were an ocean, and no one was cheering.

I only boo a Met in the most extreme conceivable circumstances. But I must tell you that the crowd I was sitting in at Shea on the afternoon of June 12 was not really booing in the destructive way we've sometimes seen in the past. They were moaning with bitterness and sadness. They were angry like loving parents or children or lovers who have been betrayed. They were crying to the heavens about the cruelty of fate, crying to the DIRECTV blimp that just kept going back and forth and back and forth. What made the crowd different from real booers is that they were behind Billy Wagner 100 percent. You could hear this in their pleasure when a runner was forced at home. You could hear it in their cheers for Wagner's strikes on the next hitter. And if the game had ended where it should have ended, with a double play so that the tying run wouldn't have scored, the shouts of joy and relieved appreciation Wagner would have heard would have made everything all right. We weren't telling Billy Wagner that we wanted him to go away and not come back. We were telling him how sad he was making us. We were asking him why he was doing this to us when we needed him so badly right now. And so, when he ended the inning with a strikeout that seemed to suggest that there was nothing actually wrong with him, the warm boos he got for his inning's work were intended to tell him how hurt we were, and how depressed, and how helpless we felt. Just as he felt helpless. Except he was making us feel this way. We weren't doing anything to him. Why was he doing this to us?

We were back in the same situation we had been in the previous evening. We had gone from watching a game that would redeem us to watching a game that could not be lost. The four-run lead was gone. The score was tied. Okay, I thought, so let it be like last night. Let there be the redemption that only a win in the final turn at bat can provide. Jose Reyes made it to first on a ground ball that would have been an out for anyone else. He clapped his hands with joy three times. Endy Chavez bunted him over. Then in a split second, David Wright's game-winning double down the left field line turned into a groundout. Beltran was walked intentionally. And Carlos Delgado, who must have been insulted, came to the plate. The crowd made a committed effort to cheer him. At just this moment, two very confused birds flew over my section, looking to escape this loud curved place. Delgado walked, and Damion Easley came up. He grounded out, and a disheartening number of people got up to leave. I have never left a game at Shea before it was over, but I understand that other people do. What I want to know is why does anyone leave a tie game after nine innings? Those who were leaving would not be beating any rush hour traffic. It was already 4:30 p.m. Why do you pay the money to go to the stadium if you're not going to stay to see the end of something like this? I noticed that only half of the original crowd was still in the stadium at the top of the tenth. Why? What did this mean?

Those of us who stayed felt the terrible symmetry of this game and the one the night before. When Justin Upton doubled off of Heilman to start the tenth inning, there was almost no crowd reaction. No "awwwwww." No boos even. There was just a steady simmer of anguished boredom and discontent. And yet there was still excited "lets have a strikeout" clapping when the count on a hitter went to 0-2. When the go-ahead run scored on a sacrifice fly, more people headed to the exits. I had the sense that we were all thinking that Beltran's home run the night before had only been a cruel reprieve. Now we were going to have the doom that had originally been intended for us. In the bottom of the tenth, Ramon Castro, a hero of the game, fouled out. Pinch-hitting Luis Castillo beat out a strange, weak infield hit. The new guy, Chris Aguila, had the chance to be our hero. I always love it when the new guy is the hero. Aguila grounded into a double play. Everybody got up really quickly.

The game, I felt, told me everything about what the 2008 season was so far. Mets fans were still with their team. But we were basket cases. And so were the Mets. We expected disaster. We had love and hope but we did not have faith. We were ill and therefore deserved sympathy and not contempt. Our booing was not the sound of spoiled brats. It was the sound of something deeper, something that a big crowd of people cannot put into any more nuanced form. It was "oh hell," "oh shit," "oh woe." We knew that we could bounce back if the Mets could manage to bounce back. But there had been so much bouncing over the past two years. Everybody knows that when a ball bounces too much, it eventually loses its ability to bounce.

The Firing of Willie Randolph

It screws up my schedule to stay up past midnight, but when there's a West Coast night game, I usually allow my schedule to be screwed up. I can't always last the whole game, but I like to stay up for a big chunk of it. The house is quiet. Everyone's asleep. There's a weird sense I have that I am keeping Gary and Ron company. Is it my imagination or is there a kind of late-night intimacy to their West Coast broadcasts, as if they know they're talking to people who are watching the game all by themselves, with the volume down, in quiet houses?

I made it through most of the first game of the Angels series on June 16. I decided to pack it in after Heilman got out of the seventh. The game was still close, but I was tired and I had a sense, if you know what I mean, that I had put in my watching of the game.

So I woke up the next morning and was having breakfast when my wife Sheila, on her way out of the house for a yoga class, told me that the Mets had fired Willie Randolph. That can't be, I said. I was up until 1 a.m. and they hadn't fired Randolph. What were they going to do, fire him in the early morning hours so that nobody would notice?

To show me that she hadn't misunderstood what she had heard, Sheila went and turned on SNY and said that "yes, they had fired him." There was a banner that said so across the bottom of the screen. I finished my breakfast and went into the study and turned on my laptop. They fired him. At 3:15 in the morning, eastern daylight time.

What in God's name were they thinking? Was there a universe in which this made any sense? If so, I didn't want to go there. It was one thing for the Mets to be perennial underachievers. I couldn't handle a "what could be worse?" joke.

The dynamics of the Randolph situation were fairly simple by mid-June. Mets fans were divided between those who wanted Willie to go and those who would have liked for him to stay but had fully accepted that he was on his way out. I was in the latter group. I did not think that Willie Randolph was the main or even a particularly significant reason for the team's mediocre performance over the past year. But I understood that when baseball fate bends in a certain way, the traditional remedy is human sacrifice.

I was prepared for the sacrifice. Like most Mets fans, I felt for this decent, skilled, strong, and solid man. But firing the manager when a talented team is underperforming is not a judgment. It is a tactic. It is pushing the reset button, going out and coming back in. It is a blind expunging of the whatever, since you can't surgically remove exactly what you know to be wrong. I was looking forward to a purely psychological sense of renewal, for the players and the fans. There would be blood. But the blood would do useful work.

Now look at what they had done. They had made a mess of it. The story was not that Randolph was finally fired. It was that Randolph was fired at 3:15 a.m. New York time. The story was that after four encouraging games, what was probably but not necessarily inevitable was done in the middle of the night way the hell out in Anaheim. This didn't feel like the dignified, considered removal of a fine man willing to offer himself up for the greater good. It felt like a rubout. It felt as if Willie had been taken for a ride at 3 a.m., bumped off, and thrown in the Pacific. I felt sick. A decent man had been treated badly and an opportunity had been lost. I supposed that we could afford the rudeness to a decent man. But I wasn't sure we could afford to lose many more opportunities to make the team feel new again.

Tuscany Tile and the
Wisdom of the East

As I read through all of the reactions to Willie's firing on the Internet, I saw that everyone felt pretty much as I did. I turned on SNY to see what they had about the story. The commentators didn't say anything different from what the people on the Web were saying, but the network had footage of Randolph himself, shocked more than you'd expect, leaving his hotel to fly home. The saddest thing, Willie pointed out, was that he now would never have his redemptive victory with the Mets.

The Mets could still have a good season, but Randolph could not be a part of it. He lived, but we were still in the station wagon and he was not. Even if the most wonderful things were to happen in the long run, here is where his story ended. You could say that it didn't matter, that nothing wonderful was likely to happen. But it did matter, because all that kept us from getting out of the station wagon ourselves was the fervent, at times pitiful hope that we were going someplace where they had ice cream.

There were speculations all day in the press about whether or not Omar Minaya had really wanted to do this, or whether or not this was worse than what the Steinbrenners had done to Torre. And as a fan trying to be fair-minded, I had to live once again with the indeterminacy of all situations like this. I didn't know who or what to get angry at or about because I had no solid information with which to direct the flow of my venom and bile. And I feel crappy getting mad at people when I have a sense in the back of my mind that there is a possibility that they don't deserve it.

So I just watched, without much emotion, as SNY CNN'd the thing into a whole afternoon of programming.

Most of what I watched was boring. There was some good analysis by journalists, but they had only about ten minutes of stuff to say and were recycling it in a loop.

What was not boring was Rick Peterson, who was calm, smart, and eerily secure. It made me wish that I had gotten to know him better. As Rick observed, in a statement that deserves to be remembered, "Homes go through renovations, and sometimes you have to make changes when things don't go that well, and I'm part of that change. I totally understand that—I grew up in the baseball business. I'm the hardwood floor that's getting ripped out, and they're going to bring in the Tuscany tile. It'll be great . . . I wear this bracelet because I'm very in tune with Eastern philosophy and universal law. [The bracelet rings signify] faith, compassion, equanimity and love. . . . The Eastern language writes in symbols, and the symbol for crisis they also use for opportunity. I've been given a great opportunity here, and as I walk out that door, I seek my next opportunity. I walk out in peace, and I wish everybody else here the best. . . . Hopefully, the Tuscany tile will do a lot better than a hardwood floor."

As Gary and Ron were to observe later, this metaphor works. The Mets had commissioned a new floor, although what they may really have needed was a new ceiling. The new floor might not be great. But it would be different. Sometimes when we make a change, we can trick ourselves into being different. And if we don't change, and things don't happen as we would want, there is always faith, compassion, equanimity, and love, qualities Mets fans have always had, if not always in the requisite abundance.

The bald guy who does the *Beer Money* filler show on SNY made fun of Peterson for talking as he did. This man doesn't do metaphors. And what's this, he asked, with "Middle Eastern philosophy"? And "equanimity," what the hell is that? He says he was an English major and he doesn't know what the word "equanimity" means. He was an English major? Great. The next time I was advising students about what they could do with an English major, I could tell them that they could do *Beer Money*.

Was it my imagination or did SNY hire its civilian analysts mainly according to how well they could be heard without a microphone, in a sitting position, from a distance of 500 feet? You know, I don't want to sound like a snob, but how many beefy male dolls does one city need, who, when you pull a ring at the back of their necks, will bark with a Hollywood version of a New York accent that the team has no heart and that they're sick and tired of it? Why couldn't FAN and SNY recognize that the people we liked to hear from were people like Gary, Keith, and Ron and Howie and Eddie? We don't know what to make of and we certainly don't warm up to the parodies of simple-minded middle-aged male sports fans they were always throwing at us. Are these guys supposed to look like us? Have they ever met us? Do they understand that some of us speak without barking and can maintain two possible alternative ideas in our heads at the same time without exploding?

The bright spot of the afternoon was not Omar Minaya's moving and unconvincing effort to take it all on himself. It was the poise and intelligence of Jerry Manuel, Randolph's bench coach, who had been appointed interim manager. Manuel was African-American, so no one could be tempted to do anything with the racial issue. I enjoyed Manuel's first press conference. He had a schmoozy ease you never saw from Willie. I wished him well. And I was intrigued when he said that he was inspired by the ideas of Mahatma Gandhi and Martin Luther King Jr. I was curious to see how the ideas of Gandhi and King could be applied to baseball management. This was, after all, a little counterintuitive. My feeling was that Mahatma Gandhi and Eastern philosophy, with all the stuff about patience and acceptance and calm and living in the moment, might be more helpful for Mets fans than they would be for the Mets.

The changing of the guard did not make any immediate difference. The Mets were 34-35 when Manuel was named as the manager on the morning of June 17. On July 5, they were 43-44 after beating the Phillies in a 9–4 game in Philadelphia. The malaise was continuing, and Manuel's cool wit and flair for colorful language and interesting metaphors was not getting the Mets any further than Willie Randolph's steadfast and stolid calm. Maybe nothing was going to happen this season. It was almost half over. Maybe we just had to live through it.

In the Booth

One interesting thing that happened to me during the unpleasant Mets' spring of 2008 is that I got to meet Lynn Cohen, Gary Cohen's wife. Lynn, it turned out, was a reader of my blog and she e-mailed me after I sent an invitation to my book launch to everyone who had left comments on the blog. I only had her e-mail address. I had no idea that Gary Cohen's wife was reading my blog. Lynn said that she planned to come to my book launch party, but in the end her son's football practice got in the way. I sent Lynn a copy of *Mets Fan* when it was published. She read it and enjoyed it. We had e-mailed a few times since then, and when Lynn decided, in the spring of 2008, to start selling t-shirts and other items to benefit charities chosen by Gary, Keith, and Ron, I helped her out by giving her a list of reputable bloggers, forums, and podcasts that could help publicize the project. To thank me, she invited me to meet her at the Diamond Club for dinner and to watch a game as her guest.

So there I was, on the way to the Diamond Club to meet Lynn. I was very excited about finally getting to go to the Diamond Club. When I first heard about the Diamond Club, when I was a kid, I figured that it had to be one of the most glamorous places on earth. I loved the idea that there was this exclusive club-like restaurant in the hidden recesses of the stadium where celebrities and reporters and announcers rubbed elbows and ate prime rib and drank martinis. I imagined it as a swanky nightclub, glittering with lights, like a diamond. I thought it might be like Toots Shor's, a once-famous restaurant in Manhattan where ballplayers used to hang out together after they put on their suits for their night on the town.

The Diamond Club is not like this. It's a very nice place and the food is genuinely good. You see a lot of casually but decently dressed older men and some very pampered grandchildren. There was a great view of the big green field. Still, the Diamond Club was in the thin level of Shea that separated the mezzanine from the loge. Ever since I saw my first game at Shea in 1964, I had dreamed of the lives that were lived in that level. I had imagined great things: the Mets executive offices, sky boxes like executive suites in Manhattan skyscrapers, the long, curved, continuous desk where reporters sat jowl to jowl, chomping on their cigars. In my mind, though, the most glamorous places of all in that horseshoe of wonder were the booths: the little spaces right behind home plate from which the game was broadcast. I remember how I focused my binoculars in the 1960s and saw Lindsey Nelson, Ralph Kiner, and Bob Murphy, in shirtsleeves with ties. I saw them talking to each other, suspended above home plate at the exact center of the stadium, like the emperor Flavius in the Colosseum in Rome. How many times had I looked at that space, in the navel of Shea? The booths connected the field to the immense world beyond the stadium, where millions watched the Mets in living rooms and listened to them in cars. The booths were not where it happened, but the booths and the men in them were the eyes and mind of the whole thing. They were awesome, magnificent places, even if they appeared to be just tiny little booths.

I met Lynn and her son Zach, and Zoe Rice, one of the bloggers I recommended, in a seat by the window of the real Diamond Club. I had a terrific dinner and a fine time. Lynn was something else. I immediately felt as if I'd known her for a long time. We had similar backgrounds and many of the ideas and perspectives associated with those backgrounds. We lived somewhat similar lives in the same area of Connecticut, with adolescent children going through a lot of the same bullshit. (Zach reminded me a lot of my daughter's nicer male friends.) We had the same favorite movie theatre and fifties-style diner. The biggest difference seemed to be that her husband had this incredibly demanding job which required him to be away from home a lot, leaving her with the bulk of the work of the Connecticut parent (driving, being in specific places at specific times to watch specific things). My wife has a less demanding schedule, so we get to go places and do stuff. Lynn and Gary have to squeeze their vacation into the All-Star break.

One thing that really struck me was how curious Lynn was about the world that fans like me know and take for granted. For all that her life is like mine, Lynn lives, on a daily basis, in the world of the ring between the mezzanine and the loge. She said to me that she'd love to just walk around the parking lot and get a sense of the flavor of the tailgate parties. She liked to read the blogs and used to read the mets.com board until it started to upset her, and Gary asked her why she was doing that to herself. So I told her about such kinder, gentler, more reliably smarter forums as thehappyrecap.com and grandslamsingle.com. Lynn had a great curiosity about the world of the fan. It was as glamorous to her as her world was to me. And the "Gary, Keith, and Ron" charitable t-shirt project that she'd organized seemed to be an effort to connect the worlds. She wanted to be a part of what we had. And in return, we, as fans, were to be given a chance to be part of Gary, Keith, and Ron's humanity. We could go to the garykeithandron.com website and learn that if he hadn't been a baseball announcer, Ron would have liked to have been an expatriate living in the south of France. We could learn that Gary was a fan of Phillip Roth and that he took his pillow on the road with him. We could learn that Keith would like to learn how to waltz. Or at least that he said he would. Meeting Lynn, I had a vivid sense that at the core of this whole Mets thing were real people you'd actually want to know. At the center of it all was a noble, festive human enterprise that had none of the whiny anger or crassness or greed that sometimes seems to have taken over everything.

After dinner, we went to our seats in the loge behind home plate. The game was one of the good ones, and the crowd seemed positive and hopeful. Cowbell Man came by wearing one of the Gary, Keith, and Ron t-shirts, and he stopped to tell Lynn about how much he admired and respected Gary. After the seventh-inning stretch, Lynn flashed her pass and took us up through the Diamond Club bar into a narrow hallway leading to the SNY suite, which was like a hotel room with a lot of free food lying around. We watched the rest of the game from seats suspended from this hotel room, with a couple of guys whom Lynn explained were sponsors or prospective sponsors. There were TVs in this hotel room, and when *Post Game Live* was over, we walked down the narrow hallway back to the Diamond Club bar where Zoe, Zach, and I sat down at a table right by the entrance to the hallway. Lynn disappeared for a minute or two and then waved to us to follow her. We went back into the hallway and turned right into an even smaller hallway. We then stepped down into a little place with a view out to the field where there were a desk and some guys with headphones picking stuff up. There too were Lynn's husband and two big men around my age who were unmistakably Ron Darling and Keith Hernandez.

I was in the booth.

My instinct in a situation like this is to retreat into respectful silence. My existence was briefly but pleasantly and politely acknowledged. More outgoing and better prepared Zoe had a camera and got pictures. We were introduced as bloggers who had helped with the t-shirt project. I stood without a camera and just felt the incandescence of a reality that was really just down a hallway from the one in which I lived. My brain received impressions that will never get less distinct than they are right now. How small and ordinary the booth was. It was a workplace, and here were the guys who worked in it, with their eternally familiar voices. But they were not voices or projections. The men I met in that booth were real. They were human beings. That is obvious, but you know it is not. The booth was not a shrine with infinite depths. The only depths it had were in time, not in space. I thought of Murph. I thought of all the years this tiny space had played a role in my life. How much had happened here. How much had been viewed and seen and felt by so many. How soon this would just be airspace above a parking lot.

Zoe and I went down the elevator with the Cohen family, Gary wheeling his stuff like airplane luggage. We stepped out of the stadium and Gary was greeted by fans, including Cowbell Man, who obviously knew that this was where he always came out. I said goodbye to Gary, Lynn, and Zach and walked with Zoe to the subway and then to my car, in which I would, like the Cohens, drive over the Whitestone Bridge and home to Connecticut.

The Guys in the Booth

If there is one undeniably great thing about being a fan of the New York Mets, it is the fact that we have a tradition of great announcers. No matter what was happening to our team, Mets fans have from the beginning experienced it in an atmosphere of down-to-earth poetry, wit, and knowledge. This has been extremely important in shaping the character of Mets fandom at its best. If you listen to announcers for most other teams, you know that there's a common assumption across the land that baseball announcing should be flat, dreary, and inoffensive. It is supposed to be conducted in a universe in which irony and sophistication are unknown and in which knowledge of anything other than sports is suspect. Fans of the New York Mets have never had to deal with these assumptions. I can't imagine what it would be like to have to watch and listen to baseball games that have been stripped of vitality, interest, and wonder by having to be filtered through unexceptional brains. Every Mets fan knows the sinking feeling of learning that a game is going to be broadcast on Fox or ESPN. When that happens, I get my radio, turn off the TV sound, and listen to Howie Rose.

To watch a game and experience it in its proper Mets atmosphere, Mets fans need the Mets announcers. We admire them because they are so good, but our admiration becomes a need because the best of our announcers last so long. We can't recognize a Mets game without them. When we don't have them, we sometimes even wonder why people take the trouble to follow this sport. Our original broadcasting team, Ralph Kiner, Bob Murphy, and Lindsey Nelson, took me all the way through my childhood. Kiner and Murphy have taken me practically to my dotage. By having been around so long, their thoughtful, gentlemanly, optimistic personalities have become part of my own. Everyone who grew up with these guys feels that they have been uncles and role models. Their voices are forever in our heads. In life, and in baseball, we do not begrudge others their achievements. We give people the benefit of the doubt. We are hopeful that things will improve. We savor the good things that happen with a perceptive enthusiasm.

In the 1980s, great announcers like Howie Rose and Gary Cohen came forward to continue this tradition, while adding some elements that are more characteristic of the generation to which Howie, Gary, and I belong. Rose and Cohen were just as generous, hopeful, and enthusiastic as Kiner and Murphy, but their wit was sharper and their criticisms were more direct. Their vocabularies and their ranges of reference were also broader. They had also grown up as Mets fans. They not only knew what they were talking about, they knew what we were. They were of us. They knew that for the most part, we Mets fans are demanding and critical, sometimes whiny. But they also knew that we were desperately loyal. We wanted to know about what we were seeing so that we could judge it fairly, make suggestions if we needed to, or be patient if that was what was called for. We didn't want announcers who would praise everything. We wouldn't tolerate excessive bias and cheerleading. We wanted guys who would let you know when they had a problem. We wanted announcers who gave us the deepest possible appreciation of this very complex game.

Howie Rose keeps this alive on the radio broadcasts. Tom McCarthy did a fine job of keeping up with Howie during the 2007 season. The sound of his voice, eerily similar to Gary Cohen's, reminded Mets fans of the many years we had Howie and Gary together broadcasting games on the radio, while Kiner and Murphy and various others broadcast on TV. In 2008, McCarthy defected to the hated Phillies and was replaced by the pleasant, somewhat conventionally professional announcer Wayne Hagin. As the year went on, Hagin seemed to be developing, under Howie's tutelage, a deeper understanding of how you do Mets announcing and how it is different from, say, broadcasting the Brewers. I hope he finds his Mets persona. As Ralph and Murph would say, I'm sure he can do it, he's got so much talent. But Howie, on the radio, is the

Man. Howie uses the full resources of the English language to describe ordinary things in a way that no one else has ever thought of. Howie remembers more of his childhood and adolescence with the Mets than any of the rest of us aging baby boomers do. Howie can smell horseshit as soon as it enters a room and no matter how hard someone is trying to hide it. Howie makes you feel a great play by Jose Reyes or a home run by David Wright with all the intensity with which you once felt a great play by Buddy Harrelson or a home run by Rusty Staub. Howie, I hope, will forever be my friend of the highways, the guy who is with me when I'm pulling weeds or spraying the Roundup on the poison ivy.

When I can watch the Mets on TV, though, I do. And here Mets fans have something extraordinary: the best television broadcasting team in the history of baseball. Let me give you an idea of what I mean. I was listening to Gary and Ron broadcasting a game from Los Angeles. They started to talk about Sandy Koufax and instead of talking, as generic broadcasters would, in obvious ways about the pitching accomplishments everyone knows about, and about what a nice guy he is and how nice his wife is and how nice his kids are, Ronnie talked about the kind of aura Koufax has for pitchers, and how meeting him is like what it would be like for a deeply spiritual person to meet the Dalai Lama. He then goes on to praise Koufax for his important role standing up for all players, and not just for himself, by insisting on labor justice for ballplayers more than a decade before that became a movement. Gary, in the meantime, explained what would strike modern fans as the peculiar fact that Koufax was on the World Championship 1955 Dodgers but didn't really come into his own as a pitcher until the early 1960s. You learned about the rules that governed bonus signings, how Koufax, by signing for a bonus, had to be on the major league roster for a designated period of time.

This is what I'm talking about. Do you think you would have learned any of this from other announcers? Do you think other announcers would know how to use the Dalai Lama in a sentence? We Mets fans are such a privileged group. We know and understand more about baseball because we get to listen to this kind of commentary. I know that a big part of our identity is our affectionate attachment to the over-the-top silliness of life at Shea. We're like kids because we respond to Mr. Met, the apple, Cowbell Man, and the Curly Shuffle. But we're like grown-ups because we expect and get a "word picture" with this much life, character, and dimension.

One thing I particularly love about Gary, Keith, and Ron is that they're all knowledgeable but they know different things because of the different perspectives from which they've experienced the game. Ron, of course, teaches us so much about pitching, just as Keith teaches us so much about hitting. But I get a great vicarious pleasure when Gary answers Ron and Keith's questions about things like when Jon Matlack joined the team, or which minor player broke up which Mets almost no-hitter. A lifelong Mets fan like Gary knows these things. You see that the Mets need us, to teach them about the Mets. It is in the memories of the fans, even more than the players, that the Mets exist.

Just as the announcing is great, the dynamic of this broadcasting team is very entertaining. Representing the Mets fan, Gary is charmingly nerdy. He has arched eyebrows and a crooked mouth and he makes little jerks of his head, at the very top of which is just a little tuft of hair. He doesn't actually look like George Clooney, as you might have expected from listening to his magnificent voice. He's the responsible one, the one who keeps things moving, who keeps things solid, even though he can also be moved to lyricism. If Nelson Figueroa starts an April game, Gary will tell us that "as a fog descends, a specter from the past takes the mound at Shea." Gary has a relaxed, respectful rapport with Ron Darling, who is, as he's always been, impossibly cool, but in a refreshingly accessible way. Darling shows you that jocks can be as wonky as fans but even more sophisticated than newscasters. I've never seen a player in the booth as good as Darling. No one ever has. It's as if Christy Mathewson had gone into broadcasting. Darling probably doesn't like the awe he inspires in people, with his looks, his name, and his talents. And this is probably why he's so self-effacing. It's as if he's saying, "Hey, this is just what I am. I'm relaxed, so you relax."

In this trio, Keith's role is to be a little bit of the class clown, someone who can shrug and make fun of himself, who throws

Tootsie Rolls out of the booth, who will complain about a long promo being like a novella, who will let the Mets have a day to honor his mustache, and who is willing to serve as the spokesman of a company that sells the hair dye he uses. He's a middle-aged version of the guy you see on the Seinfeld episode. He doesn't seem to pick up on everything right away. He has this way of asking funny questions. Answering his questions, Gary and Ron have fun playing around with him, with a little bit of mockery but a lot of respect and affection. I know this is going to sound a little funny, but Gary and Ron are so smart that you almost lose sight of how incredibly smart Keith is. Keith is incredibly smart. He is amazingly smart and articulate for an ex-ballplayer. But he is not as smart as Gary and Ron, because who is? The great thing about Keith is that he acts as if he knows this but doesn't give a shit. Why should he? He's Keith Hernandez.

The spirit of these three is perfectly evident in the way they look when you suddenly see them all together on *Post Game Live*. Are they looking great in their suits or is it goofy matching t-shirt day? They look as if they're going to be serious, but they also look as if they think there's something very funny about it being *Post Game Live* again. And there is, especially if they have to squeeze together for the camera in the t-shirts, with Gary between the sky blue or black or white matching guts of the athletes. As Gary offers his overview of the game, Ron nods as if he agrees and as if he's waiting to say something really important. Keith nods too, but with a little smile, as if he's trying to keep it under control. Gary turns it over to Ron, who offers his sage perspective. Ron gives it back to Gary, who moves things forward to the next game detail so that Keith can talk about it. Keith offers his insight, usually talking to the little screen on which the replay prompt is playing instead of talking to the camera as he's probably supposed to. Keith often says really insightful things, but he rarely, if ever, says them with the authority Darling musters so easily. Although he's older, Keith almost seems like a little brother in relation to Ron. This impression is reinforced by the fact that Darling looks and sounds a little like Wally Cleaver. Keith, you realize, is the Beaver! He means well, but he has a tendency to get into trouble. And with his paternal voice and his bemused curiosity about what's going on up there in the boys' room, Gary Cohen is like Ward Cleaver.

That's what they feel like to me. I think of them as a family I've known a long time. Gary, Keith, Ron, and Howie feel like brothers to me. They are so much fun and I've learned so much from them. You want to be with them, as much as you can, as long as you can. What you hear most often, when Mets fans talk about this TV team, is the hope that they'll be with us for many years, as Murph and Kiner were. You yearn for this kind of stability, through decade after decade, just as you'd like to have it in your life and family. These guys give us something that we don't want to live without. They give us our sense of being at home with the Mets. By shaping our experience of our baseball team, they give shape to our memories. I can't imagine what my memories of the Mets would look like if they had not been shaped by Ralph, Murph, Gary, Howie, Keith, and Ron. I am at home in the place they've made for me. I would really rather not have to watch a Mets game anywhere else. Ever.

Subway Series: Going to a Yankees Game at Shea

On Saturday, June 28, 2008, I saw the Mets play the Yankees at Shea for the first time in my life.

I had always avoided Mets-Yankees games. They'd always been sold out, and I wasn't interested enough to spend a lot of extra money to see them. I guess a part of me didn't want to see Shea with a lot of Yankees fans in it. I didn't want to see fights. I didn't want to risk seeing enemies exulting on our turf.

Yet since both teams had gotten off to mediocre starts, the Mets-Yankees thing was not as big a deal in 2008 as it had been in the past. I was able to get tickets on StubHub for only $13 more than face value. And so, forty-five years after I exulted in the Mets' 6–2 triumph over the Yankees in the first Mayor's Trophy Game, I finally saw the Yankees play the Mets at Shea.

I have to tell you that I enjoyed the experience more than I thought I would, even though the Mets lost the game. It was very interesting, and a little surprising.

The first surprise came as I was trying to find a parking space. They had let me into the lot, but tailgaters were filling up so many spots that there weren't any spaces visible. I drove up and down a few aisles until finally some tailgaters motioned to me that I could come right into the space where they were tailgating. They were very nice and accommodating, and although it was perfectly obvious to anyone paying attention, I didn't realize until I got out of the car that these nice people who looked like ordinary Mets fans were festooned with Yankee regalia. Okay, I thought. Whatever.

Then I walked to the stadium and was shocked to see something I was going to see all day. I saw a guy in a Posada jersey with his arm around a girl in a Reyes jersey. I saw family groups where brothers with nearly identical faces were wearing shirts with antithetical logos. This was totally bizarre. How did this happen? How could it happen so frequently? I know that Cro-Magnon Man coexisted with Neanderthals for a few tens of thousands of years and we still don't know if they interbred or if the Neanderthals just died out or were killed off by the Cro-Magnons. This reminded me of that. Seriously. I felt as if I were witnessing an ancient and impenetrable mystery. It didn't look like normal New York diversity. It looked like the strangely intimate coexistence of irreconcilable opposites. The completely obvious fact that there were no distinguishing differences between Mets and Yankees fans except for the caps and jerseys they were wearing somehow bothered and amazed me. I mean, shouldn't there at least be physiognomic differences? Shouldn't we be able to see the arrogance on the faces of the Yankees fans? Shouldn't we be able to see the eager philosophical hope and sweetness on the faces of the Mets fans? If I used some sort of selective imagination, I could see these things. If I was honest with myself, I couldn't.

One thing I enjoyed was the way in which the opposing fan groups gave each other an audience to cheer for and boo at. This made me realize what a lazy experience it is, normally, to watch a game in your home stadium. You cheer and boo, but if you're busy talking or putting mustard on your hot dog, it doesn't matter if you don't make any noise because everyone else is making the requisite obvious noise. But when Shea has all these Yankees fans, you feel you have to make a lot of noise when something good happens for the Mets because the Yankees fans are making a lot of noise when something good happens for the Yankees. You want them to hear you because they are trying so hard to make you hear them. It takes a lot of extra energy to go to a Subway Series game.

And everybody seems to love the theatricality of the whole deal. There is much generally good-natured striking of violently hostile Kabuki poses. People even take pictures of staged scowling face-offs. People whip themselves up into a frenzy, holding onto $8 bottles of bad beer. One hand is always full and the other hand is waving around. And it's always funny that the lout in the Jeter shirt has in his hand a cobalt blue bottle with a Mets logo commemorating the last year of Shea.

Throughout the afternoon, in the familiar stands of my beloved Shea, I heard Yankees fans chanting "Lets Go Yan-kees!" a chant that seemed to create a natural space for an answering chant of "Yankees Suck!" The Yankees fans were only able to muster a weak "No" after "Lets Go Mets!" in the space in which younger fans like to put the "Woooo!" We definitely had a more effective and persuasive counter-cheering situation, even if it did not exactly reflect well on us.

Around the seventh inning, it began to rain and everybody took shelter, just like Cro-Magnons and Neanderthals, in the cave-like promenade behind the stands. There were endless lines for the bathrooms. People streamed by, slapping the hands of those who had the same colors and logos as they did, ignoring those who didn't. It was hot, steamy, and close, and there were claps of thunder that rattled the long-echoing space filled with sweating bodies and the sounds of talking and laughing and shouting into cell phones. Right next to me was a group of three mothers, two in Mets outfits and one in a Yankees outfit, and a big, mixed-loyalty brood of their young. One of the men associated with this group, a guy with a Mets jersey who was apparently the husband of the woman in the Yankees jersey, showed up with two blue bottles in his hand, drinking from both of them in a way that would only have made sense if he had had two mouths. A domestic quarrel ensued, a foot and a half from my head. "I called you four fucking times!" "I didn't fucking hear the phone! It's too fucking loud!" "You should have been listening for the fucking phone!" "I can't take any more of this fucking bullshit!" As all this was going on, my daughter was beside me, texting on her phone. And people kept up the chants and the silliness. I worried that a quarrel between a Mets fan and a Yankees fan might lead to something unpleasant, but no one was paying attention and this was obviously a couple having an intimate fight in each other's face. So I just stood in wonder at the scene, which eventually floated away. And gradually things grew lighter and you could see the bay and Manhattan off in a hazy orange distance, everything looking indescribably serene and calm beyond the streaming crowd on the promenade and the people smoking illegally off at the last edge of the stadium.

When it was light enough and dry enough for the game to re-sume, Sonia and I walked up into the bright bowl and saw that the lights were turned on and that they were beautiful reflected on the white tarp covering the infield. Wiping off our seats with tis-sues, we heard "Somewhere over the Rainbow" on the stadium sound system and excitedly turned to see a big, fuzzy rainbow over Flushing. Was it a symbol of the season? You know, when re-ality pulls something like this, I become full of cynical fear. That rainbow, I knew, was not really a sign of the revivification of the Mets. It was just a rainbow, and if the Mets were going to win this game, Jose Reyes wouldn't have been picked off at second with David Wright at the plate.

Play resumed. Sonia and I left our pleasant seats in the breezy upper deck at the end of the eighth inning because the Yankees contingent had become dominant after too many Mets fans went home because of the rain delay. At that point, the Mets were be-hind 3–2. We went down and watched the last inning in an area of the mezzanine where glum and tired Mets season-ticket holders sweated under the overhang to no purpose. I got to see Mariano Rivera's cutter in person. There were a few Yankees fans down there but only a few, including a woman in a Williams jersey who did some kind of weird little dance every time one of Rivera's pitches got by a Mets batter. When the game ended, the Yankees fans gyrated and I felt for the first time all afternoon how much I disliked them and how much I wanted them to go away and not come back. Still, I thought, it was the Mets who lost that game, and all by themselves. The craziness of the season was continuing.

But at least I saw this very strange thing: this unending, cen-tury-old family quarrel that will continue as long as there is base-ball. This fissure in the city that is not a real division so much as an occasion for enjoying the pleasure of battle and contempt with-out any real meaning. This exciting excuse to get all worked up and to chant and gyrate and be pleased to see rainbows. Oh, what fun it would be, I thought, if both teams could turn it around and the season were to end with a big, dramatic New York smashup, in the final year of the two old stadiums.

The Mets' Bar Mitzvah

From June 17, when Jerry Manuel became the manager, until July 4, the Mets lost one and won one, won one and lost one, won one and lost two, won two and lost two, won one and lost one, won one and lost one, and won one and lost one. They were not merely playing .500 ball, they were defining .500 ball. Mets fans felt as if they were walking through a featureless landscape halfway between heaven and hell. There was no music, just a repetitive hum, like an engine warming up, getting ready to start moving. Or maybe it was like some deadeningly repetitive torture technique. One or the other.

Then, from July 5 through July 17, the Mets did not lose. They won ten games in a row.

After a year of flat and often foolish baseball, maybe it was time to start getting excited about the Mets again. I was ready, because I was sick and tired of not being very excited. I don't follow baseball because it is boring and doesn't engage my emotions. Most other things are boring. Most other things don't engage my emotions. Baseball was supposed to be exciting. The Mets didn't have to win to make me happy. But they did have to interest me.

Maybe it was time for Mets fans to put behind them the sour disappointments and futile anger of the previous thirteen months. With their win streak, the Mets were so close to the division-leading Phillies that it was possible that they could go into first place during the series between the two teams in late July. And if the risible saga of A-Rod and his mind-controlling, mystical girlfriend ever settled down long enough, it might even become possible to read about the Mets on the back pages of the tabloids.

In the middle of the winning streak, Gary, Keith, and Ron took a moment to point out that July 9 was the thirty-ninth anniversary of Tom Seaver's Imperfect Game, the 1969 game in which

Seaver gave up only one hit and nothing else, with one batter out in the ninth. The reason this game is remembered, and needs to be known by all generations of Mets fans, is that it marked the moment at which the Mets became something different from what they had been before. They didn't become good on that July evening. They had been good for a couple of months. They didn't become the Miracle Mets. They wouldn't really become miraculous for another month and a half. What happened on that evening, and in that three-game series against the division-leading Chicago Cubs, was that for the first time in their eight-year history, the Mets were playing games that mattered in the eyes of a respectful world and wildly enthusiastic fans, challenging for the division title, led by a young man who showed every sign, in his mid-twenties, of being a shoo-in Hall of Famer.

Seaver's almost perfect game was, as Gary Cohen said, a "legitimizing game for a franchise." Interviewed by Marty Noble for an article on the mets.com website, Howie Rose said something similar: "I remember thinking . . . 'We've got one now, the Mets have their Mantle or their Koufax.' They'd been around almost eight seasons, and they had their superstar and they were in a pennant race and the focus of all baseball. That was the Mets' bar mitzvah."

A bar mitzvah is a perfect analogy. Every culture has such rites of passage, symbolic moments that elevate the awkwardness and inconsistency of adolescence in such a way that we see past them to what they promise. Nothing is more absurd, more unsure, more funny-looking than a thirteen-year-old kid. But what you are looking at is a transition of greater importance than anything else that happens after the first two years of life. You're looking at a hand that will stop trembling, a voice that will stop cracking and quavering. You're looking at energy that will eventually do the world some good and you're looking at an innocence that will settle into something seasoned and competent.

Here, in July, in this winning streak, was the 2008 Mets' bar mitzvah, or confirmation, or whatever you wanted to call it. Here was the end of the dumbass first half of the season. Maybe we'd just been looking at a goofy kid who didn't know what to do, a kid who could surprise you but who couldn't do anything consistently. We'd been looking at somebody so unsure of himself that he was tripping over his own feet, falling flat, getting up, and taking a few seconds to remember where he was going. Now we were beginning to see something that resembled adult competence. The games mattered. The world was becoming respectful. The fans were becoming wildly enthusiastic. The team was challenging for all available titles. Could they be led once again by a young man, or even a couple of young men, who showed signs, in their mid-twenties, of being shoo-in Hall of Famers?

Winning Ten in a Row

It is a great thing to win ten in a row. I know. I've had the experience of playing blackjack in a casino and winning ten hands in a row. I enjoy playing blackjack. And I understand that if I have an excellent mastery of the basic strategy that has been developed according to the probabilities calculated by a computer, I can't win much, but I won't lose much, as long as I bet small amounts of money and bet very conservatively. When I go to a casino, I go to the $10 tables and bet $10 each time. Allowing myself $100 in chips, I find that I will always reach a point at which I will be $60 ahead. When I reach that point, I play until I am back down to $50 or until I decide to get up from the table, whichever happens first. Normally I make $50. I know that the odds are that every once in a while, I will lose $100 before I'm ever ahead by $50, but that hasn't happened to me yet. I know that no matter what I do, I am ahead of the game if I make $50. Fifty dollars is enough. I say that I get a free dinner. I get a free dinner.

Anyway, what happens when you win ten in a row is that, no matter what you know, and no matter what you've experienced, you start to wonder if you can quit your job and live off blackjack. You really do wonder that, even though you know perfectly well that you can't. I'm not saying that you think it, but you wonder it. You feel the power and majesty of a moment in which the world seems to be asking you to make three wishes. This feeling has accomplished wonderful things for many people. It is a feeling that you are not tied down by necessity or fortune or any of the stuff that keeps us from being gods. All it takes to get there is winning ten times in a row.

Baseball is not blackjack. It is, for the most part, not a game of chance. But it can act like blackjack, being made as it is of shoulders and elbows and hamstrings and skulls, and malaise and stupidity and unheralded rookies and inexplicable streaks and slumps. Every once in a while, you will keep getting face cards and the dealer's up card is reliably a four or a five. Every once in a while, you'll average seven runs a game, while the other side is averaging less than one. And no matter how much you know that *a* does not equal *b*, you somehow start to believe that it does or it could and that you'll make it all the way to the World Series, averaging seven runs a game and averaging one given up.

I went to one of the Mets games in the middle of the July streak. It was one of those afternoon travel day games in the middle of the summer. It was hot, but boy were people happy. There was none of that now familiar stench of the expectation of defeat. It was as if we had all gone to some other place. There were only the good feelings that community and family and shared enthusiasm and winning a lot of baseball games can bring.

Neither I nor anyone else had forgotten the bottom of the previous September. I hadn't forgotten Adam Wainwright's curveball. I wasn't forgetting any of the other things Mets fans never forget (Scioscia's homer, Rogers's walk, Templeton's homer, Piazza's ball caught at the wall). But I was having fun remembering this other Mets thing that I hadn't felt for awhile: the losing of the mind and raising of the spirit, the sense of blue cotton candy good fortune promised in the sunlight of a summer afternoon.

The Last Play at Shea

As we rode the wave of the July streak into the All-Star break, Billy Joel gave two concerts at Shea, each of which was at some point supposed to be the last concert ever to be performed at the stadium. The first concert, on July 16, had sold out. So a second concert was set up for July 18, to the chagrin of those who had managed to score tickets for the first one. Both concerts were called "The Last Play at Shea."

I've always liked Billy Joel. I didn't love him the way I love Springsteen or Dylan, but I've always liked him. And I agreed that he was the right person to play the last concert. The composer of "New York State of Mind," he was a New York guy, and he was a New York guy in the way that the Mets are a New York team. He was of the great city, but he looked towards the east. As Joel said during the first of his concerts, Shea was kind of the border between New York City and Long Island, which is where Joel grew up and where he lived. Although Mets fans can be from anywhere, the Mets heartland is the island that extends to the east of Shea, the island Walt Whitman called by its original Indian name, Paumanok. The Yankees might be more popular elsewhere, but the Mets ruled the fish-shaped island the English divided into the counties of Nassau, Suffolk, Kings, and Queens.

Joel was the right guy to play the last concert because he was like Shea in a number of ways. He was a little the worse for wear and kind of past his prime, but he had seen and done great things. As he mentioned at the concert, Joel began his career in music in 1964, the same year Shea opened. Like Shea, Billy Joel connected us with a valued past, but he was cool enough not to begrudge the future. Like the Mets, Joel was local and familiar, but well-known everywhere. And like the Mets, he had had his ups and downs, but he never lost the love of his fans. He could still bring people to their feet and draw tears from their eyes.

As everyone knew, the only thing that would have been more appropriate than Billy Joel playing the final concert at Shea would have been the resurrection and return of the Beatles. On the evening of August 15, 1965, right here at Shea, the Beatles had invented the stadium concert. Until there were the Beatles, no one had ever imagined that it might be possible to fill an entire stadium for a concert. The Beatles changed everyone's idea of what was and wasn't possible. When I first heard their music in 1964, I felt this immediately. I felt as if the world was being thrown violently forward by their exciting and unfamiliar harmonies. There were these moments in all of the Beatles' songs when you heard this world-changing sound. A key changed or the voices of Lennon and McCartney would suddenly come together in a louder, quickening surprise, a sound that seemed to be between that of an adult and a child, between that of a man and a woman. The appeal of this sound and the songs was immediate and universal and it swept the world. Everyone wanted to hear it.

On the evening of August 14, 1965, everyone in America had watched the Beatles on *The Ed Sullivan Show*, and on the following evening, everyone in the world was paying attention as the Beatles traveled by helicopter from the East Side of Manhattan to the Port Authority Heliport at the New York World's Fair. They flew over the Triborough Bridge and the Grand Central Parkway, which were clogged with the pilgrimage to see them. They landed at the fair and were driven across the parkway and through the lot and into the bullpen and out onto the field. They leaped from their van and ran to the stage in shallow center, where they played under the big Mets logo at the top of the scoreboard. In their light brown jackets, they waved and smiled with amusement and awe at the wall of screams that came towards them like water bursting a dike. No one had ever seen anything like this. This was the largest crowd that had ever assembled to listen to music. What happened at Shea that night would eventually lead to the crowd of half a million at Woodstock. But the crowd at Woodstock would not scream like this. This was a sound that could only come from decorous teenagers who have had nothing to drink. It was a sound of pure astonishment, intensified by anticipation. After this, there would be plenty of stadium concerts with enthusiastic crowds. But what happened on the evening of August 15, 1965, would never be new again.

Of course, the concert wasn't what we imagine it to have been, just as Woodstock wasn't what we imagine it to have been. The Beatles could not hear themselves play. The crowd could not hear them. The soundtrack you hear on the documentary that was made by Ed Sullivan's production company had to be rerecorded in secret. But the images of the screaming, crying kids and the two thousand sweating policemen intercepting those who, in a kind of delirium, ran with such terrifying speed towards the stage, became part of everyone's memory of the 1960s. Shea became the place where people strained at boundaries and sometimes overran them. I think that the image of the running kids, who knew they would not make it to the stage, but who had to get onto the field and as close as possible, was part of what impelled the crowds to burst onto the field when the Mets won their first division title and championship five years later. At the Beatles concert, Shea Stadium became a symbol of all that was new about the 1960s. It became the place where the sound of the crowd could make the giant building tremble.

The "Beatles at Shea Stadium" was a shower of stars that blessed the earth on which it fell. It took a lot of guts for Billy Joel, or for anyone, to dare to commemorate it.

Billy Joel was not the Beatles. He was not an object of worship and he was not a suitable endpoint of a pilgrimage. His message to the crowds that filled the stadium for his concerts was that he was simply one of them. He was a New Yorker. He remembered the New York that had welcomed the Beatles, the New York of the Ed Sullivan show and the 1964-1965 New York World's Fair. He knew our highways and beaches, our great buildings, our rivers and bays, and our Mets. Images of these things were projected on the screens behind him as he sang songs to which everyone knew the words.

As Billy Joel sang his long, nostalgic set, people in the crowd on July 18 began to notice that he was taking his time, that he was singing for longer than they thought he was supposed to sing. And after his first encore on the evening of July 18, you could make out that something was happening. You saw Joel pause and then you heard him shout into his microphone, "Please welcome . . . Sir Paul McCartney!" Each of the hundreds of people who taped this and put it on YouTube shakes wildly at this introduction. You see darkness and people's heads and the blurred tracks of lights and then finally the image steadies and you see McCartney and Joel and you hear the roar of rapture from the middle-aged crowd. There is Joel at the piano and McCartney standing at the microphone with his guitar. They sing "I Saw Her Standing There," a song that I used to sing to myself all the time in 1964. It was one of my favorite songs, one of the songs that the Beatles seemed to have written about me. It was all about awe, about crossing that room. It was about the promise of happiness and love. These were the feelings I felt whenever I thought about Shea Stadium, the World's Fair, and the Beatles. They were the feelings I expected to have when I would finally be allowed to enter the promised world of love. How wonderful it would be to go beyond the constraints of childhood. How wonderful it would be to know what was way beyond compare.

McCartney wore a white shirt with a loosened dark tie. Singing into the microphone, he moved his head and neck exactly as he had moved them forty-three years earlier. He bounced back on his heels in the same way and sang up into the microphone in the same way, with his big cheeks and his bright, friendly eyes. It looked as if he were singing on *The Ed Sullivan Show*, sweating once again in the bright lights on the black-and-white TV in our living room. The rap against rock at the time was that it would never last, that the Beatles were a passing craze. This the grown-ups got completely wrong. Of course, we kids disagreed. We said, without confidence, that the Beatles' music would last forever. But no one in 1964 thought they would ever see Paul McCartney singing "I Saw Her Standing There," with all the energy it deserved, at the last concert ever played at Shea Stadium. People really have no idea what will last and what won't, what will happen and what won't. No one ran out onto the field at "The Last Play at Shea" because fans were already sitting on the field, on seats set up on a platform that protected the grass. Fans were right in front of the stage, behind which were the screens that turned Joel and McCartney into giants.

After "I Saw Her Standing There," Billy Joel sang "Piano Man," playing his own piano and looking out in wonder, but without surprise, at thousands of people singing along with him. Sometimes he would stop and just watch them, with his cool grey beard and his handsome, ordinary guy face. "Piano Man" was Joel's choice for a final song and he sang, with particular emphasis, the lines about playing a memory that was sad and sweet and he knew it complete when he wore a younger man's clothes. After "Piano Man," McCartney and Joel hugged on the stage and McCartney addressed the crowd, saying "It's so cool to be back here on the last night. Been here a long time ago—we had a blast that night, and we're having another one tonight." That was the thing about pop stars in their sixties playing a final concert in a stadium where they sang as young men. Sure, they were having a blast. They could still do it. They were still here. They were not young any more, but so what? Maybe there should have been something sadder about "The Last Play at Shea," but if we were going to get something sadder, it wasn't going to be from these guys.

McCartney's elegy, and the final song of the evening, was "Let It Be." If you had to choose one song that would be the most appropriate final song to be played at Shea, you could not have chosen anything other than "Let It Be." All the broken-hearted people living in the world of dreams. That was all of it right there. McCartney sang the song as a strangely inspiring blues piece, and the crowd sang along as if it were an anthem. Only McCartney could have sung the blues with so much optimism. In spite of his full head of dark hair, he looked his age. He didn't look like an object of worship, or Dionysian passion, or any of the other things that might have come his way in 1965. He looked as if he was singing a song on the earth. And it looked as if he was perfectly happy with that. When he was done, McCartney lifted his arms high in the air and then spread them and waved them around as if he was touching everyone from a distance. Then he waved, just as he had waved as a Beatle, and the concert was over.

It was great. This was life. This was music. And I couldn't help but feel that this was what it was like to root for the Mets. You see her standing there and in the end, you let it be. What happened in between was what was most important. But you couldn't enjoy what happened in between unless you could see her standing there and unless you could let it be.

I didn't go to the concert. I saw it through the jiggly, blurred, yet startlingly real windows of YouTube. And I heard about it from other Mets fans. I would have liked to have gone, but while it was happening I was on vacation. I was with my wife, Sheila, on our first extended trip together since our daughter was born seventeen years before. We were in Burguete, Spain, at the Hostal Burguete, where Mike and Jake stay on their fishing trip in *The Sun Also Rises*. We had the same meal as they had, the vegetable soup and the trout wrapped in ham. We saw the piano Mike had played to keep warm. We kept warm in our sweet little room on that summer night high in the mountains. There was an enormous moon out our window, in a deep blue sky. You may not think this is relevant, but I do. I thought nothing about the Mets. I felt full of life, and when Paul McCartney took the stage at what would have been four in the morning Spanish time, I was soundly and happily asleep.

The World's Fair

Let me tell you something. Once upon a time, New York looked very much the same as it does now, but it was also very different. All the highways and the bridges and the airports were there. Manhattan was a loud, exciting cluster of skyscrapers and neighborhoods, just as it is now. The cars were bigger and differently shaped, but they were still cars, and if you were a kid sitting in the back seat, they were pretty large and comfortable. New York was New York. People didn't have as much money, but they were much better dressed. The suburbs were already the suburbs. The houses were a little smaller, the shopping malls were outdoors, and there were these wonderful drive-in movies.

I was a kid in the back seat of one of those big cars that would pull into gas stations and be filled up by a friendly guy in a uniform whom my dad would call "Chief." I loved it when the whole family would get into the car and drive over the George Washington Bridge and then down the Harlem River Drive to the Triborough and cross the Harlem River to get to that immense elevated toll plaza that was so bright, so lifted high above the city in the sunlight. I remember how we'd drive past the hospital with the tiny barred windows, with the spectacular sky road of the Hell Gate Bridge on our left, onto the bluish-green span of the Triborough that would lower us into Queens. We'd descend into Astoria and then there would be the graveyard and the Bulova watch company on the right, and then there was LaGuardia Airport on our left, and then I'd be watching straight ahead, through the space between my parents' heads, to get my first glimpse of the beautiful new stadium of the Mets, the gateway to the 1964–1965 New York World's Fair.

In 1964 and 1965, my family and I drove this sacred route from New Jersey to Flushing at least thirty times. We went to the fair exactly twenty-four times. You could buy an expensive single ticket, or you could get a great deal by buying a packet of twelve tickets that you could use all year. I thought that the 1964–1965 World's Fair was the most wonderful and the most amazing thing I had ever seen. I was very proud of it because I assumed that the whole world was impressed by it. I was proud of its association with my city and my baseball team. In 1964 and 1965, because of the World's Fair, it seemed as if Flushing, Queens, was the center of the world. Normally, Flushing was an obscure portion of New York City, but when it was fair time, every twenty-five years, it became enormously famous. I knew all about the 1939–1940 World's Fair. I loved to see pictures of its Flash Gordon buildings, its still stunning yet antiquated image of the future. I loved the one picture my family had of the 1939–1940 fair: a little black-and-white snapshot of my eleven-year-old mother with her parents and teenage brothers and the Trylon and Perisphere in the background. It was so strange to see my grandparents, whom I associated with the infinite distances of the past, standing awkwardly in front of these giant geometric symbols. As Hitler was about to invade Poland, here were these little Jewish owners of a candy store in Brooklyn taking a rare day off to visit the world of television and superhighways and self-cleaning kitchens.

Despite Hitler's interruption, the future did come. And the new future I saw at the 1964–1965 World's Fair seemed glorious beyond belief. My grandparents were still alive. We would visit them often. They had just moved out of the Park Slope brownstone apartment above their store where they had lived for half a century. Now they lived in the modern high-rise towers that had been built on the site of Ebbets Field. Their gleaming new apartment in the sky brought my grandparents into the modern age, but it still smelled exactly the same as the apartment in the brownstone. In 1964, I was nine. The past and the future were coexisting in a kind of balance that was more precious than I realized. In the middle was me.

I loved everything at the World's Fair. One of the great things was the General Motors Futurama ride, where you rode smoothly through the history of transportation, ending up in the world as it would look when I was an adult, a world of strangely shaped tall glass buildings with cars moving steadily through them on many levels of highway. My very favorite was the Bell Telephone ride, with the immense armchairs with stereo headphones that took you through the history of communication from "Tom Tom to Telstar." Sometimes at the fair, instead of riding through time in your own cozy gliding nook, you would be with the rest of the crowd on a rotating or elevating "people mover." You'd visit the steadily improving decades of the twentieth century on General Electric's Carousel of Progress, and you'd visit the steadily more elaborate electrified holidays of the year with Ben Franklin and Reddy Kilowatt at the Tower of Light. At night, the clustered columns of the Tower of Light were lit up in primary colors. At the center of the rainbow of columns, the brightest searchlight in the history of the world shot straight into the sky over Flushing. This looked unbelievable in the middle of the other brilliantly illuminated pavilions on the avenues beside the leaping, spraying colored fountains. I wish I could have seen all this from a plane. I would have loved to have seen it when there was a night game, when Shea would have been visible on the edge, a sparkling semicircle around an emerald lawn. Whether it reflects well on me or whether it doesn't, I will admit that nothing I have ever seen has impressed me as much as the 1964–1965 New York World's Fair at night.

I still remember the names of everything at the fair. I would have remembered them without consulting the guidebook or the infinite resources of the Internet, which no one who designed the World's Fair foresaw. The Tower of Light, the guidebook explained, was a pavilion jointly operated by investor-owned electrical utilities. Not to be outdone, the natural gas companies had their Festival of Gas. Everything was a Tower or a Festival. Buildings weren't buildings, they were Pavilions. The pathways between the pavilions were Courts and Avenues. Even a place designed for old people to sit down was called the "Pavilion of Dynamic Maturity," which caused me and my sisters no end of mirth. I remember all of the songs of the fair. "We're on a Holiday, a happy Holiday, we're on a Holiday with Light!" You know some of those songs too, because Disney carted a couple of the pavilions they had designed out to Disneyland. "It's a Great Big

Beautiful Tomorrow, Shining at the End of Every Day! It's a Great Big Beautiful Tomorrow, Just a Dream Away!" "It's a Small World, After All!" It was indeed. A small world in a good way, a big beautiful tomorrow in a good way. At a couple of points I wondered what it was going to be like to take my kids to the 1989–1990 World's Fair, or go with my grandchildren, in my dynamic maturity, to the 2014–2015 and the 2039–2040 World's Fairs.

The 1989–1990 fair didn't happen. The 2014–2015 fair and the 2039–2040 fair won't happen either. But we didn't know that in 1964. We thought they would happen. We expected a lot of things to happen in 1964 that never ended up happening, and a lot of things did happen that we did not see coming. In 1964, I thought that there was a reasonable chance that I'd be living on the moon by 2008. I also hoped and even kind of expected that the rotating carousel of medical science would grant me the privilege of eternal life. I loved the World's Fair for its cool shows and sweeping forms and brilliant colors. But I loved it most because it suggested that everything that wasn't possible was going to become possible. At some level, I still believe all of the bizarre, wonderful, untrue things it taught me.

It wasn't, you must know, really a World's Fair. The world largely stayed away because people in other countries seemed to think that the whole thing had developed into a display of shameless American corporate propaganda. I didn't think about this at the age of nine. Although I know better now, I still resist caring about this. The people who made what I saw in those pavilions were all lying. But I could not see how anyone could not love the fair and its promise of the future. The real geniuses of America weren't the people who ran those companies, alas. They were the people who made those shows. They were the people who filled me with an excitement about the future that has gone away but will echo in my head for as long as there are echoes in my head. There was something beautiful about my excitement, something that was in a certain way superior to what came after it.

The New Stadium

When Shea opened in April of 1964, it was considered a part of the World's Fair. On programs and on posters you'd see it called "Shea Stadium at the New York World's Fair." I remember that there was an ad in one of the Mets' programs or scorecards which said that the fair was just a "dinosaur's throw" from the stadium. The ad was for the Sinclair Oil Company, whose fair exhibit featured models of dinosaurs. The stadium was right next to the fair. You could walk or take a shuttle bus. Shea was a part of the fair that would fulfill the promise that the future would be better than the past. The fair would close after two years, but Shea would go into the future with us.

Shea looked like the fair. I know this is hard for younger fans to believe because in the last years of its life the stadium had the architectural equivalent of 1980s hair. I mean, I loved it and all, but the exceptionally deep Mets blue and the elaborate stylishness of the neon sculptures of ballplayers, the photo montages of the championship years, and all the Pepsi and Budweiser stuff that had been stuck onto the scoreboard made Shea look very different from the way it had looked in its youth. When it opened, Shea wasn't blue. It was a kind of sand color, a pinkish tan. The first new stadium built in over thirty years, it didn't look like the older stadiums. It didn't have any wood or brick or columns. It didn't look like the sort of place in which you might as well be watching a horse race. Shea looked monumental across a parking lot, yet it made no reference to the monumental architecture of the past. Immense and relentlessly modern and round, it looked like a flying saucer that had just landed. I suppose, in a way, it also looked as if it could take off at a moment's notice. In 1964, there was this idea that it was a good thing to have nothing to do with the past, to look as if you were a visitor from outer space.

The main decoration on the exterior of Shea was squiggly blue and orange aluminum panels suspended on thin, almost invisible cables. The panels had the same audacity of color you saw everywhere at the fair. They looked like the cozy, futuristic Howard Johnsons that were scattered all across the country at the time. The panels were part of something that was happening right at that moment in history, on television, in movies, and everywhere. Everything that had always been in black and white was suddenly in color. The blue and orange panels at Shea were like the brilliant animated opening credit sequences you saw at the beginning of movies in 1964 and 1965. They were asymmetrical and irregular. They looked as if they were about to change their shape, or change from one thing into another. Since you could hardly see the cables to which they were attached, they appeared to be floating and perhaps rising. I always thought they looked like the bubbles I loved to watch as they rose inside a glass of Coca-Cola. The panels made Shea look cool, hip, modern, and friendly.

Contributing to the sense of Shea's colorful hipness was the fact that the seats in the stadium were a different color in each level. The field boxes were a soft yellow, the loge was bright orange, the mezzanine was a pretty dark blue, and the upper deck was old-fashioned baseball park green. Stadium seats were normally only one color at that time. But Shea was like a rainbow with an arc of 300 degrees. The scoreboard too was striking. Seen from behind, it was sleek, sweeping, and white, like something on *The Jetsons*, or like the TWA terminal at Kennedy airport. It looked like a big white vampire with a big square head and an immense white cloak. From the front, it offered state-of-the-art information with little electric lights on a dark display. It didn't talk or make noise, but it gave you what you needed, such as scores and stats, welcomes to civic groups, birthday wishes, and warnings not to throw objects on the field. It would also proudly tell you when you were listening to Jane Jarvis, Shea's Queen of Melody, on the Thomas Organ.

At the top of the scoreboard, on the right, was a big black clock with white hands. It was a real clock that said Longines on it. Time wasn't digitized yet. There were ads on the scoreboard, but they didn't overwhelm it the way the Pepsi-Budweiser blotches did in the stadium's final years. There was a Rheingold logo at the top and a Rheingold ad at the bottom. I loved Rheingold and had already decided that it would be "my beer" when I was an adult. From the lovely waltz jingle of the commercials, I gathered that adults had specific beers. My parents didn't drink much beer so I hadn't known that. I liked the idea presented in the jingle and the ads that Rheingold was "extra dry." I didn't understand what this meant, but I liked the way it sounded and I liked the name Rheingold a lot too. It made the beer sound as if it was a golden liquid that somehow came from a winding river with romantic castles along the side of it.

At some point in the 1960s, the Rheingold ad at the bottom of the scoreboard acquired a picture of a glass stein with an enormous head of foam. The Rheingold ads and commercials always had these glass steins with beads of moisture on the side of them and with enormous white foamy heads. People who argue that ads for alcoholic beverages make young people want to try them should understand that they do in fact have this effect. I imagined that it would be wonderful to drink such a beverage. I could imagine how wonderful the foam must taste. The ad on the scoreboard said, "The Ten-Minute Head, Haven't You Timed It Yet?" It was as if there was something wrong with you if you didn't time your beer head to see how long it would take to flatten out. Did you have to wait for it to be gone before you drank your beer? I hoped not. It looked delicious. It looked like foamy melting ice cream that rose up out of something golden. I couldn't wait to grow up and drink my beer, Rheingold, the dry beer, the beer of the New York Mets.

The feeling of old Shea was not just created by architecture and ads. There was also this funky Mets thing that everyone was into. There was a universal sense that we were rooting for a last-place team that had little hope of being anything but a last-place team for quite a while yet. So to compensate for our team's mediocrity, we had to be the most enthusiastic and colorful fans in baseball. The franchise had to have something that made it distinctive in a good way. Being what Casey Stengel had called "the New Breed," we Mets fans played the part for all it was worth. We channeled the legendary nuttiness of Dodgers fans and the stubbornness of

Giants fans. We screamed and cheered for players who did not deserve the extravagance of our affection. We hung our scruffy banners from the balconies of the immaculate new ballpark, and on windy days they would look like laundry flapping on a clothesline. With the noisy crowd and the flapping sheets, you could almost imagine hearing the cries of vendors with their pushcarts. New York's working class, abandoned by the Dodgers and the Giants, moved into the new palace of a stadium as if it was meant for them. It was. We were New York too. Our team didn't win as much as the Yankees. But the Mets had better, more passionate fans. We liked how we were supposed to be so over the top. We liked being nutty, but warm and generous. We liked rooting for something that people in other places couldn't see the point of. We liked being New Yorkers.

Because of the way memory actually works, I can't tell you for sure when I first went to a game at Shea. I know that I celebrated my tenth birthday with my family at the Fan Appreciation Day doubleheader that was played against Cincinnati on Sunday, September 27, 1964. I remember Charlie Smith getting three hits and Tracy Stallard losing his twentieth game of the season. It was at that part of the old Mets seasons when the statistics would start getting really ugly, when we would pass a hundred losses and some of the pitchers would get their twentieth losses. I have a sense that we went to a game earlier than that, but I can't remember which one it was and neither can my mother, who is the only person I can ask. I remember that on the first game I went to at Shea, I looked through the binoculars my father bought in Tokyo when he was fighting in Korea, and saw Casey Stengel on the dugout bench, his head in his hand, asleep. I thought I remembered Sandy Koufax on the mound at that game. I do remember Sandy Koufax on the mound. I remember him very vividly. But the only appearance Koufax would have made at Shea in 1964 was a Thursday night game, and we wouldn't have gone to a Thursday night game. I see Koufax in the daylight. I see his intensity and his lean face and black stubble through the binoculars. But the game I am remembering has to have been his Saturday afternoon appearance on June 12, 1965. My memories of Shea, in the early years, like your memories too, I would guess, are not neatly ordered in a list of box scores. They are a soup. Things come floating by. They sink down, they surface. More is there than you see at first, but things aren't connected. I remember what I felt, I remember impressions, but I don't remember who fouled out to end the ballgame.

We always brought food to the game and we never parked in the parking lot. My parents could have afforded to buy food at the stadium and park their car in the parking lot, but as a matter of economic principle they never did. They had grown up poor in Brooklyn in the 1930s and had gone to Ebbets Field plenty of times, and this was the way they liked their baseball. You could spend money on other things, but with baseball, the idea was just to be there with everybody else. If it mattered so much to you to see the players close up, you could stay home and watch the game on TV.

We always parked our car for free under the Whitestone Expressway, carrying the hamper with food that they wouldn't let you take in now. We never bought anything from the vendors, but I remember how excited I always was to see them, shouting with their boxes. I wanted to be a vendor someday. I also would have loved to have had a hot dog from a vendor, but I never asked for one, and I never believed my mother, who told me that they weren't as good as the hot dogs we were used to from places like Katz's and Nathan's at Coney Island. They looked so good. Sure they were expensive. Maybe they weren't as good as Katz's or Nathan's, but I bet they tasted as good. I bet there was nothing that tasted as good as a hot dog you ate in the stands at a ballgame.

We always sat in the upper deck. Those were good enough seats and we were a family of five. The players were far away, but you could still see what they were doing. You couldn't see their faces, but you could kind of make out that the players were the people that the numbers on their backs indicated. Ballplayers still wore those old fashioned uniforms with the knickers-type pants and the socks that were stirrups. They were just like my little league uniforms. And so, when you saw them playing on the green grass and on the smooth infield, they looked like the very idea of baseball players. That silhouette, that form, could belong to nothing but a ballplayer playing their game far away. And it could be 1920 or it could be 1935 or it could be 1964. You were watching baseball.

Going to a Mets game was pleasure from the moment we drove out of our driveway to the moment we drove back into it. Even a boring game was wonderful. It was hard to explain why going to the stadium was so much more fun than listening to the game on the radio or watching it on TV, because at the ballpark, you often didn't have a clear understanding of what was going on. Why was that an error? What are they taking so much time to talk about on the field? What did this guy do the last time he came up? But when you were at the game, you were in the place where it was happening. You saw that it was real, that it was not rehearsed or scripted. It was a joy and a festival and it didn't need any special hype to make you feel that way. The scoreboard was enough, the organ was enough, the giant crowd in the enormous bowl was enough. It was enough to be in the open air, in the famous place, with all these people you would probably never see again but with whom you had an intense and eternal bond. It is still like this for me. It is still the same. I don't know what it must be like to be the fan of a team that sells out all of its seats for every game. They didn't have teams like that in the 1960s. The stadiums were always big enough for everybody. Anybody could go to a major league baseball game whenever they wanted to for not all that much money. How can this be preserved in the future? This can't be lost. This shouldn't be lost. For all of its costs and all of its inconveniences, there is nothing like being at a ballgame. It offers a high that it is impossible to get from any other source. We spend enough time in our living rooms. We spend enough time in our cars. We spend enough time at our computers. We need to go places. We need to be open to the sky and to be lifted up on the sound of so many other voices. We need to know what it feels like to be there, to be in the place where it is, where our senses can be filled and even flooded by the things that we love that are happening.

Shea will always be the 1960s to me, the decade in which my spirit took shape. It was part of my original conception of the world, my original idea of perfect fun. And since I no longer think that the great, big, beautiful tomorrow is shining at the end of every day, and since I have a somewhat more complicated understanding of what life and love entail, when Shea is gone all I will have left of my original conception of the world is my love of the Mets. There will be nothing big and physical. There will only be this living fossil inside my soul. I will miss Shea so much. Shea was cool. Shea was kind of old and rickety in the end. But in the beginning it was a glamorous present that promised a spectacular future. It was the Gateway to the World of Tomorrow. It was in Technicolor and in Cinerama.

Shea Memories

When Shea opened, nobody thought that having a new stadium was going to mean that the Mets were going to play any better. In fact, the first Mets team to play at Shea was just about exactly as good or bad as the last team to play in the Polo Grounds in 1963. In 1964, the Mets won fifty-three games. In 1963, they had won fifty-one. We did not have a good team. Yet this fact was not experienced in the same way as you might experience it now. If you were a new team in 1964, you didn't think you were immediately entitled to competitive balance, any more than you thought you were entitled to competitive balance with grown-ups if you were a kid. I used to play chess with my father all the time and I would have killed him if he lost to me on purpose. But I was so happy if I could last an hour against him, or if I could take a pawn of his when he didn't expect it. This was what it was like to be a fan of a team that regularly lost 110 games, at least from my child's perspective. You were satisfied with any sign at all that your team deserved to wear a uniform and have a stadium and have its name printed anywhere in the standings. You didn't often get such signs, but when you did, it was wonderful.

Rooting for the Mets in 1964 was like being from one of those countries that sends a team to the Olympics and does win one bronze medal, or maybe one silver and one bronze. You had so little that everything meant more. And you could dare to dream of a future where the New York that was so firmly anchored at the bottom of the National League standings would float up a little and rest on top of the names of a few other cities. Rooting for the Mets in 1964 was just like being a kid. It was knowing you couldn't compete then but that you would someday. It was taking what you could get. It was waiting to grow up.

Shea didn't help the Mets to win, but it made our losing team seem different. We were no longer in the crumbling home of giants who had once walked the earth. We lived in a place that was glamorous and new. We were a bad team because we were a young team, and there is nothing shameful or dingy about the incompetence of youth. And the Mets who inaugurated Shea were a young team, much younger than the Mets of 1962 or 1963. Frank Thomas, Roger Craig, and Duke Snider were gone. Our biggest star was the runner-up for the 1963 Rookie of the Year: twenty-three-year-old Ron Hunt. Our other "stars," Joe Christopher, Jim Hickman, Charlie Smith, Al Jackson, Jack Fisher, and Tracy Stallard, were all in their twenties. And at first base, we had a star of the future, nineteen-year-old Eddie Kranepool. The crowd was young, too, or so it seemed to me. My generation, the largest generation in history, was all born and ready to start loving baseball. We weren't old Giants fans and Dodgers fans, like the grown-ups. We were Mets fans, a new kind of fan in a new stadium.

My family went to a bunch of games throughout the 1960s—not that many, but three or four a year, I think. Going to a game was something that would happen when it would happen. I don't know what the pattern was. I was a kid. I received the result of the plans. I didn't make them. One thing I know is that every year, around my birthday, which was at the end of the baseball season, we would go to the last Sunday doubleheader at home, which was Fan Appreciation Day. It was always festive and, strangely enough, never ironic. Of course the Mets appreciated us and of course we appreciated them, even as they were losing their 106th and/or 107th game. It was always the five of us, me, my mom and dad, and my two sisters, way high up. The first time I ever saw a game from the box seats was when I went to a game with a friend and his father, who owned some kind of meat refrigeration company and therefore had a seat right behind the visiting dugout. From this close, a baseball game was an entirely new experience. It was not better, it was just different. You felt that you had snuck into the home of some famous people and you were hiding in a closet or under a couch. The players were so close, and you had so little sense of the crowd or the stadium because it was all behind you. I remember I saw Larry Stahl hit a home run. I remember hearing his voice as he talked to his teammates waiting for him at home plate.

When I was thirteen, my parents started to let me go to games without them if I went with a friend who knew how to get there. Me and my friend Michael would walk to the bus that would take us over the George Washington Bridge. Then we'd take the A train down to 42nd street, where we would get the 7 train to Willets Point that would rattle its way through Queens. How exciting it was to be on my own, with just one other kid, navigating the tunnels of the subway, past all the people dressed for work going home, tired with their briefcases and their newspapers. There I was, virtually alone, out in the world. This was the world, what I saw from the 7 train. New Jersey, where I was reluctantly growing up, was not the world. New York was the world. The old buildings the train would pass with the blinds drawn, the streets filled with cars, the sidewalks filled with people and signs and fruit. At the end of this long, elevated trip through the world were the Mets. The Mets were part of the real world as much as they were part of my ideal world. What an amazing thing the Mets were!

On an afternoon in April 1969, I remember that Michael and I saw something that would someday become very famous. We saw Tommie Agee hit a home run into the upper deck. It was the only time in the history of Shea that a home run was hit into the upper deck, and it is officially counted as the longest home run ever hit at the ballpark. I remember that when Agee hit the ball, it just looked as if it was climbing up into the sky. As with a lot of home runs, I didn't really see where the ball was, I just knew from the sound of the impact that it was going far. But then I saw it land in the upper deck and I could not understand it, because I did not think it was possible that a ball could be hit there. Was that the ball or some other ball? There were not very many people in the stands that afternoon. It was 1969, but we didn't know what that meant yet. Agee was just this guy who had had a really disappointing first season, and a lot of us wanted him to be traded. Nothing about this moment was what it would later become. And the few people in the stands were not cheering so much as they were turning around and asking each other in disbelief if a ball really had just been hit into the upper deck.

I saw the 1969 Mets several times. I've racked my memory but I can't pull out individual games. I just remember fragments, some of which may not even be from 1969. I remember the privilege of seeing Seaver pitch. I remember how incredibly fluid Donn Clendenon's swing was, how graceful and big and smooth. Not until Strawberry would I ever see a swing like that again. I remember Agee's surprising speed and the way in which Tug McGraw would come into a game and you would feel as if you knew him better than anyone else on the team. I remember how, having been such a die-hard fan during my childhood, I began to wander away from baseball some in my late teens. It was the early 1970s and the Mets were still good, but my late adolescence was filled with all sorts of new distractions. My sisters became enormous fans right around that time. In the 1960s, I had been a 1960s little boy being a 1960s little boy. In the early 1960s, I wore my Mets hat and my Mets shirt all the time. I even had a shirt that said "Shea Stadium, Home At Last." I was far and away the biggest fan in my family. But that changed in the early 1970s as my sisters built themselves a sisterly Mets culture around their favorite players, listening to all the games and all the postgames, and going to lots of games together. I wasn't part of that. Part of me regretted this and part of me didn't. Now I regret this of course, because they share memories of the Mets that I don't share with them. I would take a break from whatever else I was doing and come back into the family fold to enjoy things like the great pennant drive at the end of the 1973 season. The whole family involvement with the Mets never went away and it never lost its attraction for me. But at this particular point in my life, I wondered if I was beginning to outgrow baseball.

I remember getting back into a closer relationship with baseball in 1977, as the Mets suddenly got really bad, and not just bad in the way they had been bad before. The Mets were shameful because they were being run by shameful people who did not treat our wonderful players with respect. M. Donald Grant and Dick Young drove Tom Seaver out of town because he dared to ask to be paid a fraction of what he was worth. I was coming back to baseball because I had fallen in love with Sheila, a Red Sox fan from Massachusetts who was as passionate about baseball as I was. I was friendly with a bunch of other baseball fans in graduate school, where we felt the need for something that would link us to the human race in ways that graduate school didn't. My involvement with Mets baseball at different points in my life has rarely had anything to do with how the Mets were playing. Sometimes I have needed baseball and sometimes I've just wanted it, and sometimes I have been too content to push it towards the periphery. It has come to me and left me in waves, and each time it comes back it hooks up with what was there before. Being a baseball fan is a permanent thing in my soul, but it is not a constant flame. It's like a fire. Sometimes I put some more wood on and poke the embers until it flares up. Sometimes it goes down low. But it has never gone out.

I really got to know Shea during the dark years of the Mets between 1977 and 1983. Shea wasn't as it had been. I would show up at the stadium when I felt like it, even on Opening Day. I would buy an upper deck ticket and go up and sit there for the first inning or two. Then I would take the escalators down and sit wherever I wanted to. If somebody showed up to claim the seat I had chosen, I would just move. Nobody cared and nobody bothered me or anyone else. The stadium could get depressing when it was too empty, but there was actually something nice about it. You didn't have an awareness of a crowd, as you had in the days when the Mets were either new or good. You didn't hear a swelling roar, but you could hear individual people cheering. And everyone was as true and loyal and as blue and orange as I was. Only the crazies were left and we loved being crazy together. We were like the people who hated disco at the time. We didn't care if the Bronx was burning. Nothing could make us care about what was happening in the Bronx. All there was was Queens and our stadium, which now seemed weirdly old before its time in the middle of the ruins of the World's Fair. And the foolishness of the owners of our team could never make us forget the unimaginable glory we had seen in this very place.

In 1977, I was at the game where Tom Seaver returned in a Reds uniform and I rooted for Jerry Koosman to beat him. I was at the game where Bebe and Whitney de Roulet introduced our new mascot, a mule named "Met-Al," which was supposed to make you think of the Mets as having "mettle." Who used a word like "mettle" in the twentieth century? Who could think that what the Mets needed was more "mettle?" Who could think that what the Mets needed was a mule named "Met-Al" as a mascot? The only metal the Mets needed from these people was their gold, which they weren't coming up with. Anyway, I think it was Opening Day, and the de Roulet girls proudly rode down the right field line in a carriage drawn by this mule, as 25,000 of the purest possible Mets fans hid their faces with embarrassment.

Years later, I read that those wild and crazy de Roulet girls had been doing you-know-what with some of the Mets players. If you had told me that, as I was watching them in their beribboned carriage riding down the right field line behind that mule, I would have fallen out of my seat and laughed until I was dead. Who knows whether we won that game? Who knows what happened to that poor mule?

In 1980, Nelson Doubleday and Fred Wilpon bought the team and vowed to bring it up to a level where more than a million people a year might want to pay to see it. They put a sign up that said "The Magic Is Back." It wasn't, but it was a good thought. This is when the plastic seats were put in. The Home Run Apple and the Diamond Vision were put in shortly after that.

One of the most vivid memories I have from this time was the Opening Day of the 1983 season. It was the day Tom Seaver came back to us, and almost 50,000 people, probably the largest crowd since 1976, filled the stadium to see him. I remember when he was announced, when the public address announcer intoned, "And pitching, for the New York Mets, number 41, Tom . . ." I remember the roar of the crowd as we saw "41" jogging in from the bullpen. I remember how the sound just rose to the skies and grew and grew. It was full-throated, joyful, and loving. Inside we were also crying and mad about the six years of his career we had been deprived of. And then I remember how the sound system played the theme song from "Welcome Back, Kotter" and almost drowned out the crowd. I also remember a day about a month later when my family and I, the five of us still, went to see the major league debut of Darryl Strawberry. We were celebrating my mother's fifty-fifth birthday. In his first at-bat he struck out. But we had seen him hit a long foul ball that one could not deny contained all of the elements of Hall of Fame greatness.

Shortly after this, Shea became the center of the New York baseball world again. It was no longer the home of the Miracle Mets. It was the place where you were supposed to "Catch the Rising Stars." The exterior was closed up, painted the deepest imaginable blue, and the giant neon sculptures were installed on it. There was the Home Run Apple, and the Diamond Vision, and all the new recorded music, which I originally hated because I loved so much to hear Jane Jarvis on the organ. The stadium, after its full makeover, didn't feel new, but it felt renewed. It was as if it had had a dye job and an infusion of monkey glands. It looked old. It looked done over. It was now the Very Big Blue Thing. But it hardly mattered whether it was funny looking or no longer in the greatest shape. The baseball that was played there in the mid- and late 1980s was sublime.

This was the time of the Curley Shuffle and the curtain calls and the occasional brawl and an unbelievably exciting and intimidating team that won more games than any other Mets team had ever won and that played before crowds that were bigger and louder than any New York baseball crowds had ever been. I loved this period of the Mets. Sometimes I just stop and think of how happy that team made me, even when crazy things were going on within the team later in the decade. There was nothing like the sublimity of a Strawberry home run, or the intelligent intensity with which Keith Hernandez played first base. There was nothing as sublime as Dwight Gooden's "Lord Charles" curveball and nothing as endearing as Gary Carter's eager, earnest desire to excel and be loved. There was nothing like the dangerous men at the top of the order, the marvelous hitters in the middle, each with entirely different talents. There was nothing like rooting for a team with a superb offense, five excellent starting pitchers, and a fabulous bullpen. The Mets of the 1980s played like they really hated to lose. And they rarely did. This made for happy crowds. And it is so much fun to be part of a happy crowd.

When that big, long Shea party was over and my daughter was born, in 1991, I didn't go to Shea for a few years. I knew I wasn't missing a great deal. I still paid attention and I had a few brief moments of excitement about ballplayers like Rico Brogna and Paul Wilson. But the next time I went to Shea was the first time I brought my daughter. There are two pictures of this game on my mother's refrigerator. They're from my family's celebration of my mother's sixty-eighth birthday. My mother is standing up tall on her own two feet, with her arm on my daughter's shoulder, as Sonia looks like she's swinging an imaginary baseball bat. There's a picture of us sitting in the stands of the upper deck, me and my sisters, with my daughter kissing my mother. My dad must have taken the picture. I have more hair and there is no white in my beard.

This was the beginning of the new good Mets era, when Shea had its last moment of extended vitality without the shadow of its replacement looming over it. This was the period when I started to go to ballgames more than I ever had before. I mainly went with Sonia. We went what seems like a million times, though it is probably only twenty-five or thirty. We called them "Daddy-Daughter Days," which is something Homer Simpson once said to Lisa. We'd get into the car in Connecticut and have these really intense, lyrical, philosophical, meaningful discussions until we got off the Whitestone Expressway at the Northern Boulevard exit. We'd park in the lot and go through the people with the wands and go into the store and not buy anything. We'd go to batting practice and she'd get so excited if she saw Mike Piazza really close up. We'd eat our supper of hot dogs and a knish from the kosher stand. We weren't kosher, but these were the most wonderful hot dogs and knishes. We'd sit in our seats and talk about how much we loved baseball and the Mets, and then we'd watch the game and she would cheer and holler for everything and everybody, and she'd always know which baseball cap had the ball under it, and she'd always get really excited about whatever dumb race or whatever was up on the Diamond Vision. She didn't realize that all those things were ads. Or maybe she did and it didn't matter to her any more than it mattered to me that the World's Fair was an ad. She'd eat all kinds of wonderful, horrible expensive food that my parents never bought for me. At the end of the game, she'd love to go down the ramps and chant "Lets Go Mets," and she thought it was hysterical and cool whenever anybody started a chant of "Yankees Suck." She'd join in with a look on her face as if she was enjoying getting away with something. I told her it wasn't nice and she would smile like she didn't care. We'd get into our car, and she'd call home to tell her mother when we'd be home, and then we'd do some kind of silly comedy routine and then she would fall asleep. This is the way it always was and these are some of the happiest memories of my life.

I never went to a game alone with my own father. I know that going to the game with your father is something that a lot of people do and it means a lot to people to have done it. But in my family, we always went everywhere together. There wasn't this splitting up that people now do so that individual parents can develop individual relationships with individual children. The thing is that it was easy enough for each of us kids to establish individual relationships with our mother because she was there all the time. She was home when we came home from school, and until I left for college I would often talk with her, by myself. I never had much of a chance to do this with my father because he would leave the house at 6:30 in the morning at get home at 6:30 at night. I was with him a lot, in the evening and on weekends, but it wasn't just me and him, it was always everybody.

My dad was a big baseball fan, a big Mets fan, and I know that he always knew what was going on. A couple of people at his memorial service even mentioned what a big Mets fan he was, and they remembered how he and my mother were always part of a big group from the Anesthesiology Department at Columbia-Presbyterian that would go to Opening Day every year together.

What's weird is that I can't honestly remember having a discussion about baseball with my father. This is so strange because I remember often talking about Mets baseball with my mother and each of my sisters. I don't know why this is and I will never know why it was, because my dad died in 2001. My sisters don't remember talking about baseball with him either. My mother says she does, but they were together all the time after we kids were out of the house, and during the season they watched every game together. They must have talked about it. But I don't remember talking with him about it.

It's not as if we didn't talk to each other. A few of the conversations I had with my father count for me as the most meaningful and intimate conversations I've ever had with anyone. We were close, even if we weren't often alone together. Maybe it was because we were together so rarely that we didn't take up any of the time we did have together to talk about baseball. There were other things we had to say.

This is a mystery and I don't know what it means. Maybe baseball was not a part of my relationship with my father. Maybe it was part of the general connection that brought together all of the members of my family. I don't know. My father was a gentle, generous, and thoughtful man. I think that in his prime, he thought baseball was diverting but not much more. It was not something to be passionate about. It was a healthy recreation. I do remember, though, that as my father lost most of his mind to Alzheimer's, he developed a more emotional relationship to baseball than he had ever had. He recognized what he was seeing and he responded as he always had, but with a deeper, almost mournful engagement. He took his cues from the rest of the family and the rest of the crowd, but he had lost the distance that had once insulated him from the game. He behaved as if it were not a game. At the very last game he went to, my father and my sisters and my mother were watching as the Mets clinched a tie for the Wild Card as Melvin Mora raced home on a wild pitch. The stadium exploded. My father appeared to be frightened for a moment and then he seemed much more pleased than he would have been if he hadn't been suffering so much.

Mets baseball in the late 1990s was wonderful and exciting again, and the crowds were big and filled with love. This was the era of Mike Piazza, whose quiet charisma filled the stadium. Nothing I have ever seen in baseball was as endlessly beautiful to me as Piazza's lightning-swift short swing. I would look at him when he came to the plate and stare almost without blinking so that I would never miss the sight of that swing when he connected. It thrilled my soul. It was like what I imagine it would have been like to have heard Maria Callas. Oh, how I loved the big, winning, smart, and sloppy teams of the late 1990s into the great year of 2000. I loved to see John Olerud play, and Edgardo Alfonso and Robin Ventura and Al Leiter. I loved how they had a more mature version of the spirit of the 1980s team, without having quite as much talent and nowhere near as much pitching. These were the guys who entertained me and Sonia.

I didn't go to games just with Sonia. I went by myself and with friends. I loved going to the game by myself. I loved just hearing my own inner voices. I loved it when it was just me and the giant spectacle and the Mets. I also loved going with friends and watching everything and talking the whole time and having these conversations that went back and forth between the Mets and everything else. Every year, I would go see the Pirates play with my friend Lee who grew up in Pittsburgh. Lee and I were colleagues who sometimes disagreed at work, and when we did, we weren't very happy with each other. But going to a game at Shea to root for different teams, we were always happy and always close, and the stadium would seem more real than the hallways and offices of our department. I went to a lot of games with my sisters as grown-ups and their friends. I've sat with Stefanie in her Saturday plan seats among the people of her little village in the mezzanine, the people she'd known for years and the kids she'd seen grow up. Sheila has come with me from time to time and she has enjoyed the carnival. When she comes, I try to imagine how this all looks to her. I know that she understands what there is to love about all this and I know that she remains loyal to the decision she made to give up baseball forever, a decision she made the morning after the evening when we had seen the ball go through Bill Buckner's legs. After I wrote *Mets Fan*, I was able to go to games with other Mets writers and bloggers who love the game and the team in the same strange, difficult, and incoherent way that I do. Most of all, I have loved the strangers, the people in the seats around me, the people who are jumping to their feet for the same reason I am. Nowhere have I felt the warmth of strangers as much as I have felt it at Shea.

I remember that there were terrible disappointments here. I remember this vividly. When I think of the stadium though, all I seem to recall is how wonderful everything was, how happy we all were.

I love whatever Shea has given me. I love how it has touched all the eras of my life. I love how it has marked my time. I love its powers to bless, to excite, and to reconcile. I have loved all the things I have had in it. I still love all of the things I had hoped for, whether I got them or not. In some mysterious way, this thing that has so often disappointed me has never let me down.

Crowds

When I look at Shea, I see my life. I also hear the crowds. I hear the crowds that cheered the lousy Mets when they would every once in a while clobber an unsuspecting team. I hear the crowds from 1969 who could not believe what was happening to them. I hear the crowds that loved Steve Henderson and Bruce Boisclair, and the girls who screeched for Lee Mazzilli. I remember the happy hum of the big stadium and the explosive chortle of the crowds in the middle of the 1980s. I remember feeling the big bath of noise and the stadium trembling when Todd Zeile hit a double to clear the loaded bases to give the Mets a 6–0 lead in the final game of the 2000 National League Championship Series against the Cardinals.

I remember how those crowds sounded because I remember that they sounded exactly like the crowds I hear now, cheering a game-winning home run by David Wright or an inning-ending strikeout by Johan Santana. The sound of a human crowd is the sound of a human crowd. Of course there are variations in volume and there are variations according to the proportion of people of different ages, genders, and social classes. But a big crowd that makes a sound of triumph, joy, or love has a family resemblance to every other crowd that has ever expressed the same emotions through a pure, loud sound that has not been shaped into words.

When you're in a stadium with 55,000 people, it can feel as if you're with everyone in the entire world. If you actually were with everyone in the entire world, it would look something like this. It would certainly sound something like this. This is as close as we get to being with everyone in the world, or everyone who has ever been in the world. And the sound of a big crowd is so loud and so overwhelming that it makes the idea of everyone in the world seem as if it is not abstract. Here in the overwhelming sound is the concrete reality of all other people.

This has always been understood. The ancient world loved to build stadiums and amphitheatres. In medieval paintings, Heaven is often represented as a stadium. The main players are down on the field, the saints are in the field boxes, and the saved souls are in the upper deck. Everyone is singing or praising. Perhaps they're cheering. There is the crowd and there is the sound. There is a vast circle of rows around a glorious center. The self is lost in a communal hymn of praise. This kind of thing would get boring if you did it for an eternity, but I know from experience that it is a wonderful thing to do for a few moments. I know that this isn't entirely a good thing. I've seen the Nuremburg rallies in *Triumph of the Will*. But I still think this is something to celebrate. It's all good when it's just about baseball. As long as nobody is hurt, and as long as it doesn't involve having to believe something that isn't true, it is wonderful to have occasions for mass ecstasy.

The crowds in the Colosseum in Rome must have sounded like the crowds I've heard at Shea. When I've gone to the Colosseum, like all the other tourists, I imagine that I can hear the ancient crowds. I hear their big explosions and the ordinary chattering cacophony that you have when nothing so important is happening. Having been so many times in a crowd in a giant circle around a spectacle, I feel as if I know what they sounded like.

Stadiums can last forever if nobody quarries them to build other buildings. But Shea will never be a ruin like the tower and giant cupola of the New York State Pavilion from the 1964–1965 World's Fair, which have been falling apart for decades right next to Shea. Shea will be one of these New York buildings that gets torn down and replaced. It won't be a place you can walk through and imagine that you can smell the frying sausages and onions and see the brilliant lights and the kids with the foam fingers and the guys with the jerseys and the moms with the bags. Nobody will ever try to make sense of the pipes that ran along the top of the concourses. Flowers from all over the world won't bloom in the passageways because animals from all over the world were brought here. Shea won't become a tourist attraction with trained guides, a long literary tradition, and guys dressed up like gladiators who will pose for pictures with you. Where Shea is now will become a parking lot, and eventually the stadium will be forgotten.

Going to a Game with My Teenage Daughter

Soon after I got home from vacation, I went to a game with Sonia. It was August 11, a makeup of a rainout against Pittsburgh. We did all the things that we always do, since our game-going rituals have been the same, more or less, for the past ten years. We had our deeply serious talk on the way down. Then we saw the stadium and glided into our Mets discussion and happily found a place to park. We watched batting practice and got our hot dogs and knishes from the kosher stand. We sat in our seats and soaked it all in. Sonia and I started going to games together when she was seven. Now she was seventeen. Although the point of significant parent-child rituals is to keep certain things exactly the same, the reason you do that is because in the meantime, everything else has become different.

The teenager does not need to get cotton candy anymore, but she still needs both the cracker jacks and the curly fries. Her high-pitched holler is the same but it is louder. The between-innings amusements on the Diamond Vision have changed over the years, but she still finds them enormously amusing and never doubts that they are worthy of her full attention. As when she was little, Sonia is still a relatively indifferent baseball fan. She goes to ballgames with me and she will watch one with me on TV every once in a while. But she never listens to games by herself and she is entirely uninterested in statistics. I don't even want to ask her what she knows and doesn't know. She does know the names of all the players and their positions, and she seems to have a very definite idea of their individual quirks and personalities. According to her, they're all wonderful, but in very different and very cute ways.

One thing that has never varied is that Sonia always absolutely loves to go to a ballgame with me. And being a teenager right now, she has ways of intensifying this pleasure that were not available to previous generations. Now, whenever a Met does something wonderful and dramatic, or whenever the Mets screw up, she sends a text message either to her friend Lindsey or to her aunt Stefanie. She doesn't do this in order to inform Lindsey or Stefanie. If they are sufficiently interested, they can watch the ballgame themselves. Both are big Mets fans and are often watching or listening to the ballgame at the same time. But Sonia doesn't ever text Lindsey or Stefanie when we watch a ballgame together on TV. The point of her texting is to show them that she is actually at the ballgame and therefore has a particularly close relationship to the home run that David Wright has just hit. Texting allows her to bring Lindsey and Stefanie into the aura of her own proximity to this exciting thing. They hear about it on their phones just as they would hear about whatever Sonia would choose to tell them about whatever happened last Friday when she went to the multiplex with fill-in-the-blank. Sonia assures me that this is kind of a girl thing and I can imagine that it is. I don't want to sound like an old fart, but I don't even want to learn how to text. I still think of cell phones as things that are good to have in case of car trouble.

I make sure that Sonia understands that open-minded daddy is tolerant of the texting. If she was texting because she was bored, then I would have a problem. But her texting is a way of making a trip to the ballgame with dad even more meaningful. So I'm okay with it.

The biggest difference between a teenager and a kid is self-consciousness. Kids are in their experiences. Teenagers are in their experiences, they are watching themselves have the experiences, and they are making sure that others are watching them have the experiences as well. So our games together not only get broadcast by text message now, they also end up on Facebook, where they become the subject of sentimental favorable comment from friends of hers who are not Yankees fans. The Yankee fans make the obvious comments.

I tolerate the texting and the Facebook, but the aspect of Sonia's self-consciousness I really enjoy is the part that is the beginning of her own nostalgia. Sonia has the same love she has always had of David Wright, Jose Reyes, Pedro Martinez, curly fries, cracker jacks, hot dogs, knishes, the color of the field lit up at night, Mr. Met, the Home Run Apple, the games on the Diamond Vision, and the human waves. But now she likes to reminisce about how much she used to love Mike Piazza. She also loves to see fathers with their kids at the ballgame, particularly if the kids are little girls. It reminds her of the way we used to be. Sonia as a teenager still wants to make sure we do everything at the ballpark exactly the way we've always done it. She doesn't want to leave anything out. She wants her friend and her aunt to know that she's at the game with what she calls her "Daddy." I used to be "Dad" but my recent evolution into "Daddy" is itself a part of her nostalgia. I don't complain. This is all cool. She is who she is, my buddy with whom I go to ballgames. I don't have a problem with her not knowing that there are 162 games in a season or her being fuzzy about who, exactly, is in the Eastern division of the National League.

Because I've been puzzled that Sonia's never developed her own independent love of baseball, I've asked her why she loves baseball so much. She says she likes having a team and she likes sharing the team with me, and with the rest of my family. It makes her feel a part of us. She says that being a baseball fan is like being in a family and she loves how a team and their fans have to be like a family. We aren't always happy with each other, but we always make up. And we always have each other. Sonia loves the fact that baseball extends backwards into the glamorous past and she tells me that she wishes she could have seen Ron Darling and Keith Hernandez, "when they weren't guys in their fifties" playing baseball on the field. She wishes she had been around for the 1969 Mets, which, according to her, sounds like the plot of a movie. She wishes she could have gone to a Brooklyn Dodgers game in the 1940s, which, as she imagines it, was like *Citizen Kane* or *Casablanca*, with people in hats and big emotions and colorful ways of speaking.

Sonia says that the main reason she loves baseball is because she loves me. A knish, she says, and blue and orange, and the word Mets will always make her think of me. She wishes Shea Stadium would always be around so that it could always remind her of me. She says these things and I understand what I've been for her and I understand what I will become for her. I start to think of how in some ways I have already become a memory for her. But that's only right, because in lots of ways Sonia has already become a memory for me. We'll have each other, of course, for many more years and we'll go to many more ballgames together. In the seventeen-year-old beside me, I do see all the Sonias I have brought to Shea for the past ten years. But I don't see them clearly. I don't remember each one of them as well as I wish I did. I remember our games together because we always did pretty much the same thing. Maybe we were always doing the same thing because we knew that we would need to have something we could be sure to remember, because we knew that all of the individual details of our individual games would be lost. If they kept Shea up, it would be nice. We could do the exact things we've always done forever. We would never get tired of them. But Shea doesn't bring back the small Sonias for me. And I don't know exactly what it brings back for her. We can't ask the Mets not to tear down an old stadium because it might help people remember what they will always cherish, what they say they will always remember, but what they will for the most part forget.

A Letter to the Future

There was something here, where the parking lot is, to the west of Citi Field. I'm looking at it as I'm writing these words. It really is there. I see it. But if you are reading these words, it is no longer there. You may remember it, and you will hear about it for a long time. The last people to remember Shea Stadium will live into the twenty-second century.

This is what happens. Everyone knows this. But the reason Citi Field looks like a stadium that was demolished in 1960 shows you that people can't accept this. I can't accept this. You know what I'm talking about. Stuff is there and then it isn't. And no, it doesn't live on in your memory. Your memories may be your most prized possessions, but nothing lives in them.

Really big things that get torn down have a particular grandeur. If they can be gone, everything can be gone. Being gone is no big deal. Shea was very big, much bigger than Citi Field. Trust me. I am looking at them both, standing side by side. Shea is immense, and Citi Field looks little beside it. I'm looking at living proof that the world was bigger in the past. I remember how big everything used to be. I remember a parade on Fifth Avenue in the 1950s and how immense the buildings were. I remember the original Penn Station and the great ocean liners lined up at the docks on the West Side. I remember dirigibles in the sky. Penn Station and the ocean liners and the dirigibles are gone too. The big buildings are still there, but they don't seem as big. Everything was bigger in the past. This is a very old human sentiment, and to some degree, it is literally true. I'm looking at proof.

Why was Shea so big? Because the people who built it thought that that many people might want to come to it. The people who are building Citi Field know that that many people will want to come to Citi Field, but they won't always come and so they don't feel a need to be ready and hopeful that everyone will arrive. I am still not reconciled to this. I understand why Shea is being torn down. Still, to replace it with a stadium that has 13,000 fewer seats is a cynical calculation. I'm sorry. I think that the purpose of baseball, and of all of human culture, is to enrich everyone's life. It is not to make a small number of rich people richer than they already are. There are so many of us and so few of them. Why couldn't we have had a vote about the capacity of the new stadium? Who set things up in this way and why does everyone just shrug now and call it rational?

There are plenty of moments now when I feel that I am at a breaking point. I want to mourn the dear old stadium in a decorous way. I want to get all lyrical about the passing of time and the disappearance of big and beloved things. I don't want the destruction of Shea to symbolize something meaner than that. I don't want to have to be angry.

The Sweet Summer of 2008

After the Mets finally got it together in early July, they played superior ball through the month of July, into August, and into September. They took over first place from the Phillies on July 24, and although they had dropped back down into second by the end of the month, they came roaring back into first in mid-August by winning ten out of eleven games. They held on to first place, with a small lead over the Phillies, into September. Between July 5 and September 12, the Mets won forty games and lost nineteen. They were terrific, as good as they had been at any point in the 2006 season. By September 12, after their 145th game, at the exact point where they had peaked in 2007, the Mets were in first, three and a half games ahead of Philadelphia.

There were several reasons the Mets were playing so well. David Wright settled into a superb summer groove, hitting well over .300 with a steady power swing, driving in plenty of runs. Jose Reyes had returned to his 2006 form, reassuring us that his distracted play in the last couple of months of 2007 was nothing to get unduly worried about. Carlos Beltran had a few of his usual brief slumps, but for the most part he was wonderful, hitting home runs, driving in runs, catching anything that was hit just about anywhere in the outfield. Fernando Tatis, who in the previous century had had one superb season and had done little since, briefly returned to the level of that season. Daniel Murphy, a reinforcement called in from AA Binghampton, hit over .300 and held his own in left.

The starting pitchers were mostly impressive. John Maine, who was, it turned out, pitching with one of the biggest bone spurs anyone had ever seen, was obviously not his usual self, but Oliver Perez was pitching well and Pedro Martinez was contributing five well-pitched innings each time out. After a good but not great start, Johan Santana hit an astonishing stride, pitching better than anyone else in the National League for the second half of the season. After his 3–2 loss to the Yankees on June 28, he did not lose another game for the rest of the season. Even the middle relievers were perfectly adequate in July and August. Billy Wagner was having one of his best seasons ever. And when he went on the disabled list in August, no one thought it would be a big deal, since he would be back soon and the patchwork relief staff looked as if it would be able to fill in while he was gone.

The reliable core of the Mets was solid. But in addition to the reliable core, there were two exhilarating surprises. Mike Pelfrey was showing signs of developing into an ace, maybe even a superstar. And Carlos Delgado came back.

Long-time Mets fans know the pleasure of seeing the development of a first-rate young pitcher. Sometimes it is something that happens right away, as it did when Seaver came up in 1967, when Matlack came up in 1972, or when Gooden came up in 1984. But there is a special excitement when you see a young pitcher find his comfort and his confidence just when you were beginning to be convinced that he wasn't going to amount to much. After his lousy rookie season in 2007, Mike Pelfrey was beginning to look and feel like a disappointment, one of these prospects who wear down your faith in future prospects. In April and May of 2008, Pelf gave no sign that he was about to turn anything around. He was 2-6 by the end of May, with an ERA around 5. And then he suddenly had it. In June, July, and August, Pelfrey was 11-2, with an ERA under 3. Suddenly, without anybody having anticipated it, the Mets had a confident twenty-four-year-old pitcher who could pitch as well as anybody. With Santana and Pelfrey at the top of their rotation, and with everything else functioning more or less smoothly, it was no wonder that the Mets, over the sixty games played in those nine weeks, won twice as often as they lost.

It was Delgado who gave us the deepest pleasure of the summer. His first three months of 2008 had been particularly painful. On June 25, seventy-six games through the season, almost halfway, Carlos had a batting average of .229, with eleven home runs, thirty-five RBIs, and a slugging percentage under .400. What had looked, at the end of 2006, like a plausibly Hall-of-Fame career was fading before its time. There was something wrong with him, something wrong with the way he was swinging his bat. He looked stunned. There was a mild look of fear on his face. You felt for him and you wrung your hands because you couldn't imagine what the Mets could possibly do. Thirty-six-year-old players playing like this never turned it around, or if they did, it was only for a couple of weeks, and you couldn't easily replace someone from whom you expected and needed so much. Then on June 27, the Mets played the Yankees. Carlos broke a Mets record by driving in nine runs in a single game. In three consecutive at-bats, he hit a two-run double, a grand slam home run, and a three-run homer. The film was gone from his gaze. His stroke was once again steady and sure. Carlos went on to have one of the best summers I had ever seen a Met have. In the eighty-six games from June 27 on, Carlos hit well over .300. In what was just a little more than the second half of the season, he hit twenty-seven home runs and drove in eighty runs. Throughout the second half, when Carlos Delgado came to the plate and whenever he got a hit, the crowd would chant "MVP! MVP!" It was all so wonderful and all so different from last year.

The Mets were not only playing well, it felt good to watch them. And as much as I was always a partisan and a defender of Willie Randolph, I had to acknowledge that Jerry Manuel's managing may have had a lot to do with it. I didn't know if Manuel was actually a better manager than Randolph. I can never judge these things. But the canny, involved way in which Jerry responded to problems just made me feel better. Willie set his jaw and his lips and would look as if he was determined to ride things out. Jerry looked out at that field with a questioning gaze and a what-the-$**&? sense of irony and bemusement. You saw it in the first crucial test that Jose Reyes gave him in the very first inning of Jerry's very first game. Jose didn't want to come out when it seemed as if he had strained his hamstring, and Jerry was taking him out. Jerry was completely authoritative and yet he also seemed amused. That was Manuel. He was amused and amusing. I realized from the beginning of his tenure as manager that this was something we'd been missing. It was a cool style, and it had roots in the Mets tradition. The guy Jerry Manuel reminded me most of was Bobby Valentine. Like Stengel and Valentine, Jerry wasn't scrupulously careful about what he said. When a reporter asked him about the effect booing might have on Aaron Heilman, Manuel said, "It's difficult. It's painful. But it's also growth. It's growth for him. It's very, very—I'm going to say this, and I hope y'all don't take this wrong. I know you're going to run out of here with something crazy on this. It's very, very fertile ground for growth at Shea Stadium. It's fertile ground for a team's growth and development. Sometimes fertile ground has fertilizer. (Laughter in room.) Fertilizer is a good thing. It's a good thing. You get the greatest results, you get the most beautiful plants, when you put it in that type of fertile soil. That's what we have the opportunity to do. Don't y'all take that wrong because I know what you're going to do with it."

Yeah, he knew what they were going to do with it. There even were reporters dull enough to think that Jerry Manuel had just called Mets fans pieces of shit. But I loved this. Here was a guy who was just eccentric enough to phrase things with originality, and canny enough to play around with the reporters by joking about what they'd make of what he said. Manuel's interviews were something to look forward to. With all his talk about gangstas and ladies on the bus and Mahatma Gandhi, he had immediately earned himself a place in the Mets pantheon of characters. Once again, we had the kind of guy who could get thrown out of a ballgame and wear a glasses-and-moustache disguise back into the dugout. I had a sense that like Bobby V., Jerry Manuel was a piece of work, not exactly careful, but smarter than anyone else in the room.

Whatever he had, it was working. Under Jerry Manuel, the Mets were different. The fans finally relaxed and believed that the Mets were headed for the finish that would allow us all to forget that 2007 had ever happened.

Going to the Game on August 20

In August, the Mets announced that the team would soon begin to sell 16,000 pairs of seats from Shea to the general public at the cost of $869 a pair. The price was intended to remind fans of the two World Championships in 1986 and 1969. Although I was glad to have this mnemonic device, I wasn't going to buy a pair of seats. Eight hundred and sixty-nine dollars is a lot of money. For that amount of money, you could bring your family to a game, park your car, and have a couple of hot dogs and beers.

The Mets weren't just selling the seats. They were selling everything, from the napkin holders to the foul poles. Shea Stadium would become the site of the biggest sale of holy relics since the Middle Ages. Shea wasn't going to crumble into the Flushing Meadows. It was going to be scattered through the dens, basements, and attics of Greater New York.

With all of the publicity surrounding the relic sale, it began to sink in to me that Shea was soon going to be dismembered. When I went to the game on August 20, I felt as if I were visiting a dying friend who was a committed organ donor. I'm joking about the organ donor, but I'm serious about the dying friend. I felt that with five weeks left to the season, it was time to begin to fix a final image of Shea in my head so that I could remember it as well as I could.

When you make this kind of commitment, you start to notice everything. You can't assume that you'll be coming back many more times. So just as you'd notice, for the first time, on a final visit, something about the way in which your friend's voice has a little kind of echo in it, something about the way your friend looks off to the side when speaking, something about the way your friend scratches the left cheek with one finger, I began to notice things about Shea that I'd never noticed before.

I noticed the big and beautifully old-fashioned lights above the food concourses behind the stands (except in the upper deck, where they just had fluorescent lights). They looked kind of old New York, with scalloped detailing. They were really out of place in the what-the-hell spaces they illuminated. They didn't fit in with the pipes and wires and food signs. I'd walked under those lights for four and a half decades and this was the first time I was ever really looking at them.

I noticed how much bigger the mezzanine was than the loge. It was much, much bigger. I hadn't realized that. I counted the flags flying along the top of the stadium. There were twenty-one. I noticed that when the lights were on, there was a big area behind home plate where they weren't on. I noticed how, when a Met hit a single, there was a gathering rumble and then a giddy, higher-pitched roar. I noticed how this was different from the uncertain-to-explosive steadier crescendo the crowd made when a home run was hit. I noticed the way the green and yellow and blue and orange light looked on the reflecting surfaces of the tunnels that led from the concourse up to the stands. What was I doing when I wasn't noticing this stuff? I'd been here so many times. I always took everything for granted.

I went to batting practice, down in the well of the seats with names on them. I'd done this many times before, but for the first time I felt this experience on the edge of its extinction. Batting practice would undoubtedly feel different in the new stadium. But here I was again, with the players so casual, standing around with bats and joking, with all the nets that kept the balls from hitting anyone or going anywhere, with Omar Minaya and Jay Horowitz, dressed for the office, roaming around below, with studious Howie and Gary and Ron clearly visible up above. I looked at the poster frieze that ran along below the press level and saw that it said "Believe Magic Amazin' Miracle Believe Magic," with "Mets" written in Mets script in between each of the words of the incantation. I never noticed this before. Believe Magic Amazin' Miracle Believe Magic. If there were a cataclysm tomorrow and people or aliens were to someday find this harmonious circle with 55,000 seats and a frieze with these words on it, they would be right to conclude that it was some kind of a religious site.

After batting practice, I went up to the loge level and took the Citi Field tour. I was trying. I was struggling to be fair to the new stadium. Someday I would probably love it, but right now my friend was dying, and after she was dead, I knew that her husband was going to marry that gorgeous young thing over there behind the scoreboard. What was going to happen to the kids? Was he going to be fair to all of them? I had heard rumors that some of the kids were going to be taken care of and some weren't. I went through the Citi Field tour. I marveled at the ordinary people (none of whom were season-ticket holders according to the sign-up sheet) trouping through and listening respectfully to the sales pitch for the luxury boxes and the season tickets. The guy giving the tour showed us where the apple would be and explained that it would be a new one, because if they moved the old one, "it would probably fall apart." Everybody laughed. If we had any questions, we could go over to the table near the entrance. I went over and asked what the cost range would be for individual seats in the different sections, and I was told that they didn't know yet. I asked if there would still be Saturday plans, and they didn't know yet. I was told that they were selling just season tickets at that time. I asked when they'd be selling anything other than season tickets, and I was told that it would probably be very close to the start of the season, maybe February or March. I asked if there would be an Opening Day lottery, and I was told probably not, because this was a very different kind of stadium. I could see that. It had more leg room.

I got my supper and went up to my seat high in the upper deck behind home plate. I ate, overlooking everything. There, for the only time ever, was "Citifi." It was Italian-American night and they had some Italian-American singers singing that famous Andrea Bocelli song that sounds like opera but isn't. The game began and there was an absolutely exhilarating first inning as Pelfrey, big and commanding now on the mound instead of big and rough and gawky, looked unhittable. We scored five runs in the bottom of the first, with Daniel Murphy and Mike Pelfrey hitting beautiful surprising singles and the Braves (the Braves!) playing as if they didn't really know what they were doing and were afraid of us. It was a beautiful game, real fast and lovely. David Wright hit a home run, Mike Pelfrey kept pitching like a superstar, and the crowd, festive, bouncy, and noisy, went absolutely wild when he took the mound in the ninth inning. What feels like a Mets game that feels good? Nothing feels like a Mets game that feels good. The fans were happy; the players were happy. We were only a game and a half in first. There were a few clouds on the horizon, of course. Something was wrong with John Maine. And there was some concern that Billy Wagner might be out for the season. But the bullpen was doing just fine. And the starting pitchers were pitching as if they weren't even needed.

Going to the Game on September 10

I went to the game on September 10 with a $5 ticket, which actually cost me $16 once you added various surcharges necessary to cover the administrative, labor, and material costs of sending the e-mail back to me with a PDF document attached. Still, it was a $5 ticket. That's what it said on the front.

As I got to the stadium, I saw from signs and from some people in uniforms at the entrance to the press area that the theme of the night was going to be 9/11. It was September 10, but we were off tomorrow.

I had a weird thought. It's a kind of inappropriate thought, but I wondered if anyone else had it. The events of 9/11, besides causing the murder of thousands of innocent people, also destroyed an emblematic New York landmark consisting of two buildings that every weekday held 50,000 people. The destruction of the World Trade Center permanently changed the face of New York. It changed what the great city looked like from an airplane and from many angles on the ground. Suddenly, a gigantic thing that held a lot of human life was gone.

I know that the destruction of Shea is in no significant way analogous to the destruction of the World Trade Center. But I couldn't help having this dreamlike thought. I couldn't help being struck by the apocalyptic similarities. It is as weird as hell to be sitting in a gigantic building filled with tens of thousands of people and to realize that in a couple of months it is not going to be there anymore. It's weirder than sitting in a smaller building with fewer people. Giant things force on you an idea that they will last a long time because they take up so much space. How can something so big disappear? How can something so sublimely real stop being real?

The thing is that, in New York, giant things are often destroyed. Few cities in the world have a more spectacular list of gigantic things destroyed or demolished. Shea Stadium was about to go the way of the old Penn Station, the Sixth Avenue El, the Singer Building, Coney Island's Steeplechase, New York's Crystal Palace, the Croton Reservoir, the old Madison Square Garden, the ocean liners lined up at the West Side piers, and the World Trade Center. All these big things that once contained living crowds as large as the one I was in had been dispatched to the great New York of memory. Only Ebbets Field had been allowed to come back from the dead.

My $5 seats were in the upper deck in that shadow area behind home plate. On both sides of the shadow, the right and left field stands were illuminated by the banks of lights that look like teeth at the top of the stadium. Where I was, in row N, there were a lot of birds, eerily tame pigeons that flew very low over your head the way the planes do approaching LaGuardia as they come in over the Grand Central Parkway. It was actually a nice place to sit on one of these last days of Shea. You could see the whole stadium and the whole crowd. This is where I used to sit when I was a kid, so I had a sense that I was looking out over the stadium and looking back into the life I had spent in this place. I looked towards the just fair point of the upper deck and remembered when I saw Tommy Agee hit the ball there.

There was a lot of 9/11 stuff, which people applauded more than they usually applaud the people who throw out first balls and take down numbers and stand around with Mr. Met. The Quantico Marine Corps Band played the national anthem with the brassy drama that only a good military band can give it. Somebody near me sang along with a loud, screechy, emotional voice, far off-key. And the 7 train rattled loudly through our moment of silence. But this was all right. New York is no more about perfection than it's about permanence.

I liked the feel of the crowd in the first couple of innings. I liked the spontaneous storms of affection for this team as they got hits and threw strikes and made plays. I hadn't felt so much Mets love in a Shea crowd since the first couple of months of 2007. I particularly loved the joy with which Carlos Delgado's mere existence was celebrated. I remembered my anger at how he had been booed all those months. But I was in a forgiving mood. And then the third inning, when they scored six runs, was a perfect feast. Jose Reyes (at twenty-five!) broke Mookie Wilson's all-time Mets stolen base record. Wright and Beltran hit their RBI singles. I had forgotten how beautiful singles look from the upper deck, how they pop out over the near portion of the outfield, hang for a second, and then drop and roll onto the green, to the delighted cheers of the crowd. I loved how we all booed the Nationals for walking Delgado and then how we all got to see more and more runs coming home to us off the bats of Tatis and Easley. As I watched, I enjoyed the cozy, fragrant warmth of my pretzel and the smooth, earthy coolness of my bright yellow beer. What a feast for the senses and spirit a good ballgame is! Oh, how much I love the Mets!

But of course, it was a Mets game, so there had to be some strangeness and trouble. I couldn't figure out why Elijah Dukes thought that Mike Pelfrey would have wanted to take the trouble to hit him in a 7–1 game between a first- and last-place team. But I understood that the drill was that we would all boo him real loud when he came up, which of course would eventually distract Pelfrey, and Dukes would have a terrific day at the plate. This is baseball crowd logic. It's not logical. Then I couldn't believe it when we lost a big lead for the second night in a row. And then there was "Hey-ay-ay baybee! I want to know-wo-wo, if you'll be my girl!" And the t-shirts. And then I changed my seat, moving down to where the mezzanine extends out into left field. I wanted to get a different perspective on the stadium. So I walked down the forbidding slope of the upper deck, holding the railing where so much red paint had been worn away by so many hands, stepping on people's peanut shells, reading their backs, Wright, Reyes, Santana, Coney Island Polar Bear Club.

As I walked down the aisle of the mezzanine toward my new seats, I looked up and saw how the lights of Shea illuminated each individual face. When you look at a well-lit crowd, you see how crowds don't really overwhelm the individuality of the people in them. You see how absolutely distinctive everyone's face is, especially in a New York crowd, where there is so much variety of color and feature. You also see, in such bright light, how everyone's style is also distinctive. The only thing that brought all of these sharp human impressions together was what was happening in the middle of all the greenish-yellow light. Everyone cheered, smiled, and grimaced at the same time. As I was walking, I saw all these faces grimace, and that was how I learned that Heilman had given up a home run to Guzman to tie the game.

When I found my new seat, overlooking the visiting bullpen and the picnic area, I saw how the big crowd looked different and sounded different from the other side. It was funny to see the illuminated booth with Gary, Keith, and Ron, like a little set jewel in the vast bank of seats and faces. It was funny to face the batter instead of standing behind him. It felt like a different game. And it became a different game as the Mets regained the lead, and then almost lost it. Wright hit his home run into the picnic area and right up close I got to see the Home Run Apple rise to the occasion and take its proud curtain call.

We won, 13–10. Everything felt good as we bounced down the ramps. Our hitting was good, our fielding was good, our spirit was good, our pitching had been bad, but in the end we didn't think of it. The Phillies had lost. We were three and a half games in first with seventeen to play. Of course, having lost last year when we were seven games ahead with seventeen to play, we couldn't say we were confident. But the odds were on our side. The odds had been spectacularly on our side last year too. But there was a reason we could actually feel good. In 2007, we were 5-12 for those last seventeen games and the Phillies were 13-4. In 2008, if we went 9-8, the Phillies would have to go 13-4 to beat us. How likely was it that we couldn't manage 9-8? And even if we couldn't, how likely was it that the Phillies would go 13-4? We felt good because we didn't smell defeat in this year's team. We smelled hot dogs and happiness. We smelled glory.

Everything at Stake

After the game on September 10, Atlanta came to town. In the first game of a doubleheader, Johan Santana pitched shutout ball through seven innings and then, with a two-run lead, he tired in the eighth, gave up two singles, and was replaced by Scott Schoeneweis. Schoeneweis faced one batter, giving up a single to load the bases. Brian Stokes, a September call-up, then gave up a two-run single to tie the game. The runners were bunted over to second and third. Stokes then walked the pinch hitter Greg Norton and gave up a sacrifice fly that drove in the go-ahead run. When the inning ended, the Braves were ahead 3–2.

Delgado was the first Mets batter in the bottom of the eighth and he flied out deep to left center field. Nothing else happened for the rest of the game. This kind of loss, so close to being a win, made you feel sour. You could only hope it wouldn't matter in the end. In the second game of the doubleheader, a September call-up named Jon Niese pitched eight innings of shutout ball and the Mets won 5–0. So we were all right.

But then, in the final game of the Atlanta series, on Sunday, the Mets blew another lead. Once again our starting pitcher, this time Oliver Perez, pitched seven strong innings. He left with the Mets leading 4–2. In the ninth, Luis Ayala and Pedro Feliciano gave up five runs. Brian Stokes got the last two outs, but the Mets could not regain the lead in the bottom of the ninth and so they lost, 7–4.

The Mets went down to Washington. Pedro Martinez started the first game and pitched well, as he often had in the 2008 season, through five innings. Going into the bottom of the sixth, the Nationals led 2–1. Then the Nationals scored two more off of Pedro in the bottom of the sixth, and Duaner Sanchez, the man who has to have pizza whenever he wants pizza, gave up three runs in the seventh. The Mets lost, 7–2.

In the second game of the Washington series, Mike Pelfrey looked as if he had what it would take to stop this annoying little slide. Only one run was scored on him in seven innings. The Nationals pitcher, Odalis Perez, hit a fly ball to left. Fernando Tatis dived for the ball and separated his shoulder. His season, and possibly his Mets career, were over. Perez became the Nationals' only run of the game. But there were to be no Mets runs, as Perez, pitching his best game in years, held the Mets scoreless through seven. Washington's mighty last-place rookie relief staff held the Mets scoreless the rest of the way. The Mets did have a chance to score in the sixth. Brian Schneider singled and Jose Reyes was hit by a pitch. David Wright came up with two outs and hit a ball that by all rights should have been a two-run double to left. Willie Harris, with his back to home plate, lunged for David's ball and held on to it.

Of the five games they played after their 13–10 victory on September 10, the Mets had only won one. The Phillies, in the meantime, won five in a row. The Mets had lost four games in the standings in six days. On September 17, the Phillies went back into first, a half game ahead of the Mets.

I suppose this was exciting, but it felt like hell. As the relievers began to settle into a pattern of blowing leads, the loss of Wagner suddenly loomed large. We had waved it off in the way that you ignore a sore that is growing on your back. At a news conference on September 9 at which he announced that his Mets career was almost certainly over, Billy Wagner broke down and cried, recalling how his ten-year-old-son cried when he realized that his dad's career might be over. I felt bad for the Wagners, but what about us? Were we going to be left with these other guys? Would we be able to win a pennant race without a serious bullpen? Had anyone ever done that?

The only thing that softened the horror of the Mets' mid-September stumble was the unexpected fact that we were now in two pennant races, not one. The Milwaukee Brewers had had a terrific first half of the season, battling the Cubs for first place in the suddenly strong National League Central Division. The Cubs had pulled away, but the Brewers had still been able to build what looked like an insurmountable lead in the Wild Card standings.

They were twenty-four games above .500 at the end of August, and no other second-place team was anywhere in sight. Then the Brewers lost fifteen of the first twenty games of September, and so on September 17, when the Phillies moved a half game ahead of the Mets, the Mets were a half game ahead of the Brewers in the Wild Card race. The Mets were as close and as far from first place as they had been on April 1. It was as if the season hadn't happened. There was now going to be a twelve-game playoff.

Normally a baseball team has a right not to make it to the playoffs. It's really no shame not to. But for the 2008 Mets, losing both races this year was not an option. In 2007, the Mets had finished one game behind in both the NL East and the Wild Card. They only spent one day, the final day of the season, in second place. The idea that something like this could conceivably happen two years in a row was unthinkable. I felt as if we were back in the time of the Trojan War. The Trojans couldn't lose to the Greeks, because if they did, all the men would be killed and all the women and children would be enslaved. They had to win. There was no other option. I'm not overstating this. Of course I'm talking about baseball, which is as imaginary as the Trojan War, and for many as emotionally compelling. Within the imaginative world of baseball, the Mets could not lose.

This is why it hurt in a horrible, searing, thrilling way, when Willie Harris stole David Wright's two-run double and Fernando Tatis's shoulder separated. Would a game like the September 16 game against Washington be the edge, the precipice, the border on one side of which was life and joy, and beyond which was nothing? Would this one game prevent us from redeeming the disappointments of the last three seasons? Could four years of our baseball lives disappear into willed oblivion because a Washington left fielder, doing his job for a last-place team, made one spectacular catch?

What could we do with 2005–2008 if we blew it again? There would be no story that any of us would want to remember or tell. Could there be a winning period of New York Mets history that no one would want to remember? Would we ever be able to think of the great 2006 season without the pain of contemplating what followed? If we got into the playoffs this year and didn't embarrass ourselves when we got there, there would at least be a story. There would be the story of coming back after an unimaginable disaster. There would be the rescue of the honor of the wonderful team that clinched the NL East title two years ago. There would be relief and exhilaration.

There had to be relief and exhilaration. There were no other options. The Mets understood this. After the 1–0 loss to the Nationals, David Wright observed that "we've got to dig down deep. This is what makes it fun. You've got, what, twelve, thirteen games left and that's going to decide the season? This is what you work hard for, this is what you prepare for, and as an athlete, a competitor, you love this."

This was vintage David. What was he going to say? What David always says after a tough loss is what you're supposed to say. Part of me wanted to hear him whine and wail. When somebody asked him about the double Willie Harris stole from him, David observed that it was a shame he didn't get that double, but that the real problem was that "we needed to do a better job of putting more pressure on them in more innings, not just having one opportunity and have that make or break the game." This is all very true, David. All true. You always say the right thing. Now scream. And then hold your breath until your face turns blue. Don't let it happen again. What happen again? When Pelf was asked whether the Mets were thinking about the epic collapse of 2007, he snapped to the reporter, "The only time anybody ever thinks about that is when you guys bring it up. It happened last year. I feel the atmosphere of the team is totally different. Nobody's worrying about that, nobody's playing and thinking about last year." Nobody. Nobody. Nobody at all. Nobody is thinking about it, Pelf. Everybody's thinking about how much fun it is to be competitors.

The fans buried their faces in their couch pillows as the Mets gave the appropriate answers to the reporters. But the team did dig deep. Or at least, it looked as if they did. They won their next three games. The Phillies, in the meantime, won two more but then stumbled just a little and lost one. Thanks to that one precious Phillies loss, the Mets moved back into first. They had a half game lead going into the weekend of September 20–21.

On Saturday, Pedro Martinez pitched. He gave up three runs in the first but then settled down and held the Braves scoreless until the sixth. The Mets, however, could not dig deep enough to get hits. They lost the game 4–2. The Phillies beat the Marlins and moved back into first. On Sunday, the Mets did find some hits and runs. They led 4–2 after two innings and then held the lead as Mike Pelfrey pitched into the seventh. Pelf opened the seventh by giving up a walk, and Brian Stokes was brought in to relieve him. Stokes gave up a single, a bunt, and a sacrifice fly that scored the third Atlanta run. The Mets still led into the bottom of the eighth, when Scott Schoeneweis, Joe Smith, Pedro Feliciano, and Aaron Heilman were brought in to give up four runs. The Braves led 7–4. In the top of the ninth, with the Braves ahead by three, Carlos Delgado hit a long two-run homer. Carlos Beltran then struck out, and Damion Easley did too. The game was over. The Phillies beat Florida again, 5–2. Both teams returned home for the home-stands that would end their seasons. The Phillies had a lead of a game and a half.

Good vs. Evil

Every once in a while I have a student who tells me that some great, rich, wonderful, complex book is really about the eternal battle between good and evil. That's not what great books are usually about, but it is certainly what baseball is about. The eternal battle between good and evil. The Phillies in 2008 were once again our archrivals and our nemesis. The 2007–2008 Phillies had taken the place of Atlanta as the team that was Lex Luthor, Brainiac, the Penguin, and the Joker all rolled into one. I loved the city of Philadelphia. I loved the long, straight streets with the eighteenth-century houses. I loved the homey, neighborhoody feel of the South Side and particularly a little place called the Victor Cafe, where a little bell was rung every fifteen minutes and one of the waiters or waitresses would sing an aria. I loved the Reading Terminal Market, all of the crazy wonderful Steven Starr restaurants, the collection of Eakins in the art museum, and the elegant feel of the streets around Rittenhouse Square. I liked the whole area around Independence Hall and the Liberty Bell and the Constitution Center. Philly was a fun place to visit. And I heard that their new stadium was an enjoyable place to watch a ballgame. Still, one thing was clear. The Phillies were bad. They were evil.

Jimmy Rollins liked to taunt us and Pat Burrell always killed us. And that was just for starters. The Phillies fans hated us, because smaller cities always hate New York since they think we think we're so great. Provincials. Peasants. They had a real nice city, but it wasn't New York. No place was like New York, except maybe Paris or London, and they didn't have major league baseball teams.

So we hated them and they hated us and there was all that. And of course there was always the question that I perversely ask myself whenever the Mets are locked in a pennant race. Let's say that suddenly overnight you switched the rosters of the Mets and the Phillies. Could you possibly love the players who had been on the Phillies as if they were the Mets? Could you possibly hate the players who had been on the Mets if they were the Phillies? No, you want to say. There was something quintessentially Mets-ish about our guys, and something quintessentially Phillies-ish about the other guys. Our guys were scruffy, fun, ironic, colorful big city guys. Their guys were whatever. You couldn't make the switch.

Uh huh. This is the thing. Casey Stengel was right. You root for the laundry. Look, Mets fans, at that incredible first baseman we have. Forty-eight home runs and 146 runs batted in! He had to be the greatest home run hitter in baseball now and he was only twenty-eight. And our second baseman! What team has a better right side of the infield! Our team always keeps coming back. They win when it really counts, unlike the Phillies, with their big payroll and their overrated nutcase of a shortstop who isn't anywhere near as good as our MVP shortstop. Our guy may shoot his mouth off, but he puts his money where his mouth is. That's leadership! What do the Phillies have for leadership? Just that cutie-pie third baseman, who's too young and too much like a student council president to lead anybody. Our team is a team. We've got a twenty-five-year-old ace who came up through our system and is a truly great postseason pitcher. And our other ace is forty-six and shows no signs of slowing down. It also doesn't hurt to have a closer who didn't blow a save all season long! I love this team we have now. They're the best. They're true Mets, tough and interesting and with that gritty, come-from-behind New York spirit.

You know, it's not as if this isn't a real problem. It's a problem every baseball fan faces. If you had to be objective, would you have chosen the team you are rooting for? If I were really true to my principles, wouldn't I be rooting for Pittsburgh, or Kansas City, or Tampa Bay? Isn't it corrupt of me to love an underperforming team with one of the highest payrolls in baseball? Isn't it disingenuous of me to try to pretend that the Mets still have anything to do with the colorful underdog image the New York hype machine manufactured for them back in the 1960s? It makes sense, I guess, that my loyalty is to the New York baseball team that is not the Yankees. I am a New Yorker and I can explain why I don't want Steinbrenner's Yankees to represent me. The Mets, given my background, are my natural team. But do I have to go further than this in the way that I always do? Do I have to convince myself or do I have to pretend that the actual collection of players I have chosen to root for have qualities that would have led me to choose them even if they weren't on my team?

Whenever my analytical mind penetrates all the way to the deepest absurdities of my baseball fandom, my poetic mind pushes back and says, see, there's something extraordinary here, because you don't like irrational belief, but here you are irrationally believing in something. You can't cure yourself of your attraction to it. And you don't want to. This is magic. It cannot be explained. Enjoy and experience how completely it has you. Your critical intellect is powerless against it. Then my intellect answers, "But how can that be? There's nothing intrinsic to baseball that holds me like this. Basketball and soccer, and who knows maybe even football and hockey, are also wonderful sports, but they never got into me as baseball did. Whatever hold baseball has over me comes from my own mind." Where did I think magic came from?

Oh, and by the way, do you also have to hate the teams against whom you're competing for the Wild Card? That doesn't feel right, somehow. But it's just as serious a competition. If we hate the Phillies we have to hate the Milwaukee Brewers. Who hates the Milwaukee Brewers? How could I hate a team that has a sausage race? It was not going to happen.

All of the hokum of the pennant race raised another uncomfortable issue for me. What would I think about Shea if it was somebody else's stadium? I have been to several hundred major league baseball games in my life, but I have actually only been to two stadiums besides Shea. I saw two games at Wrigley in 1970, two games at Fenway in 1978, and one game at Fenway in 1980. That's it. I never even made it across town to see the old Yankee Stadium. You may contextualize my love of Shea by understanding that I have very little basis for comparison. Sure I thought that Wrigley and Fenway had more charm than Shea. Everybody knows that they do. That wasn't a surprise. Are the other stadiums in the majors better than Shea? That's nice. I don't care.

My feelings about Shea remind me of something I've always disliked about other people. I hate it when people think that their own little town is the greatest place in the world even though they've never been anywhere else. I hate it when northerners won't go south and southerners won't go north, and easterners won't go west and westerners won't go east. I really hate it when Americans say that they don't want to ever leave America. I want to go on record as saying that I still hate it when people say these things and feel this way. But I have never taken the trouble over three decades to go to any stadium other than Shea.

I am not afraid that the other stadiums will be better. I am actually curious about what they're like, and I know that if I thought they were superior to Shea it would not change my feelings about Shea at all. The line you often hear from Mets fans is "It's a dump, but it's our dump." I guess that's what the people in the more blasted small towns think too. I guess that's what it means to be at home. But this is where the paradox is. I am not a home guy. I don't care whether I'm home or not. I feel very little when I move out of a place I've been living for a while. I'm mostly just excited about the new place. In fact, I could move anywhere tomorrow as long as I had Sheila with me. Sonia's ready to go off to college and we can meet up with her anywhere she wants. I don't need to be at home. But when I think about baseball, all I care about is being at home. Is my attachment to a crummy stadium and a disappointing baseball team a compensation for the fact that I have so few other unconditional attachments, that I have so few other homes? Is my love of baseball telling me that I need more of a sense of home and more irrational attachments? No. Let baseball be the place where I do these things. That will be more than enough. Let the other parts of my mind take seats in the stands and watch. It is September. Everything is on the line. And I am absorbed in the eternal battle between good and evil.

Going to the Game on September 22

The Mets entered their final week and I had tickets for Monday night's game. I parked across Roosevelt Avenue from the stadium, in the big long lot where I park when I have tickets down the right field line. The three remaining tickets I had for Shea, on Wednesday, Saturday, and Sunday, were on the other side of the stadium. So as I crossed Roosevelt Avenue under the elevated tracks, I thought of how this was the last time I would approach the stadium from the right field side. There it was in front of me, all carnival garish and gaudy blue. And there to the right, looking more and more like a stadium and less and less like a construction site every time I saw it, was a classy, urbane, Brooklyn brownstone stadium, out of place and out of time in the parking lot of the other one. I looked at the two of them together. To the right was 1900, the product of a long, rich heritage of architecture. In front of me, in its dying vigor, was the Coney Island of the mind: brassy, loud, bumptious, clueless, and big.

As I walked along towards gate C, I heard "Runaround Sue" blaring from the speakers. It was WCBS 101 Sixties Music Night, according to a sign I saw on an umbrella shed. As "Runaround Sue" turned into "Big Girls Don't Cry," I thought of how this was the music we had when the Mets first came along and Shea was being built. This was the music you'd hear when the Mets weren't on, on WABC, the first station that broadcast them. This is what came out of the old tan radio we had with its nubbly fake-leather skin. This was the music that went with a stadium like this. This was the music of Palisades Amusement Park and Jones Beach and Coney Island and all of the other big, brash, chaotic, fun paradises of my childhood. There was my mom in striped slacks and goofy sunglasses that would now be considered cool. There was my dad, with his pipe, looking amused but dubious on his day off. There were me and my sisters, smelling and dreaming about the food and whatever rides we could convince our folks to pay for. They'd torn down most of that world, but they couldn't tear down the music. It didn't even sound dated.

Stop it, I thought. They're tearing down a stadium. They're not tearing down my childhood. That's already gone. No it's not, I think, as I listen to the music. Not entirely. I'm on my way to batting practice.

Batting practice was what it always was. I was down in the well, the navel where I never sit, in the palace they turn over to the peasants for an hour and a half. I walked down a permissible aisle to stand behind the Mets dugout. There on the field were the Mets. Hopeful, shy kids and encouraging parents waited with baseballs. Photographers with arty hairdos walked around carrying tripods and cameras with gigantic lenses. I looked for clues in the Mets' body postures. I saw clues. The Mets were not as relaxed in batting practice as they usually are. They seemed focused, nervous, and stiff. They had every reason to be.

From down in the well I looked up at the stadium. I saw Gary, Howie, and Ron, bent over reading matter like good students doing their homework. On the long screens that show advertisements during the game I saw the long ribbon sea of blue in which there are champagne fireworks and revolving Mets logos that float to the top. Those graphics always reminded me of the opening of the Honeymooners. The Mets hit balls very far during batting practice, but so would the other team. You can't tell anything by how they hit the balls lobbed at them from that shopping cart filled with baseballs.

During batting practice you notice the planes more than you do during a game. You look up and you see two planes, one close, one far, going in different directions. You also see two seagulls, going in yet other directions. There is always a pattern, a dance of flying things in the Shea sky. This was the Shea sky. I look over at Citi Field and see that it is carving out an entirely different area of the sky. Shea's sky has the shape of Shea. It is that much further to the west. It has these clouds and not those clouds. Citi Field won't have an open end. That will make the sky look entirely different. But Shea's sky is already different from what it was. The opening to the East is now plugged by some hog trying to get into a picture you're trying to take of someone else.

There's Omar Minaya in his suit. "Mister Mina-a-ya!" people whine. The guy next to me gets all excited, telling the people around me that Omar knows his kid. Omar is coming towards the Mets dugout. Everybody leans forward. "Michael Patanzi!!!!" the guy shouts to Omar, pointing his finger up and down urgently at his son's head. Omar waves pleasantly at all of us and enters the dugout. The guy is disappointed.

It's a very big night, I think, as I walk towards the stand where I'd get my dinner. If the Mets lose tonight and the Phillies win, the Mets will have lost six games in the standings against the Phillies in about ten games. Last year, in the worst collapse in baseball history, they lost eight games in the standings in seventeen games. I was not confident and I felt helpless. I walked past the food stalls on the field level. I smelled the sweet, acrid smell of burning onions. I hate onions but I love that smell, that San Gennaro smell, that smell of the infinitely fun and interesting city. I got my two hot dogs with sauerkraut and my homemade knish and my diet Pepsi. I found my seat in the Mezzanine. I enjoyed my dinner up and out in right field, looking out at the whole stadium like a god up on Olympus. I was not down in the well. I was high up, tasting the hot dog, with that intensity with which you taste a fine hot dog in a baseball stadium. And then I have the wonderful knish for dessert. What a beautiful knish, with its warm garlic and potato center that is so cozy in its mushiness, with that soft, dense falling-apartness that Jewish cooking has at its best. The hot dogs and knish comfort me.

It was a busy night at Shea. Not only was it a big baseball night, but in addition to WCBS 101 Sixties Music Night, it was also "Flushing Community Night," "Police Organization Providing Peer Assistance (POPPA) Night," and "Voices against Brain Cancer Night." They were getting everybody in. I don't know how many people threw out ceremonial first pitches, but there were a lot of them. It was overwhelming.

Eddie Kranepool took down the number eight to reveal the number seven. I cheered him. He looked old but good. I remember how in 1962, I was seven, and he was seventeen and playing in the major leagues. I would turn fifty-four the next day. He was sixty-four. The ten-year difference made it easy for me to keep track of Eddie Kranepool's age.

The crowd at the stadium was big and enthusiastic. There were a lot of Cubs fans, but that was okay. If my team hadn't won a World Series in a hundred years, I'd follow them around too if they'd had a year like the Cubs had had. I noticed that there were a lot of infants in the crowd in just-purchased Mets gear. People probably wanted the infants to say someday that they went to a game at Shea. I thought that they ought to have some kind of "Infant Day" in this last week so that there would be a lot of people in the twenty-second century who could say this.

It got dark and there was a ballgame. What I liked best was the footage they showed on the Diamond Vision between the innings. They showed the Beatles and the World's Fair and the stadium with the seats in the right colors. All of my favorite things from forty-four years ago. The Cubs pitcher, I remember, hit a grand slam home run, and the Diamond Vision informed us that he was from Staten Island. Whoop-de-doo. The Mets bullpen only gave up two runs in the last five innings. We scored more runs than they did in the last five innings. But nobody noticed, because in the first four innings the Cubs had scored seven runs and we had only scored two.

It was a foul, sour, pus-spurt of a boring ballgame.

Going to the Game on September 24

As the Mets were losing on Monday, September 22, the Phillies were winning. Going into Tuesday, September 23, the Mets trailed the Phillies by two and a half games. The Mets had six games to play and the Phillies had five. If the Phillies could manage to win three, the Mets would need to win all six games just to tie. The Mets and the Phillies were having a pennant race. But to Mets fans it didn't feel like a pennant race. It felt more like the race of an ambulance to a hospital after a serious and probably fatal car accident.

The only reason why the Mets and their fans did not at this point collapse with despair is that the Milwaukee Brewers were still falling and had not hit bottom. Going into the game of September 23, the Mets had a one-game lead over Milwaukee for the Wild Card. This one game was all we had left. We would take it. At this point, it did us no good to care about what our team had squandered. We would take whatever we could get. The Brewers, who had squandered even more, were as desperate as we were. The Mets and the Brewers were like two survivors of the Titanic fighting over the last remaining life preserver. On Tuesday, September 23, our ace, the mighty Johan, shut down the Cubs, and we scored some runs to win, 6–2. The Brewers also won, and the Phillies lost. Now we were still a game ahead of the Brewers and a game and a half behind the Phillies.

On Wednesday, September 24, I got to Shea a little after 5 p.m. I had tickets to see the game in the picnic area as part of fellow Mets author Matt Silverman's "Goodbye to Shea" celebration, wake, or whatever. I met up with two of my favorite bloggers, Greg Prince of "Faith and Fear in Flushing" and Mike Steffanos of "Mike's Mets." We were also joined by Greg's friend Dave, a photographer who was taking a lot of pictures. We got our pink bracelets and ate our hot dogs and then found places in the bleachers.

Everybody in the picnic area was excited about seeing such an important ballgame. A lot of people in the bleachers were part of some group that did a German folk dance on the field before the game, and so there were a lot more people in lederhosen and feathered hats and dirndls than you usually see at a Mets game, which gave everything a slightly unreal but festive air. Adding to this sense of festivity was Matt Hoey, the tall guy who wears a blue and orange "Cat in the Hat" hat, who for many years was always the first in line to buy single tickets at Shea and who is featured in the film *Mathematically Alive*. I had heard that Matt was in an accident, but I was glad to see he looked okay, even though he was pale and was walking with the help of a cane.

This was my first time sitting in the picnic area, and Saturday was going to be my last. It was wonderful. I actually felt as if I was in the outfield, ready to catch a ball hit to me. I saw the whole stadium and all the people in it. I saw the broadcasting booths like little lit boxes in the center of the big curve of the crowd. And I was closer than I had ever been to the exact spot where Cleon Jones caught Davey Johnson's line drive to end the 1969 World Series.

The game started. The Cubs went ahead and we tied them. Then we loaded the bases and Carlos Delgado came to the plate and the stadium got loud. There was a great swell of jagged, hopeful sound. As I watched Carlos taking his check swings, I had that sense of time-stopping quiet you get during a noisy moment that you are trying to preserve for all time. There was something about facing the whole crowd that gave everything a historic aura. And then, sure enough, we leaped up as we saw that the ball was climbing into the bright black sky and it was climbing and heading right towards us and we were calling to it and it came to us and the sound was so loud I couldn't hear it any more. I was in it. I was in the sound and the Mets were in the playoffs and the brightness of the stadium felt like the brightness of my spirit when I heard the sound of the crowd change from hope to joy. We were four runs ahead.

Oh, how happy everybody was. Mr. Met came by to say hello and so did Cowbell Man, who, like Matt Hoey, was limping and walking with a cane that made it hard for him to bang his cowbell. I guess Mets fans are kind of bunged up, I thought. No matter. We were four runs ahead.

Looking back, I don't know why I felt as good as I did. The company was fine, the stadium looked wonderful. But around the edges of my mind there were demons who were muttering all kinds of negative things. I did say to Mike and Greg that it was so strange that a whole long season was all coming down to just a game or two that mattered completely. Normally, it didn't matter that much if we won or lost any individual game. But if we won this particular game, and the Brewers and the Phillies lost, we'd have something like a 90 percent chance of making it to the playoffs. If we lost and they won, we'd only have something like a 50 percent chance. Individual games, and hence individual innings and at-bats, shouldn't matter so much. But they did. I didn't mind this when Delgado hit his grand slam, but on principle, I didn't think it was such a good idea.

Then the Cubs tied it up, because we didn't have the pitchers to prevent them from doing so. Then they went ahead, but we tied it with a walk that brought home a run in the eighth. In the seventh, eighth, and ninth, all three times, we had runners on third with nobody out. But only one of those runners scored. The crowd cheered with a shrill urgency in the seventh and eighth, and after Daniel Murphy hit his leadoff triple and pounded the third base bag in the ninth, you heard an open-throated, happy, expectant roar. How wonderful to win a game like this, to gain a game on the Phillies! But it didn't happen in the ninth, and when the Cubs went three runs ahead in the top of the tenth and the big family group in front of us all stood up and hugged and kissed goodbye and the picnic area and the whole stadium started to empty, all you could think of was how many chances they had blown.

I saw the bottom of the tenth with a hushed, restless smattering of a crowd. I heard someone shout, "The real Mets fans are still here." We were and there weren't enough of us. How could anyone leave a game like this? What had they come to the game for, if

they could leave a game like this? Wouldn't they feel like assholes
if they missed the Mets winning a historic victory with a grand
slam or a sizzling rally in the bottom of the tenth? But nobody did
anything in the bottom of the tenth. With two outs, Jose Reyes hit
a few fouls that you watched make an arc against a bank of
empty seats. Then he struck out.

We stood up and looked around at the almost empty and emp-
tying stadium and picnic area in the bright, shadowless light. Beer
bottles were scattered everywhere, pointing in all different directions among papers and plates and wet, dirty rally towels.

I offered to give Mike a ride to his car in the lot of the train
station in Fairfield. We walked through parking lot A. Mike said,
"I can't believe I wasted four hours on that fucking game." We
got into my car and drove out of the stadium, through Flushing to
the Whitestone Expressway and then right into an apocalyptic
traffic jam that had us spending an additional hour and a half just
to get over the Whitestone Bridge. It was fun to talk to Mike for a
couple of hours. It was a better distraction and comfort than turning on the radio and listening to Steve Somers, which is what I
usually do when I leave the stadium after a night game. Although
I worship Steve, I was not in the mood for him tonight. And I did-
n't want to listen over and over to news about the bailout that
was supposed to save the worlds' financial markets from collapse,
or hear every ten minutes about the nor'easter barreling up the
coast that was supposed to begin as showers on Thursday afternoon and then develop into a steady, soaking rain.

Oy Danele

"Oy, Danele, is nicht gut, is nicht gut." My mother grew up in a bilingual household, speaking Yiddish and English. She doesn't get a chance to speak Yiddish anymore because everyone she knew who spoke Yiddish is dead. She doesn't speak Yiddish with me because I don't understand it, but she'll use Yiddish phrases every once in a while, and I can understand her when she does. She continues in English, but with a Yiddish accent. My mother doesn't have a Yiddish accent. She has a kind of Brooklyn accent. But when she's talking about the Mets and she's upset with them, she puts on a Yiddish accent. When she's happy with the Mets she just says how wonderful they are and how much she loves them in her regular Brooklyn accent. But when she's upset, you get the Yiddish accent. This isn't an affectation. It's just that, as anyone who's had any contact with Yiddish knows, Yiddish has remarkable natural rhythms for lamentation. I wish I could go into a Yiddish accent when the Mets do badly, but with me it would be an affectation, or it would sound like one of the silly comedy routines I do for my daughter.

"Listen, Mor." I call my mother "Mor." That's not Yiddish. It's Danish. When I was eleven, my father spent a sabbatical half-year doing research at Glostrup Hospital outside of Copenhagen, Denmark. This was from April to October 1966, and it is the reason I can't remember Dennis Ribant, who only pitched for the Mets in 1966, when he had the best season of any Mets pitcher before Tom Seaver. Imitating Danish kids, I started calling my mother "Mor." You don't need to know any of this, but I am telling you to make a point. It's one of these unique, particularizing irrelevancies that are a major part of life and that we leave out when we tell stories to other people. Each of us, and there are millions of us, watch the same Mets games and have something very close to the same experience as we watch them. But there are things that are completely unique about the way in which each of us discusses these experiences with each of the Mets fans we know, our parents, children, spouses, friends, and strangers. You probably don't call your mother "Mor." She probably doesn't start speaking with a foreign accent. I think that when I complain to her about the Mets, I start speaking with a little bit of a Brooklyn accent, which I don't normally have. This is us. You have what you have. We're talking about the same thing you're talking about and we're probably saying pretty much the same things. But all of our conversations are different. Everyone has their own unique names, rhythms, languages, rituals, and styles of thinking and speaking. I call my mother every day and talk to her for about fifteen to twenty minutes. At some point she'll mention my father, at some point she'll complain about her immobility and we'll talk about her physical therapy, and at some point we'll talk about the Mets. This is the way it is.

"Look, Mor, they're tied with the Brewers and a game and a half behind the Phillies. So they have about a 50 percent chance of beating the Brewers and about a 12.5 percent chance of beating the Phillies. So they have a better than even chance of getting to the postseason."

"They're not."

"Well, maybe they won't, but there's a good chance that they will."

"No."

"Look, the odds against the 1969 Mets winning the World Series were a thousand to one or something, and they did it."

"They were different. They could do it."

"But these Mets don't even have the odds against them. The odds are on their side."

"Maybe that's the problem."

"No, it's not a problem. It's not a problem when the odds are on your side. It's better."

"You with the numbers. You should have been an accountant."

I'm laughing. "Mor! Seriously, you can't lose faith. Ya gotta believe!"

"I don't believe. They're no good."

"What, Reyes is no good? Wright is no good? Beltran is no good?"

"They're good. The bullpen is shit."

"The bullpen is not shit. The bullpen is inconsistent. They were doing really well a couple of weeks ago."

"Yeah, but now they're playing like shit. Now is what matters."

"Well, they have to turn it around. They have to regain their confidence. We have to stick by them and cheer them."

"I cheer them. They don't hear me."

"Yeah, well. Keep cheering. Don't give up on them."

"I'm not giving up on them. What am I going to do?"

You're not going to do anything, Mor. You're going to sit in that big, brown chair in that den that is frozen in the 1980s except for the pictures, and you're going to watch the Mets. You're going to eat your meals and take your pills when your aides give them to you and you're going to wait for your three kids to call you every day and you'll talk to them about their lives and how busy they are and at some point Dad will be mentioned and at some point we'll talk about how you walk and do your exercises and at another point we'll talk about the Mets. But what the Mets are going to do for you this year, Mor, is give you a World Championship. They're going to stop putzing around and the bullpen is going to calm down and they're going to start amazing themselves and all their fans in the way that they do when they get it going. They're going to win. And Shea Stadium will go out in glory. And we'll always remember this year. It will be one of those years about which there is nothing bad to remember because it ended perfectly. It will be like 1986, and 1969, and 1955 when the Dodgers beat the Yankees and you were so happy and wanted to celebrate and you hugged me and kissed me but I didn't know what was happening and I couldn't help you.

"You looking forward to going to the game on Saturday?"

"Yeah. But I wish I didn't have to go in a wheelchair."

"Yeah, wel . . ."

"I know, I know. Lynn Cohen is so sweet for making it so I can go. I just hope they win. Who's pitching, Santana?"

"Yeah, they're moving him up in the rotation. He'll be pitching on three days rest."

"He can do it. I like him."

"I like him too. It'll be wonderful to get you to a game. And next year, we'll go to Citi Field and you can tell me how it's like and how it's not like Ebbets Field."

"I thought you didn't like Citi Field."

"Yeah, well what are you gonna do?"

September 25

Wednesday night's game had been one of the worst losses in Mets history. When you live through a game like that, you wonder if you'll ever see the Mets come back or come through again. It no longer seems possible for a player on your team to hit a fly ball into the outfield with a runner on third and no one out. There's no logical reason to feel this way, but this is the way you feel. Wednesday night's game had Carlos Delgado's grand slam. Rarely had a home run made me as happy as that one did. But the joy and the beauty of that home run only made what happened afterward that much worse. All I could think was that we're toast, we've always been toast, toast is our essence.

And then the Mets did the kind of thing they'd been doing all year. They played a game on Thursday night that was as glorious as the game on Wednesday was ugly. The score was tied, 3–3, in the seventh inning, when Pedro Martinez, pitching in what was probably his last regular season game ever as a Met, was taken out after giving up a hit and a walk. It was awful to see Pedro leave. It was horrible to hear him express a soft desire to play again for the Mets. It gave you a deeper sense of the urgency of this season. Please let Pedro Martinez not have spent four years in a Mets uniform with so little to show for it in the end. It was also awful to see the two runners he had left on base score when Ricardo Rincon (who?) gave up a three-run homer to Micah Hoffpauir, a rookie having a five-for-five night.

In the bottom of the seventh, Robinson Cancel scored a run after a leadoff double. Then in the bottom of the eighth, David Wright opened things up with a single, as Carlos Delgado, the hero of the night before, grounded into a double play. With two outs, Carlos Beltran singled. Then Ryan Church singled. Then, with so much on the line, Ramon Martinez singled, scoring Beltran and moving Church to second. Robinson Cancel then hit a single into right as Church, not the fastest man on the team, tried to come all the way home from second. Koyie Hill, the Cubs catcher, waited patiently for Church at home with the ball in his glove, and then Church did something you only see in dreams. In the pouring rain and on the slippery mud, Church ran around Hill without running out of the base paths. Off balance, he seemed to slip in the mud, overshooting the plate. Hill lunged to tag him as Church reached back and touched the muddy plate. The game was tied.

Then in the bottom of the ninth, Reyes singled, but Murphy and Wright struck out. Reyes stole second and Delgado was intentionally walked. Carlos Beltran came to the plate. Like us, he must have been thinking of the at-bat we will never forget, and his lifelong mission to make up for it. Beltran stroked a single to right and scored Reyes. When Beltran crossed the plate, the Mets were all out there dancing, wet and muddy in the wind and the rain, with that bounce you see only at a clinching. The small crowd of diehards was loud and tireless. This was the Shea way. The fans, as Jerry Manuel said after the game, were demanding it. Mets fans were demanding with love, demanding to see that dance again on Sunday.

Going to the Game on September 27

After Thursday's game, the Mets were tied with the Brewers and a game behind the Phillies. Each team had three games to play, and the Mets had momentum. Some people say that in baseball there really is no such thing as momentum. I don't think this is always true, but it certainly seemed to be true of the 2008 Mets. They had neither good nor bad momentum. Each game was like flipping a coin. And so on Friday, the Mets lost. Nobody hit very much, and people named Parnell and Stokes gave up three runs out of the bullpen after Big Pelf gave up three of his own. The Phillies won and the Brewers won. The Mets were, at longest last, in the very deepest trouble, a game behind the Brewers and two games behind the Phillies, with just two games to play for everyone. For the first time since they had taken over first place for the first time in July, it looked likely that the Mets were not going to make it to the playoffs.

On Saturday, September 27, I went to Shea Stadium with my wife, my daughter, my sister Jennifer, and my mother. We were all going to be there thanks to Lynn Cohen. Lynn had bought 1,200 tickets in the picnic area to resell for a fundraiser for the charity which now bore the name Pitch In For a Good Cause. Lynn had read a piece I had written on my blog about how sad I was that I wouldn't be able to take my mother to a last game at Shea because she couldn't walk well anymore and she'd never want to go to a game in a wheelchair. Lynn made me change my mind and take my mother. She found out all about handicapped access in the picnic area and she scouted out the bathroom situation. My mother was so flattered by this attention that she let us get her a portable wheelchair. We were actually going to take her to a last game at Shea.

The fundraiser was an enormous success. Lynn had sold the 1,200 tickets. The picnic tent was filled with people wearing GaryKeithandRon t-shirts. And so we were all sitting at a picnic table eating hot dogs and pasta: my mom, my wife, my daughter, and my sister. We also had with us my father's old Mets cap. He was with us, at our last game together as a family at Shea. Lynn came by and snapped our picture. Sonia got signatures from Gary and Ron on the back of her shirt.

Before the game, all of the 1,200 people in the GaryKeithandRon shirts waited behind the center field wall to be let out onto the warning track during the national anthem. Mr. Met came by as we were waiting at the front of the line with my mom in her wheelchair. I took his picture, and when I looked at it later, I saw that a smiling, white-haired Jerry Koosman had been right behind Mr. Met. He had been standing fifteen feet away from us and we hadn't seen him.

As we were waiting, I had a meltdown. There I was under a grey sky at Shea, right by the Home Run Apple, standing behind my eighty-year-old mother in her wheelchair. Here I was, for one of the last times, at a place I had been coming to since I was nine and she was thirty-five and my dad was thirty-nine and what the hell was all this and what the hell had happened? And where was big Shea going to go now and what were they going to do with it and how many things that were once real can become memories before you just want to jump off a bridge? I asked my mother how she was doing and she said she was so happy.

They opened the outfield fence and I wheeled my mom onto the warning track. There was the wet and noisy stadium and here was the smooth, soft, bright green wonder of the field. We just looked, seeing it all from this side for the first time. We were right near the spot where Cleon caught the last ball of 1969 and dropped to his knees. We were right near the wall that Endy climbed. We were right near the right field line, made so famous by a single unforgettable ground ball. Here it was. We heard the anthem and went back through the wall. Shea would live a little longer if we won today. But soon it would be finished. And none of what was right here, right now would ever be here again.

I rolled my mom into a strange little elevator that took us up to the level of our seats. We got ourselves settled and enjoyed our vista. Looking to the left, my mother asked, "That's the bullpen?" "Yeah." "They should put a lock on it," she muttered with disgust.

First we cheered for Jerry Koosman, who took down the second-to-last number. Then we cheered for Cleon Jones, who threw out the first pitch. My mother put her hand on my arm and said, "I'm so glad to be here. I love it here." Then after the first inning, when the stadium announcer told us that the New York Mets appreciated our support, my mother said, "If they appreciate our support, they shouldn't aggravate us so much."

This was true. But this is the way it was. The Mets got two runs up onto the board really quick, but how could I avoid the sense that aggravation was on its way? Johan Santana, as good as he was, had thrown 125 pitches only three days ago. He was volunteering to pitch on what was really only two and a half days rest. This is normally a bad idea. But Johan insisted on doing it, and the Mets were not in a position to tell him not to. How long could Johan last? What if the Mets could only score two runs?

As the game went on, and as the lights came on, there was a general brightening of the spirit of the people in the stands. Blessed with a particularly magical changeup, Santana held the Marlins speechless. For all that they hated us, they could do us no harm. I began to feel, and the crowd began to feel, that we were watching the gutsiest, most brilliant, and most important Mets pitching performance since John Maine's near no-hitter exactly a year ago, or maybe even since Al Leiter's two-hit shutout in Cincinnati that won us the Wild Card in 1999. We cheered every strike and booed every time an umpire failed to identify a strike. We swiveled our many hips to the Carlos Santana song they play for every John Santana strikeout. We chanted "Johan, Johan, Johan, Johan." The rest of the Mets were out there, but we were riveted by this one single superhuman effort. I watched him through the dim soda fuzz of the rain on my glasses. I couldn't believe what was happening, but I heard it and felt it in the stamping of the picnic bleachers. "We're gonna have to clone him," my mother pointed out.

We roared with approval when Johan came to bat in the seventh. In the eighth, we sang "I'm a Believer" with proud, loud belief. "Are they singing about Tom Seaver?" my mother wondered. They might as well have been. That's who it looked like on the mound. It's true that we never scored a run beyond the two we got early. But as the ninth inning began, we were convinced that this time it wouldn't matter. Endy came into the game as a defensive replacement. He stood right in front of our bleachers and we welcomed him. You could tell from the way Johan stood on the mound that he was not going to be denied a complete game shutout. He was stepping up, and in our great communal gratitude, we pounded and cheered and chanted. There was an uninterrupted wall of sound in the ninth. Everyone was standing, except my mother, who couldn't. I stayed sitting down with her and it was as if we were hiding in a meadow during a storm of locusts. All around us, people were so happy they were screaming. And then there was a double. And then a ball was hit terrifyingly deep into left field. Endy caught it against the wall. Once again he saved us. We slapped each other's hands. We slapped strangers' hands. But it seemed, in the picnic area, as if there were no strangers. All the people in those t-shirts were as much my family as the four women around me. I was so happy, so grateful, and so surprised. The Mets would live. The Mets would continue. Shea wasn't over.

At the end of the game, my mother and I went down in the sound-proof, slow-moving elevator. She was so happy. "That was a wonderful game," she said. "Thank you so much for taking me. I didn't see the end because they were all standing up. But I don't blame them. I would too if I were them. They should have stood up. It was wonderful. At least they weren't doing that stupid wave."

I was going to be there tomorrow. And if there was to be a Monday, I would be there as well. I would stand. I would go to the window. I would do whatever I could to help Shea live as long as possible. I was so hopeful; the game had given me a kind of confidence. As I helped my mother into my car and folded up the wheelchair and put it in the trunk, I thought of how, whatever happened next, I had just been a part of Mets history. I may have just been at the game we would always remember as the game that propelled us into the 2008 playoffs. Or maybe, I thought, as I closed the trunk and turned and looked at the big blue thing still noisy with the happy, exiting crowd, maybe I had just witnessed the last Mets victory Shea Stadium would ever see.

The Last Game

At eleven o'clock on the morning of September 28, 2008, I walked towards Shea in the rain from a parking spot out by Flushing Bay. The other lots were full. They'd never been full this early. As I walked under the Whitestone Expressway, I saw the outer ramps of the stadium filled with people who were looking down on a stage lit up like a studio, where Gary, Keith, and Ron were talking to each other. There were policemen everywhere. A big SUV pulled up and the police surrounded it as Yogi Berra shuffled out and everyone started shouting "Yog –i! Yog -i!" Yogi waved at the flashes of bright light coming from hands held high above the press of people. He walked into the stadium on a soggy scarlet carpet.

When I got my ticket to the last game at Shea, I never imagined that it was going to be the most significant regular season game to be played there in forty-five years. But that's what it was. The Mets could no longer catch the Phillies, but they were tied with Milwaukee for the Wild Card. To win it, they would simply have to have a better day than the Brewers. If neither team had a better day than the other, there would be a one-game playoff at Shea on Monday.

This game was more significant than the last game of 2007, because 2007 had happened and needed to be redeemed. It was more significant than any of the regular season games played in the seasons we had made the playoffs, because whenever we made the playoffs, we had almost always won our slot by a comfortable margin. We lost the close pennant races of 1984, 1985, and 1987. We won in 1973, but the last game of that season was not as significant as this game because in 1973 we were winning against all expectations. The only regular season game that might have been as significant as this was the last game of 1999, when Melvin

Mora came home on a wild pitch. But even that game wasn't quite as significant, because we hadn't lost the NLCS on the final pitch of the seventh game two years before and collapsed completely the year before. This game was going to be the most significant regular season game in Shea Stadium history and it was today and I was there and the stadium was getting torn down at the end of the season. I was overwhelmed by all this and I wasn't pleased. I hadn't expected this day to be about a do-or-die baseball game. I had wanted a day to be alone with Shea and the big crowd and my memories.

I didn't have a choice about any of this. And I was actually feeling pretty good. I was still in the dream-like euphoria produced by Johan Santana's changeup the day before. I figured that there was a 75 percent chance that there would be a game on Monday. And if there was a game on Monday, or if we won it today, the promised ceremony would not feel like a wake. It would feel like the mining of a rich vein of collective memory. It would propel the Mets, and Shea, into one more month of life.

I met up with my sister Stefanie and her friend Terri, who had won the lottery for four tickets to the last game, and who had let me have this precious ticket. The stadium filled, completely. And everything feels different when every seat is not merely purchased but filled. Everything feels different. And everything about the 2008 season, and everything about the forty-five years the Mets had spent at Shea, was going to feel different depending on the outcome of this one single ballgame. I hate this kind of thing, even though it is supposed to be one of the reasons I love baseball. I love and hate to be dangled over the pit of possibility. I love and hate knowing how much of a difference one game, one inning, one at-bat, one pitch can make.

The game started off in excruciating fashion, with five scoreless innings. Then the Marlins scored a couple of runs in the top of the sixth, one of them on a walk with the bases loaded, by Joe Smith facing his first batter as he was called in to relieve Oliver Perez. I was terrified, but then in the bottom of the sixth, Carlos Beltran tied the game with a two-run homer. In the seventh, Endy Chavez made an astounding catch, bouncing off the wall in left field to save a run. The catch was eerily similar to the catch he had made in the seventh game of the 2006 NLCS. And it was eerie that Beltran had hit the home run he had not hit at the last game of 2006.

In the eighth inning, Scott Schoeneweis gave up a home run to pinch hitter Wes Helms. Luis Ayala came in to give up a home run to Dan Uggla. At some point in the moments after this occurred, the scoreboard indicated that the Brewers had taken a 3–1 lead over the Cubs in the eighth inning. I heard a hiss of air and realized that the deep vein had been found. Nothing would stop the air and the blood. I could do nothing. It was all ruined. It could not be retrieved. I clapped and cheered and acted hopeful in the ninth. But this was because of a reflex I had developed over forty-seven years. I had looked at my palm and seen that the life line was short, and I didn't expect anything. The inning next to the Brewers-Cubs score on the scoreboard went from 9 to F. The Brewers won. The Mets came up in the bottom of the ninth and heard our loud but dispirited cheering. David Wright popped up. Endy Chavez grounded out. Damion Easley walked. Ryan Church flied out deep to center.

The Marlins celebrated when it was over. I have always felt bad for them, because they were a good team and no one came to watch them play. Now I was glad that their stadium was always empty, that they were last in the majors in attendance. I hoped that they would languish unloved and unnoticed for a very long time to come.

When it was all over and the Marlins had finally heeded our request to "Get Off the Field!" there was an entirely unreal twenty-five minutes during which the devastated crowd stood and faced legions of policemen and security guards in orange shirts as someone played a dirge-like version of "I Fought the Law and the Law Won." The law had won, all right. Behind the unnecessary army of mounted policemen, black-suited functionaries with tape measures positioned blue and white standing posters of great Mets moments. Nobody was rushing onto that field. Nobody was ripping up sod to take it home. And no one was comforting us.

Finally the ceremonies started. They showed us a movie about Shea, and they played "New York State of Mind." Then there was an old-timey version of "Take Me Out to the Ball Game," and then, with clueless fanfare, Mr. Met took down the number 1 to reveal the Citi Field logo. For the very first time in Mets history, the crowd lustily booed something Mr. Met had done. Oh, noooo! Mr. Met, of course, doesn't talk, but I crazily thought of him as Mr. Bill from the old Saturday Night Live. My brain was completely free-associating by this point. I'm lucky I wasn't hallucinating.

Then Howie Rose came out to start the real ceremony. He read a list of names of people who had been invited but didn't come. And then there was a list of people who were representing those who had died. And then Howie slowly read a list of names of men who emerged from the right and left field fences and walked down the lines to take their places in an arch that formed from first to third base.

Jack Fisher. Ron Hunt. Al Jackson. Frank Thomas. Jim McAndrew. Jon Matlack. Craig Swan. George Theodore. Doug Flynn. Ed Charles. Art Shamsky. Wayne Garrett. Dave Kingman. Felix Millan. John Stearns. George Foster. Tim Teufel. Todd Zeile. Ron Swoboda. Lee Mazzilli. Wally Backman. Ron Darling. Sid Fernandez. Howard Johnson. Bobby Ojeda. Robin Ventura. Al Leiter. Ed Kranepool. Cleon Jones. Bud Harrelson. Jesse Orosco. Edgardo Alfonzo. John Franco. Rusty Staub. Lenny Dykstra. Gary Carter. Jerry Koosman. Yogi Berra. Keith Hernandez. Darryl Strawberry. Dwight Gooden. Willie Mays. Mike Piazza. Tom Seaver.

There they were, on the base paths, these deep and close friends I had never met. There were the larger than life figures who lived in a special dream world in the minds of millions. There was a man who made me so happy when he hit a home run as I was listening to the family car radio during an intermission between features at the Paramus Drive-In Theatre. There was someone who had made me cry when he came back after six years of unforgiveable banishment. There was someone who had played on the Mets from the time I was in the second grade until the year I got married. There was a man who made me smile as a kid because he didn't look, act, or talk like any other ballplayer. There was a shy man no one had seen in years, who was the single most exciting player I have ever seen play.

There was a chunk of my life down on that field. There were the artists who made something that would always be more than a game to me. They were all lined up and I watched them through my binoculars. I saw the old teams come together again, particularly the great team of the 1980s, the team that is about my age. I saw the older team of grown men from the impossibly distant days when I first heard Bob Murphy's voice. And I saw the newer Mets, who were young enough for my daughter to have fallen in love with. Each of them stood on the field in a big jersey with the number he had worn. And then, as the music changed to the kind of music they play at the victory celebration at the end of Star Wars, I saw each of them come forward to touch home plate and wave to the crowd. The vast concourse of the wounded cheered as if nothing had happened that afternoon. All that mattered was a half century of warm and briny love. All that mattered was them and us.

Then there was a ceremony where Tom Seaver threw one last pitch to Mike Piazza. There was the last pitch that would be thrown from that mound. There was the last pitch caught. Seaver and Piazza put their arms around each other and waved and then walked out to deep center. They stopped before the wall and waved again. The blue wall opened up and took them in. It was over, and our tears of love mixed with our tears of bitterness. The Mets were gone, but people stayed, looking, sitting, standing, taking pictures. I looked around and I couldn't believe that I would never see this broad, warm, familiar sight again. It was not really there anymore. It was behind the blue wall, with Tom and Mike. Yet as I walked down the ramps for the very last time, the stadium felt eerily alive to me. It seemed as if it was dying as people actually die: with love, generosity, and an uncanny alertness. When I was finally outside, I looked up at the neon ghosts on the side of the building, hitting and fielding and pitching.

I walked towards the parking lot by the bay, turning around every few seconds. After I passed under the Whitestone Expressway, I couldn't see the stadium anymore when I turned back towards it. I walked through the darkness of the nearly empty parking lot to my car. Not wanting to get into the car right away, I walked to the promenade along the bay and sat down on a bench. I could see the lights of LaGuardia Airport and their reflections, shimmering columns in the black water. To the left I saw the top of the Empire State Building. And off to the right in the distance was the Triborough Bridge, with its lights like the strands of a necklace. I thought of how we used to drive over the bridge in the 1960s, how I used to look between the backs of my parents' heads to get my first glimpse of Shea. I thought of how I used to show the bridge to my infant daughter. We could see it from her very first bedroom, in Astoria. Standing, with my help, on my lap, she would look at the bridge as if she could see that something was there, but she didn't know what it was or what it meant. I looked at the lights in the water and against the night sky. I knew that Shea was empty, but all of its lights were still on. I couldn't see it, but I could feel it behind me.

Again

In 2006, the Mets had fallen one game short of the National League pennant. In 2007, they were one game short of the division title and one game short of the Wild Card. In 2008, the Mets finished three games out in the division and they were, once again, one game out of the Wild Card. For the third season in a row, winning the last game played would have made all the difference. For the second season in a row, winning just one more game, any game, would have made all the difference. How many games in these two seasons had been wasted, lost on a fluke, a single bad pitch, a bad swing, or a bobbled ball? There were those games lost on ordinary evenings where you thought, "So what? There's plenty of time." There was never plenty of time. There was always just the time that there was. And there was so little difference between what would bring triumph and what would bring despair that everything mattered all the time. Great. That would do for a philosophy of life. Worry about everything, feel every loss deeply, because each individual misfortune or mistake might in the end cost you everything.

Like all Mets fans, I was very upset. But I wasn't angry with the Mets. And neither were other fans. Maybe we should have been angry at them. But we weren't because the season, in the end, had been the reverse of 2007. Starting the season 34-35 under Randolph, we finished 55-38 under Manuel. Even though the Mets blew it by only winning seven of their last seventeen games, they still had an excellent second half. If we hadn't lost Wagner and Maine, we might have finished a couple of games ahead of the Phillies. There was nothing anyone could do about ligaments and inflammations and bone spurs and all of the other anatomical gobbledegook that every once in a while pops out of a box and ruins your summer.

The 2008 season wasn't a historic collapse so much as a come-back that came just short. There had been a kind of collapse at the end, but it was more of a dropping to one's knees with a wound in the side. It wasn't a falling flat on one's face. Still, the disappointment hurt like hell. Neither 2007 nor 2008 had done their job of making up for that last game of 2006 against the Car-dinals.

What was going to happen to this team I had loved? Would anything ever make me feel that the early years of Wright and Reyes and Maine, the prime of Beltran and Santana, the last few years of Delgado and Martinez were wonderful? Would I ever cherish what I remembered from those years in the way I cher-ished the fragments of memory I had from other Mets seasons? I couldn't leave the Mets now. I had to see what would happen. Good things could happen next year. But if they did, they would happen in the new stadium. Shea was going be remembered as the cavern of disappointment. Citi Field would be the home of the champions.

That upset me. But what difference did it make? As I awoke from the dream of the season, I asked myself the questions I ask myself when I wake up from every season. Why did I care? Why did I let this game run along the side of my life? Did I really think it was such a big deal to find meaning in it? I could find meaning in anything if I tried hard enough. Did I think I was so great for doing that? Millions and millions of people love this shit. How good could it be?

What distinction or merit is there in being the fan of anything? How much credit is there in liking something you do not create and on which you have no impact? I think of a pizzeria I know that has a pizza called the "Meat Lover's Pizza." It has sausage and meatballs and bacon. That's what a fan is. Something like a meat lover. You love meat. You want credit for that? Do you think you deserve credit or admiration because you love a base-ball team so much? It takes nothing to love a baseball team. It takes nothing and you do nothing.

Why cling to this when there's so much else? Why treat it as if it's an organ or a limb? It's not a part of me. I have been tricked into making it a part of me so that some people can make a lot of money. Major League Baseball is as much of a sham as the Tower of Light or the Festival of Gas. By loving baseball so much, I have become complicit in all the things I hate about it. I should leave it. It won't go out of business. It won't miss me and I won't miss it. Look at how it takes up all this space in my soul that in other times would have been taken up by magnificent things I would actually have thought were real. How did this racket manage to become such a big deal? What made me want to celebrate it? Why would anyone treat Shea as if it were a cathedral?

Shea was not a cathedral. It was only like a cathedral because it was a gigantic place and I had associated its ceremonies with the most ordinary and inevitable things in my life. Every member of the Shea crowd knew why the place was sacred. We all had our individual reasons. We all did it by ourselves. And we all did it together, with the Mets and our families and friends. It was actually better that it wasn't a cathedral. It was better that it was merely like a cathedral. It was a baseball stadium. And that was enough.

The Whale

I went back to Shea on October 22, 2008. Driving home from work, on an impulse, I didn't take the Cross Island Parkway up to the Throgs Neck Bridge. I stayed west on the Northern State Parkway and took the 9E exit off the Grand Central Parkway. I pulled over onto the side of the road that runs along the south side of the parking lot.

There was no one around. I got out of my car and I was all alone with it. There it was, across the lot, which was empty except for painted lines and stop signs. The sky was ominous and oppressive, and it was very windy off the bay and leaves were blowing around. But it could just as easily have been a clear, still, sunny day. It made no difference. What I was seeing didn't require a heavy sky or blowing leaves to have the effect it had on me.

I took a few pictures and got back into my car and drove around the perimeter as if I were heading to one of the parking lots. I'd driven this route a million times, but this time there was only me, as in a dream, and I couldn't get into the parking lots. It was eerie. It was the middle of the afternoon and I didn't see anyone. I turned right onto the road with the chop shops. There were people here. I saw that the parking lot near the grand entrance to Citi Field had a lot of cars in it. I parked my car on the road near the entrance to the lot. There was enough activity so that no one was going to notice me if I walked in there.

I got out of my car and saw that Citi Field was bright and new and filled with people in hard hats getting it ready. I saw Shea behind the new stadium, hulking and silent. During the season, Shea was full of life and Citi Field was silent and looming. Things were reversed now. Shea's scoreboard was gone and I could see that the seats had been ripped out. This made the passages to the inner concourse look like empty eye sockets. The concrete was rough and ancient-looking where the seats had been. And the passages through which we had brought our food back to our seats were now empty eyes staring at Citi Field. Or empty mouths, dark and open. Without the scoreboard, you could stare directly at them. The only other sign of life was the giant blue mural commemorating the 1969 Championship, with Seaver pitching, Koosman leaping, and Hodges looking at something over in the distance.

There were plenty of cars in the Citi Field lot, and there was a long line of black SUVs. A few of them had license plates that suggested some kind of connection to the Mets. I walked as close as I could to Shea and took some pictures. No one stopped me. No one even acted as if they saw me. There were ominous rattling sounds somewhere over on the field at Shea. I couldn't actually see what was happening because there was this "Almost Home" Citi Field bunting draped over the metal fence that kept you from walking too close.

The chop shops were all open and busy. Usually they're closed when you go to a ballgame. I heard a lot of random hammering and cutting sounds. I heard the low-pitched, familiar rumble of the subway cars. I heard the high, sharp caw-caw sounds of the seagulls. And there were still, as always, the planes.

War of the Worlds

On December 8, 2008, I visited Shea again, this time around 5:30 in the evening. I parked where I had parked before, on the street of the chop shops, right up against Citi Field. I walked into the parking lot. It was dark, but there was still a lot of activity. Something was happening in the old stadium, which was intact, although only the ramps were lit. It was very cold and the only lights in the old stadium were red ones along the top to let planes know that something large and dark was still there.

I got as close as I could to Shea and looked through the metal fence at a spot where the plastic Mets bunting had blown open. I saw something moving, a yellow steam shovel, lit by a garish construction light that also illuminated the smoky dust that rose from where it was digging. It moved with the scary grace of machines. I don't know what it was digging or what it was doing. It was in the bullpen, right under the mural commemorating the 1969 Championship. There was light and darkness and dust and dim orange clouds and the faces of Seaver, Koosman, and Hodges, but the only thing moving was the slow neck of a steam shovel. I felt as if I were in that part of the movie *War of the Worlds* where some people drive up to the place where something has landed with a bang from the sky. They see smoke and the long neck of a machine rising up out of it. They don't know if the neck can see them. They don't know what it is doing. They don't know if it comes in peace or if it will turn towards them with sudden destructive force.

Over to my right, through the links of the fence, I saw Palladian windows opening into the Jackie Robinson Rotunda. I could see the big, lit space and the escalators. I could imagine the crowds entering in the spring.

Visiting Shea on January 21, 2009

My last visit to Shea was on January 21, 2009. I drove down in the morning and took my usual route into parking lot A, getting off the Whitestone Expressway at the Northern Boulevard exit, taking the right towards the bay, driving past the World's Fair bus shelters, and then swinging left under the expressway on the road that led straight to the stadium. I was approaching Shea in exactly the same way as I had approached it at the last game. This time I was in a car and not on foot. I stopped and got out of my car at the stop sign. You could no longer turn left into the parking lot. There was Shea in front of me, and for the first time I could imagine that it would not be there very much longer. I could see that it was not going to be there very much longer. I had thought that maybe I'd come by next week to see it again. But when I saw it, I knew that I would not be coming back.

Shea Stadium looked like something that had been hit by a car and that birds were eating. It had that bland silence of a dead thing, waiting for the next bite or blow that it would not feel. The right field upper deck was mostly gone and for the first time ever, the stadium looked lopsided. It was cracked and open to the emptiness of sunlight and wind. Things were hanging. Things were sticking out. It was no longer Shea. It was hurrying to be gone.

The day before, I had watched the inauguration of Barack Obama as the forty-fourth president of the United States. There were 2 million people on the Mall. The day was filled with references to the 1960s, to Martin Luther King Jr.'s speech at the Lincoln Memorial, to the Freedom Riders, and to the Civil Rights movement, and there were all of these comments that always make me so uncomfortable about people in heaven looking down and watching. Young people listened with respect, just as I used to listen with respect back in the 1960s when older people would talk about the struggles of the 1930s and the 1940s. Aretha Franklin, a star from the 1960s, sang "My Country, 'Tis of Thee." It was amazing to see a crowd of 2 million people on the television, all of them bundled up and waving flags in the cold. I think almost everybody, regardless of their politics, must have been moved by what they were seeing. Whatever was happening, something was beginning, something that had roots and was growing up out of them.

And here I was, on the very next day, alone except for the construction workers, mourning a baseball stadium. A highly educated man, with a keen interest in history, at an important moment in history, I was out in the morning sunlight and wind making a big deal of the death of a fucking baseball stadium. It wasn't even a particularly notable or good baseball stadium. It was Shea, which, as you will read in the future, did not exist in 2009, and did not exist during the presidency of Barack Obama.

But I saw that it was still there. Next to it, Citi Field was doing its own thing as if Shea had already left, as if Shea were taking a little longer to leave the stage than it needed to, as if it were having trouble getting its things together. The past always yields to the future, by definition. I tried to look at Citi Field as if I didn't know what it was and as if I had never seen it before. I didn't like the red arch in the Citi Field sign, which connected the first two i's, as if the whole building were a bank. I didn't like how the stadium was completely closed in. But I did like the arches and windows of the exterior, and I was curious about the inner space, about the rotunda and the new stands and the idea of seats above the outfield wall. I had just read that they were selling ticket plans that were not full-season tickets. Maybe there would be room for me in Citi Field. And maybe there wouldn't. It was like the future in general.

Citi Field was never going to mean as much to me as Shea had. It never could, even if it was a million times better. Shea was so wonderful because I had lived in it and dreamed about it since I was ten. Citi Field can't become as wonderful to me because I don't have the imagination I used to have. What I mainly have now is nostalgia, which is imagination backwards, and my nostalgia was just going to add more and more luster to Shea.

But I have more than nostalgia. My mind still comes up with new things and I feel as much vigor in my body as I ever have. The new stadium is here. I am tired of resenting it. I meant all the bitter things I said about it, and I am still critical of all the things I criticized. What I feel about what is gone is too deep to be cleared out by any easy gesture of reconciliation. Still, I don't want to spend what I have left on something that is gone. I want to enjoy myself. I want to enjoy the Mets and baseball. Shea isn't here anymore.

I am going to try to imagine being a kid now, in the back seat of a car coming over the Triborough, or maybe the Whitestone, or on the Grand Central through the ruins of the fair. Or maybe I'll come in on the Long Island Railroad or on the 7 train that still rumbles and rattles through Queens. There is the beautiful new stadium with the arches and the windows and the long row of columns. There is the Citi Field Fanwalk with all of the bricks that people have paid $195 for. There is my family's brick, "Mets Fans Forever—The Brands." What does forever mean? It means this. It means the Brands have been coming here from the beginning, and so have all of these other families and people and groups of friends. It means we're still coming. We're parking where Shea used to be, or maybe under the Whitestone Expressway. We're entering the big rotunda and going up the escalators. We're doing the same thing over and over again, so that we won't forget anything. We love the new apple. And we always love the Mets. They have our money. But they have so much more than our money.

We're still coming. And if we aren't still coming, we greet you from the Fanwalk. You know what we sounded like. You know what we felt.

INDEX

Brand, Dana.

The last days of
 Shea.

4110

$16.95

DATE			